Preaching Parchments:
Sermon Manuscripts Volume II

Troy Shaw

Preaching Parchments:
Sermon Manuscripts Volume II

ISBN: **978-0-9983245-4-8**
Copyright © June 2020
By Holam Books & Media
First Edition

All rights reserved. No part of this publication may be reproduced or transmitted in any form or by any means, electronic or mechanical, photocopy, recording, or any type of information storage and retrieval system without permission from the author and/or publisher.

Preaching Parchments:
Sermon Manuscripts Volume II

Troy Shaw

ACKNOWLEDGEMENTS

I am more than appreciative for my proofreaders Cathy Palmer, Arnetta Hodge, Kelly Shaw, and the entire Holam Books Publishing family.

DEDICATION

I dedicate this book to the God of Abraham, Isaac, Jacob, my father, and my father's father. With great love, this book is dedicated to my mother; she loves both me and God's word.

HOMILETIC

hom i let ic

/ˌhäməˈledik/

noun: **homiletics**; noun:

the art of preaching or writing sermons.

HERMENEUTIC

her me neu tic
/ˌhərməˈn(y)oōdik/

adjective: **hermeneutic**

concerning interpretation, especially of the Bible or literary texts.

INTRODUCTION

This work emerges from a year of sermons that speaks to a variety of themes and issues. These sermons are not Saturday night specials, in fact each sermon developed over a period of two years. Preparation, thought, and intentional over all continuity come together within the skeleton of each reflection.

Love is a central theme throughout the manuscripts as a profound respect for God the Father, Son, and Holy Spirit has been embraced to bring the central power of preaching to the apex of sermonic delivery.

The sermon manuscripts have been lightly edited and redacted to maintain the original oratory stability and veracity. The language and voice have been preserved to the speaking tone used to reach a broad audience, while at times dealing with complexed issues and terms.

Scripture is intentionally used throughout each sermon to provide both foundation and focus to each message. Using scripture throughout a manuscript brings life to the sermon and congregation. Christians need a greater appreciation of scripture and a sermon should bring us to embrace God's word as we strive to be both hearers and doers of the holy writ. Finally, reading scripture during a message provides a time of reflection and slows the pace of the sermon. When preaching, scripture should be recited with great respect and intention.

Hopefully you will appreciate the experience of preaching through these manuscripts.

Shaw's Sermon Question[1] Homiletic Taxonomy

Remembering: can congregants recall or remember the sermon? (define, duplicate, list, memorize, recall, repeat, reproduce state)

Understanding: can congregants explain ideas or themes from the scripture and sermon? (classify, describe, discuss, explain, identify, locate, recognize, report, select, translate, paraphrase)

Applying: can congregants use the information toward pragmatic spiritual and physical lifestyle alteration? (choose, demonstrate, dramatize, employ, illustrate, interpret, operate, schedule, sketch, solve, use, write.)

Analyzing: can congregants distinguish between the different points of the sermon, and clearly separate the divine aspects of the text? (appraise, compare, contrast, criticize, differentiate, discriminate, distinguish, examine, experiment, question, test.)

Evaluating: can congregants justify a stand or decision? (appraise, argue, defend, judge, select, support, value, evaluate)

---

[1] These are questions that I maintain in mind during sermon preparation.

Creating: can congregants build renewed perspective or point of view? (assemble, construct, create, design, develop, formulate, write.)

Preaching Parchments:
Sermon Manuscripts Volume II

Troy Shaw

Preaching Parchments: Sermon Manuscripts Volume II

TABLE OF CONTENTS

HOPE FOR THE HELPLESS	17
REJECTING THE BURN,	28
EMBRACING THE BARN	28
THE CHURCH NEEDS WATER	39
THE POWER OF PREACHING	52
PLANNED PARENTHOOD	62
SOME WAYS TO PRAISE AND WORSHIP	75
SOME WAYS TO STAY BLESSED	87
HOW TO HANDLE WHAT YOU DISH OUT	95
HOW TO REJECT BEING MYSTERIOUS	105
HOW TO AVOID A SETBACK	114
HOW TO AVOID A SELLOUT CHURCH	125
NEVER SETTLE FOR LESS	141
THAN GOD'S PROMISE	141
RESURRECTION WORK	151
FREEDOM: READY, SET, GO	162
HOW TO GET PAST CRYING	175
LIVING THE BIBLE TOGETHER:	186
THROUGH EDUCATION	186
HOW TO BE GRATEFULLY CLEAN	198
HOW TO AVOID WORD BURN	208

LIVING THE BIBLE TOGETHER:	223
THROUGH MISSIONS	223
GOD WILL ALWAYS PASS THE TEST	234
YOU CAN TAKE IT TO THE BANK	245
HOW TO SERVE	254
RIGHTEOUS RISING	266
Lovely Day	278
THERE IS A COMEBACK	291
TROUBLE DON'T LAST WITH	299
A TURN IT AROUND GOD	299
DON'T GIVE UP	313
BE READY: THE KING IS COMING	322
READY FOR A NEW WORLD ORDER	333
JUST WAIT	342
SELFLESSNESS	350
HOW TO ACTIVATE THE GUARANTEE	357
GOD DOES NOT FORGET	377

Any road will lead you away from God, only one will lead you to God – Jesus is the only way.

SERMONS

HOPE FOR THE HELPLESS

SCRIPTURE

Psalms 72:6-9 He shall come down like rain upon the mown grass: as showers that water the earth. 7 In his days shall the righteous flourish; and abundance of peace so long as the moon endureth. 8 He shall have dominion also from sea to sea, and from the river unto the ends of the earth. 9 They that dwell in the wilderness shall bow before him; and his enemies shall lick the dust.

OUTLINE

1. There is Relief for the Mowed v6
2. Blessings Will Linger (Shower Puddles) v6
3. Dust Meals are Available v9

PRAYER

Great God, our heavily Parent – creator and sustainer - Your name alone is worthy. God, great God – Your name is holy. Our God in heaven, hallowed be Your name. Hallelujah, salvation, and glory to Your name. We embrace Your will, word, and way – Your kingdom come and Your will be done in every aspect of our lives and in every corner of the world – on earth as in heaven. You've wonderfully clothed the lilies and kept watch over sparrows, we take no thought of ourselves without You, our great provider – give us this day our daily bread. We appreciate Your divine forgiveness fortified through Your blood sacrifice on the altar of Calvary – please Lord, forgive us our trespasses as we forgive those who have trespassed against us. Glorious

God our protector, provider, hope, and shield – lead us away from temptation as You deliver us from evil. You are the hope of all ages, eternal love, peace, and joy – You are the salvation of all generations, peoples, and families – indwell us to be as Christ fulfilling Your purpose to serve the least and lost. All honor and glory with never ending authority is Yours – the kingdom and the power and the glory forever. Empty me, fill me with Your presence, use me - let now the words of my mouth and the meditation of my heart be acceptable in Thy sight. Benevolently gracious God, You alone are worthy of our praise and worship. We know it's all true, Amen.

MESSAGE

Each United States presidential candidate embraces a platform from which an overall theme emerges, from the New Deal to the challenging urgency of change from the Barrack Obama Campaign. During the 1980s many of us witnessed Jesse Jackson as he became the second American of African heritage to candidate for president of the United States, second to Shirley Chisholm. Notably Reverend Jesse Jackson concluded all of his speeches with the words "Keep Hope Alive."

It seems that Reverend Jackson's directive timelessly reminds us that we need to continually fuel hope. Hebrews 11:1 says, "Now faith is the substance of things hoped for, and the sign that the things not seen are true." We need hope as an active ingredient for faith – which requires us to materialize the desire to please God, the substance of things hoped for.

We need hope, nevertheless in reality there are a number of people that seemingly live helplessly without hope. Yes, there are helpless people living as sheep waiting to be slaughtered. Helpless people, like many of the half million homeless Americans. Helpless like some of the over 43 million that live in poverty. Maybe even helpless like the thousands of asylum seekers at our southern boarders, fleeing from the terror of drug cartels fueled by American money and greed.

Oh, I wish you could agree with me this morning that we live amidst people in helpless situations. People that cannot help themselves often blamed, although, they are the victims. Helpless people that cannot get ahead no matter what they do, just like Good Times with JJ, Thelma, and Florida, two steps forward only equals six steps back – never getting a break no matter what you do. There are helpless people in helpless situations. In fact, I think most if not all of us have been in helpless situations – in need of hope.

Now, allow me to be clear – thank God, the helpless are not hopeless. No, the helpless are not hopeless – because God cares, God loves us, God hears us! The helpless are not hopeless.

The psalmist chords within the 72nd Psalm melodically tune our hearts to praise, worship, and hope, as there is great hope for the helpless.

Focus with me on Psalms 72:6 it reads, "May he come down like rain on the cut grass; like showers watering the earth. "

There is relief for the mowed, no matter what you're going through, no matter the situation that has mowed through your life – there is hope. There are times in life where it seems that situations have mowed us down. Mowed down by financial mowers, by health, relationship, and sin – mowing us down spiritual, physically, and emotionally. Mowed down by drugs, sexual promiscuity, greed, or hatred – mowed down. Yes, there are times when the situational elements of life seem to mow us down.

Edgar Allen Poe said, "I became insane, with long intervals of horrible sanity." There are times when the reality of helplessness renders nearly unbearable pain, heightened by the dramatic stage proctored by subversive storms. Oh, I wonder is there anybody here feeling mowed down by one situation or another. Surely most, if not all, innocent prisoners feel mowed down while waiting appeals – feeling helpless, unable to afford adequate defense. We can be confident that many Americans feel mowed down while their health care insurance is indefinite, as greed and politics arrest wellbeing. Homeless, before one's children must breed a feeling of helplessness – struggling before those you are innately poised to protect, emotionally wrecked by the humility fueled by abject poverty.

Certainly, there are helpless, mowed down people fraught with fears, desperately seeking asylum through our U.S. southern border. Death and certain terror in their homelands motivated by gangs that thrive on gruesome behavior.

There is a plethora of situations that mow us down, rendering us powerless, helpless, and often emotionally dead. From foreclosures to job loss. Life comes with some difficulties, ups and downs, some good and bad elements as the tragedy of sin manifests crime, hatred, and evil. We need hope; I wonder do you know we need hope. We need hope for the helpless.

Thankfully the scriptures remind us that we have hope, as we can glean from the psalmist as he articulates the prophetic hymn that rain shall come and fall down upon the mowed grass. Restoration, revival, and renewal is on the way – rejuvenation rings within the ear of the helpless as the graceful power of God is embraced even when God is not seen.

Aren't you glad that God is working on our behalf even when we cannot see God, faith enriched by hope is actively delivering blessings. There may be times when you can't see God – but you best believe that God is working on our behalf. All things work together for your good, when you love God – I know I'm right about that.

Psalm 72 thought to be penned by King Solomon, the wisest person to live before the time of Christ – brings us to praise and adoration toward God the giver of rain, our provider, our protector, sustainer, and giver of abundant resources. Can I get a witness of God's greatness, is there a praise in the sanctuary for revitalizing rain – divine resources emerging from the throne of God. Happy to know that God's eye is on the sparrow and surely God watches after us. There is hope for the helpless, revival for the mowed down.

Jesus said it like this in Luke 12:27-32, "Consider the lilies how they grow: they toil not, they spin not; and yet I say unto you, that Solomon in all his glory was not arrayed like one of these. 28 If then God so clothe the grass, which is to day in the field, and tomorrow is cast into the oven; how much more will he clothe you, O ye of little faith? 29 And seek not ye what ye shall eat, or what ye shall drink, neither be ye of doubtful mind. 30 For all these things do the nations of the world seek after: and your Father knoweth that ye have need of these things. 31 But rather seek ye the kingdom of God; and all these things shall be added unto you. 32 Fear not, little flock; for it is your Father's good pleasure to give you the kingdom."

We need to embrace the fact that God's got us, the Lord has prepared the Earth for us and the fullness there of – it's okay to be helpless as long as God is actively working on our behalf. Hallelujah, the Lord is worthy of our praise – just think about it, you don't have to worry about a thing.

Adam and Eve lived in a place of residual resources, their sin ejected them from paradise, but no need to worry – you have been invited back to a greater utopia, invited by the blood of God the Son to worship and live in the presence of God's throne where peace will be sustained forever. No longer mowed down, no longer servants but children of God, anybody excited about that? Excited to go with Jesus all the way that love might abound through eternal praise and worship, Good God Almighty – just the thought of that day brings healing hope like a salve for the soul. There is hope for the helpless.

2 Corinthians 4:5-9 says, "For we preach not ourselves, but Christ Jesus the Lord; and ourselves your servants for Jesus' sake. 6 For God, who commanded the light to shine out of darkness, hath shined in our hearts, to give the light of the knowledge of the glory of God in the face of Jesus Christ. 7 But we have this treasure in earthen vessels, that the excellency of the power may be of God, and not of us. 8 We are troubled on every side, yet not distressed; we are perplexed, but not in despair; 9 Persecuted, but not forsaken; cast down, but not destroyed;"

I'm so glad that trouble don't last always – trouble don't last always.

Focus again on verse 6 it says, "He shall come down like rain upon the mown grass: as showers that water the earth."

Blessings will linger, as the text first says the "rain shall come down" – but then says as "showers that water the earth" – in the original Hebrew the word showers is best translated to say that the rain puddles. Please don't miss it – remember as children most of us were fascinated with puddles and if you've ever walked with a child after the rain, you know that children have a way of walking through every puddle. The text is telling us that not only will it rain but there will be enough to puddle. Hmmm, don't miss it!

God doesn't just bless us, but when God blesses – there is an abundance, there are puddles! I wonder is there anybody here expecting to play in the puddles! Thank God for overflow – praise God for puddles, blessings upon blessings. Glad because God may not come when you want God, but the Lord is always on time – knowing that when God shows up, God shows out. God can top your wildest imagination.

"That he would grant you, according to the riches of his glory, to be strengthened with might by his Spirit in the inner man; That Christ may dwell in your hearts by faith; that ye, being rooted and grounded in love, May be able to comprehend with all saints what is the breadth, and length, and depth, and height; And to know the love of Christ, which passeth knowledge, that ye might be filled with all the fulness of God. Now unto him that is able to do exceeding abundantly above all that we ask or think, according to the power that worketh in us, Unto him be glory in the church by

Christ Jesus throughout all ages, world without end. Amen."

As we stand in the shadow of noon – look with me at Psalms 72:9 it reads, "They that dwell in the wilderness shall bow before him; and his enemies shall lick the dust."

There is relief for the mowed, blessings that linger, and **dust meals are available.** We have hope and as we trust and depend upon God, leaning on the everlasting arms – our enemies need to come on in the house and genuinely join the family. You can stay hateful if you want to, you can persecute God's people – but don't think you're getting the same meal that's prepared for the righteous.

David said the Lord prepares a table in the presence of enemies. Well enemies may make it to the table, but they don't get to partake from the prosperity of God's delights – you can get a dust meal. A box lunch with a dust burger – there is no benefit in attacking God's people. The Lord will bring vengeance upon those that oppress the family. We are the family of God, connected by the blood of Jesus – and that's good enough for me. "The ungodly shall not stand in the judgment, nor sinners in the congregation of the righteous. For the LORD knoweth the way of the righteous: but the way of the ungodly shall perish."

Yes, God cares for us and provides for us – but thankfully God protects us, God will get "em", God will settle the account. Hallelujah for the lamb. "Therefore, the ungodly shall not stand in the judgment, nor sinners in the congregation of the righteous. For the LORD knoweth the way of the righteous: but the way of the ungodly shall perish."

Our enemies can kick rocks, they can walk in or drive up for a dust meal. Don't you know God manifested hope for all of us in Christ, God the Son was sacrificed to save us, providing hope while fortifying faith.

God's track record should spark jubilation within the helpless – I'm so glad I got my religion in time, I'm so glad Jesus is a friend of mine – glad, so glad trouble don't last always. The vacated cross reminds us that weeping may endure for a few nights, but joy comes in the morning – there is hope for the helpless, trouble don't last always. Christ was crucified, wounded for our transgression, bruised for our iniquity, He was buried – mowed down if you will, but early one morning He arose from the grave with all power in Heaven and on Earth. His blood was shed so that the waters of baptism could flow freely for us – I wonder have you been to the puddle, celebrating like children. The eternal blessings of God call us to worship. Dancing like dervishes, stepping through the puddles, symbols of God's grace, peace, love, mercy, and everlasting provisions. There is hope for the helpless – so glad, so glad that trouble don't last always. So glad there is relief for the mowed down – hope for the helpless.

Somebody ought to be glad that the rain is falling as you study God's word, rain falling as you serve like Christ. But, be glad that enough rain falls to create puddles, and abundance of blessings – puddles so you can splash some blessings on someone else by feeding the hungry, giving relief to the thirsty, taking in the stranger, visiting the sick and imprisoned – clothing the naked. There is hope for the helpless, enemies are eating the dust while we dance in the rain, enjoying the puddles – hallelujah to the Lamb, there is hope for the helpless!

REJECTING THE BURN, EMBRACING THE BARN

SCRIPTURE
Luke 3:17 Whose fan is in his hand, and he will throughly purge his floor, and will gather the wheat into his garner; but the chaff he will burn with fire unquenchable.

OUTLINE
1. Expect to be Processed v17
2. Embrace the Barn v17
3. Reject the Burn v17

PRAYER
Great God, our heavily Parent – creator and sustainer, Your name alone is worthy. God, great God – Your name is holy. Our God in heaven, hallowed be Your name. Hallelujah, salvation, and glory to Your name. We embrace Your will, word, and way – Your kingdom come and Your will be done in every aspect of our lives and in every corner of the world – on earth as in heaven. You have wonderfully clothed the lilies and kept watch over sparrows, we take no thought of ourselves without You, our great provider – give us this day our daily bread. We appreciate Your divine forgiveness fortified through Your blood sacrifice on the altar of Calvary – please Lord, forgive us our trespasses as we forgive those who have trespass against us. Glorious God our protector, provider, hope, and shield – lead us away from temptation as You

deliver us from evil. You are the hope of all ages, eternal love, peace, and joy – You are the salvation of all generations, peoples, and families – indwell us to be as Christ fulfilling Your purpose to serve the least and lost. All honor and glory with never ending authority is Yours – the kingdom and the power and the glory forever. Empty me, fill me with Your presence, use me - let now the words of my mouth and the meditation of my heart be acceptable in Thy sight. Benevolently gracious God, You alone are worthy of our praise and worship. We know it's all true, Amen.

MESSAGE

God designed the human body to produce. Our physical bodies consume and produce. Although most of us would view the main animal byproduct as waste, antithetically what we would see as waste is actually energy ready to reinvest into the Earth as fertilizer. God designed us to produce, designed us to bring return on investment, we're designed to produce, to mature, designed to grow.

In fact, the scriptures teach us that God will prune or cut away nonproductive or dead elements both naturally and spiritually. Scientifically we have come to understanding natural selection or simplified as, survival of the fittest, brings strength to the ecologically balanced collective life emerging from God. There are natural checks and balances that prune us and our environment. God requires evolution, growth, and maturity. Seed, time, and harvest are divine elements of our life cycle.

Genesis 8:21-22 says, "And the LORD smelled a sweet savour; and the LORD said in his heart, I will not again curse the ground any more for man's sake; for the imagination of man's heart is evil from his youth; neither will I again smite any more every thing living, as I have done. 22 While the earth remaineth, seedtime and harvest, and cold and heat, and summer and winter, and day and night shall not cease." God expects maturity, yes God expects, in fact, requires growth and maturity.

Luke chapter 3 seems to direct our attention toward the requirement to grow and mature, especially chapter 3 verse 17 – as we pontificate this single verse as spotlighted support toward the idea of "Rejecting the Burn, Embracing the Barn"

Look with me at Luke 3:17, "Whose fan is in his hand, and he will thoroughly purge his floor, and will gather the wheat into his garner; but the chaff he will burn with fire unquenchable."

In order to reject the burn to embrace the barn or in parallel reject the enemy to embrace God – we must **expect to be processed**. Don't ever get so comfortable with God's graceful love that you determine that our lives will not be ultimately judged by God under God's established law. We must expect to be processed. The text says, God will thoroughly purge the floor, with fan in hand – we will be processed, we will be judged against the standard of Christ our example righteous in every way under the law of God. In Matthew chapter 22 Christ said we must love God with all of our heart, soul, and mind – loving our neighbor as we love ourselves.

One day we will be judged, you can expect to be processed – expect to be separated.

Matthew 25:31-46 says, "When the Son of man shall come in his glory, and all the holy angels with him, then shall he sit upon the throne of his glory: 32 And before him shall be gathered all nations: and he shall separate them one from another, as a shepherd divideth his sheep from the goats: 33 And he shall set the sheep on his right hand, but the goats on the left. 34 Then shall the King say unto them on his right hand, Come, ye blessed of my Father, inherit the kingdom prepared for you from the foundation of the world: 35 For I was an hungred, and ye gave me meat: I was thirsty, and ye gave me drink: I was a stranger, and ye took me in: 36 Naked, and ye clothed me: I was sick, and ye visited me: I was in prison, and ye came unto me. 37 Then shall the righteous answer him, saying, Lord, when saw we thee an hungred, and fed thee? or thirsty, and gave thee drink? 38 When saw we thee a stranger, and took thee in? or naked, and clothed thee? 39 Or when saw we thee sick, or in prison, and came unto thee? 40 And the King shall answer and say unto them, Verily I say unto you, Inasmuch as ye have done it unto one of the least of these my brethren, ye have done it unto me. 41 Then shall he say also unto them on the left hand, Depart from me, ye cursed, into everlasting fire, prepared for the devil and his angels: 42 For I was an hungred, and ye gave me no meat: I was thirsty, and ye gave me no drink: 43 I was a stranger, and ye took me not in: naked, and ye clothed me not: sick, and in prison, and ye visited me not. 44 Then shall they also answer him, saying, Lord, when saw we thee an hungred, or athirst, or a stranger, or naked, or sick, or in prison, and did not minister unto thee? 45 Then shall he answer them, saying, Verily I say unto you, Inasmuch as ye did it not to one of the least of these, ye did it not to me. 46 And these shall go away into everlasting punishment: but the righteous into life eternal."

Jesus fortifies that we will be processed, we will be separated based upon what we did and what we failed to do for the least of humanity. We will be judged against what we did and what we fail to do for others – the law of love calls us away from eternal retribution, consequence, and burn.

The threshing floor was a place of separation, where grain was processed for use – where the usable was separated from the unusable. God requires our growth, maturity, and usability – the previous verses warn that repentance is necessary, a turning point, a change – turning away from our proclivities toward the will of God.

Landscapes will change, nonproductive trees are purported to be cut down at the root. Grain will be processed and the Lord will fully purge the threshing floor – only the usably productive, only the good will survive.

We must expect to be processed and get ready through adherence to the way of God the Son – Jesus the redeemer through love. Work while you may – as faith without works is dead. Our belief in the love of God should motivate us to love as Christ loved, bringing healing and relief to the world. Loving our neighbor through service as prescribed by Jesus. We must be ready, expecting to be processed – evaluated by God. Hallelujah.

Focus again with me on verse 17 as it says "Whose fan is in his hand, and he will throughly purge his floor, and will gather the wheat into his garner; but the chaff he will burn with fire unquenchable."

We should **embrace the barn**, as a symbol of eternity with God. The passage should bring joy to our hearts as we can visually view the text as it illustrates an agriculturalist, selecting the best part and gathering the return on investment – collecting the good part. Some day when these troubling days have past, God is going to gather us close – put us in the garner, in the gathering sac, gathering us to be inseparable from God and each other as an agriculturalist gathers the harvest, processing grain suitable for collection into the barn.

In spite of the trials, temptations, and tribulations – God is preparing us for eternity. He is gathering us into the garner, gathering us into the glory of grace through the power of God's loving protection. I don't know about you, but I want to be gathered, I want to be positioned in the presence of God throughout all of eternity. I don't want to be left in the field or left on the threshing floor – I want to be gathered into the barn – called up to the city of God, to worship forever God the Father and God the Son through the indwelled power of God the Holy Spirit residing in us forever.

Oh, what precious thoughts – to be with God forever. We're going to have a good time, a great time – with Jesus, the King of Kings, called to the welcome table, a good time, oh what a great time. No more debts or worries, nothing but peace with God the source of all things and giver of all that's perfectly good – joy without end. No more troubles, no more cancer, no more tears, no more fears, hatred, separation, racism – I want to be gathered, collected for the barn, I want to be with Jesus! Oh, how I love Jesus – He first loved me with His own blood as God sacrificed God. Hallelujah!

Just as Jesus came to show us the way, help us to see the law of love in action – just as we are gathered, we must follow Christ into the process of seed, time, and harvest – we must follow Jesus to gather others through our personal and collective witness. Our testimony should shine the light so that others may grow and mature. We are challenged to take up the cross and work of Christ – loving others into the barn, the kingdom of God. We must mature to gather others, to cultivate, lead, and help others as we are motivated by love. We must be producers to avoid the burn, to avoid being cut at the root. We must serve as Christ served, bringing healing, peace, love, and compassion to the nations.

Sowing in the morning, sowing seeds of kindness,
Sowing in the noontide and the dewy eve;
Waiting for the harvest, and the time of reaping,
We shall come rejoicing, bringing in the sheaves.

Sowing in the sunshine, sowing in the shadows,
Fearing neither clouds nor winter's chilling breeze;
By and by the harvest, and the labor ended,
We shall come rejoicing, bringing in the sheaves.

Going forth with weeping, sowing for the Master,
Though the loss sustained our spirit often grieves;
When our weeping's over, He will bid us welcome,
We shall come rejoicing, bringing in the sheaves.

Bringing in the sheaves, bringing in the sheaves,
We shall come rejoicing, bringing in the sheaves,
Bringing in the sheaves, bringing in the sheaves,
We shall come rejoicing, bringing in the sheaves.

We must reject the burn, embracing the barn by expecting to be processed, embracing the barn, but finally focus with me again on verse 17 reading Luke 3:17, "Whose fan is in his hand, and he will throughly purge his floor, and will gather the wheat into his garner; but the chaff he will burn with fire unquenchable."

We must **reject the burn**, as failure to grow and mature will result in separation from the peaceful presence of God. The scripture presents a future of unquenchable fire for the chaff — for the unusable, for the nonproductive. Don't wait to allow the power of God the Holy Spirit to prepare you for threshing. We should be cleansed through Baptism, the cleansing flood that confirms our commitment to obedience as Christ leads us – then we must be baptized by the spiritual fire of God the Holy Spirit. The burn of the Holy Spirit prevents the burning fires of eternal consequence.

Coming now to Thee O Christ my Lord,
Trusting only in Thy precious word
Let my humble pray'r to Thee be heard
And send a great revival in my soul

Send the Holy Spirit now within
Burning out the dross and guilt of sin
Let Thy mighty works of grace begin
Oh, send a great revival in my soul
Send a great revival, Lord, in me
Help me that I may rejoice in Thee
Give me strength to win the victory
And send a great revival in my soul

Help me go for Thee, dear Lord, today
To some lonely soul that's gone astray
Help me lead them in the homeward way
Oh, send a great revival in my soul.

Send a great revival in my soul
Send a great revival in my soul
Let the Holy Spirit come and take control
And send a great revival in my soul.

We need the power of God to lead us away from eternal doom to eternal joy, from destruction to delight, from persecution to power, from violence to victory, from burning to beauty – I wonder is there anybody here that knows God will turn it around. We worship God, our God – a turn it around God, what the enemy tried to use to destroy you, God can turn it around and save you. We need to reject the burn and embrace the beauty of God's gathering – collecting all the saints of God, the family of God to worship forever without end.

Christ died to save you, to free us from eternal damnation, Christ died for love – what or who could separate us from the love of God in Christ Jesus. Oh, nothing can separate us, God's children from love. Hold on to the love of God with hope, peace, and firm faith. God is working, can't you feel God the Holy Spirit working it out for us through confirmation of the truth, the word of God, can't you see the scriptures unfolding before us. The enemy is busy, but God is powerful – supreme over all.

Take up the cross and follow Jesus, embrace the example of Christ and devote your life to the collective, living upon the way of God the Son. You are called to love, born to grow and mature – existing to please God through your purpose to love. Work while you may before the day of judgment when God will call and we must all answer. Someday every knee shall bow and every tongue confess that Jesus is Lord.

Oh, "when did we" was the answer
The hour of fear and trembling
Before God in need of Christ resembling.

The sheep from the goat was the way
The Shepherd seeks the pure
The light of judgment in that day.

Will you be ready with your work all done
The least and lost await your service
God the Father, Son, and Spirit have already won.

THE CHURCH NEEDS WATER

SCRIPTURE

John 2:1-11 And the third day there was a marriage in Cana of Galilee; and the mother of Jesus was there: 2 And both Jesus was called, and his disciples, to the marriage. 3 And when they wanted wine, the mother of Jesus saith unto him, They have no wine. 4 Jesus saith unto her, Woman, what have I to do with thee? mine hour is not yet come. 5 His mother saith unto the servants, Whatsoever he saith unto you, do it. 6 And there were set there six waterpots of stone, after the manner of the purifying of the Jews, containing two or three firkins apiece. 7 Jesus saith unto them, Fill the waterpots with water. And they filled them up to the brim. 8 And he saith unto them, Draw out now, and bear unto the governor of the feast. And they bare it. 9 When the ruler of the feast had tasted the water that was made wine, and knew not whence it was: (but the servants which drew the water knew;) the governor of the feast called the bridegroom, 10 And saith unto him, Every man at the beginning doth set forth good wine; and when men have well drunk, then that which is worse: but thou hast kept the good wine until now. 11 This beginning of miracles did Jesus in Cana of Galilee, and manifested forth his glory; and his disciples believed on him.

OUTLINE

1. Because of Shortage v3
2. Sometime We Must Act Beyond Time v4

3. The Servants Know v9
4. Beyond World Order v9-10
5. The Disciples Believe v11

MESSAGE

John chapter 2 reveals the first recorded miracle presented by God the Son – Jesus, as many of us are familiar with the miraculous turning of water into wine during the wedding feast at Cana of Galilee.

The narrative directs us to understand that Jesus is attending a wedding reception where His mother and possibly other family members are attending. The host family ran out of wine for the celebratory feast and customarily this was beyond unacceptable and embarrassing. The family would have been disgraced, talked about, and possibly socially segregated had they run out of wine.

With the heart of compassion, it seems that Mary the mother of Christ - compelled her Son, Jesus to do something about the shortage of wine. Long story short, Jesus calls for water - the servants bring water and Jesus turns it into wine.

Water seems to be one of the purest, cleanest, refreshing resources that God provided for us from the foundation of the Earth. In short, think about it - they brought nothing to Jesus, they brought flavorless water that Jesus turned into favored wine.

Although water is necessary for life it's not flavorful, attractive, or spectacular compared to other beverages. In fact, water is more the base model, the building block to other beverages.

You know that most of us would prefer a Pepsi, Coke, or Red Kool-Aid, by the way, red is a flavor. Others have to have coffee before starting the day or even put a smile on their faces.

I wonder is there anybody here that knows God can turn it around, taking the base and making it complex. God can add flavor to the flavorless, sparkle to the unspectacular, glory to gloom, and life to the lethargic. Jesus turned water into wine, lack into lingering celebration, problems into praise. That wedding reception was about to be disastrous, but Jesus fixed it.

It didn't take much, just water. In fact, Jesus didn't even call for clean water. The investment was nominally simplistic yet abundant – it don't take much for Jesus to make a way out of no way. The church needs to return to a place of deep faith and simple dependence on God to fix it, understanding with God all things are possible. We simply need to be obedient – and watch God work.

The church needs water, the church needs resources that depend on God, expecting the miraculous. The church needs to turn toward God and surrender what we have in order to experience the excellency of God's resource management – as little becomes much in the Master's hands.

Look with me at John 2:3 it says, "And when they wanted wine, the mother of Jesus saith unto him, They have no wine."

The church needs water **because of shortage**, as the world seems to run out of compassion, love, and peace just as wine ran out at the feast. Humanitarian resources run short as compassion is often traded for the tenants of greed. We must realize that people are hurting in need of God's salvific work flowing though the church, as our collective should present a place where love meets need.

There is a shortage of compassion toward children, women, the poor, the sick, addicts, the hungry, homeless, and helpless. The world seems to be running low on love.

The church is challenged to take up the cross of Christ and follow. Follow the Savior to care for others, giving ourselves to please God. Following to turn water into wine – sadness to happiness, sickness to wellness, pain to joy, following Christ to meet needs, yes, we are challenged to follow Jesus into the miraculous.

Christ said that the harvest is plentiful but the laborers are few. Nevertheless, just as Jesus turned water into wine – God can take a few, a remnant and do the work of companies, battalions, the work of armies. God didn't save us by committee or crowd – we're saved through the love of one that gave up life for us, as God the Son was sacrificed at Calvary. One man can change anything through the power of God – even in the shadow of Dr. Martin Luther King Jr. Day, we can embrace the power of a few persevering while empowered by God.

The church needs water – we need to give our little to God and celebrate the movement of our divine creator. There may be a shortage for the world, but look up and see the windows of Heaven open with abundance for us. Praise God, we're beautifully blessed.

Focus with me on John 2:4 it reads, "Jesus saith unto her, Woman, what have I to do with thee? mine hour is not yet come."

Sometimes we must act beyond time, holding to faith – realizing that there are times when God will work against time. Don't ever forget God can do whatever God wants to do. We can't do it – but God can. The Lord can stop time, move it forward, speed it up, slow it down, or even eliminate it.

Yes, God can do anything – you may think it's too soon or too late – we may think it's impossible, but God can grow lilies in a valley, pave streets with gold, make ice catch on fire, part the Red Sea, close lions' mouths, and God raised Jesus from the grave – all in the word of God. The church needs water – we mustn't limit God. Time, space, and matter are never factors with God. There is nothing too hard for God. We often struggle when the deadline is past, when we seemingly run out of resources – paying attention to time, plans, clocks, calendars, and schedules.

We don't have to fret over the when, as long as we know God is working – as God may not come on our time, but we can be assured that God will always be on time. God can and often will move when you least expect. When we stop trying to figure it out and let God work it out, everything will be alright.

The church needs water, the faith to believe that God can, when all the evidence seems like nobody can. Just then situations are transformed and faith in Jesus makes water become wine that we may go from sorrow to celebration.

Look with me now at John 2:5 it reads, "His mother saith unto the servants, Whatsoever he saith unto you, do it."

The church needs water as a symbol of faith so that **the servants know** – as the water brings the knowledge of Christ to the servants. We should be witnesses to the world that God is still in the miracle business. When all seems lost, when resources are spent, after foreclosure, repossession, and bankruptcy – God can bring blessings to the bruised. Every season and situation belong to God, and the world is watching to see you react – waiting on your testimony to motivate them to join the great family, to embrace Jesus, to seek the sustaining substance of salvation.

We are the salt, indwelled with the Holy Spirit to preserve others through the presence of God. Presenting faith through actions and not just words. Continually allowing God's perfect work to shine through us as we follow Christ through the scriptures under the authority of God the Holy Spirit.

Humanity needs love and love is more doing than talking. We don't become credible with words, we become trustworthy through actions. The fact that the servants witnessed Jesus should remind the church that God's work is not some big mystery to be kept secret from the world.

The Gospel is good news to be shared with all nations from sea to sea, valley to mountain, and through the planes. The old Christmas melody says, "Go tell it on the mountain over the hills and everywhere!" Yes, we are challenged to let the servants, the captives, the stranger – yes to let the world know that Jesus the Savior still works miracles.
You don't have to look far to find a miracle, this church is full of miracles – every seat is filled with a miracle. If nothing else, the Lord woke us up this morning and brought us here to worship, pray, and praise our great active God. Hallelujah, Hosanna to the Lamb! The church needs water, faith so the world may find life in God.

Focus now on John 2:9-10 as the passage reads, "When the ruler of the feast had tasted the water that was made wine, and knew not whence it was: (but the servants which drew the water knew;) the governor of the feast called the bridegroom, 10 And saith unto him, Every man at the beginning doth set forth good wine; and when men have well drunk, then that which is worse: but thou hast kept the good wine until now."

The church needs water to go **beyond world order**, after the ruler of the feast tasted the wine made from water – because serving the best for last was outside of the norm, it was opposite of the world's way to serve the best last – to decline the quality over time.

God has empowered us to move beyond world order. We don't have to be like the world, we can reject greed, hatred, unrest, and sinister survival. We can be wise like serpents, yet harmless like doves – living beyond world order.

When everybody else is slacking, backsliding, and neglecting responsibility – we can kick it up a notch, give even better in the heat of the day.

Rejoicing in recession, praising in the midst of pessimism, embracing triumph through terror. There has never been a time when the Lord has let us down. When the world convicts and condemns – we must learn to forgive and forget. When the world says leave the weak, we love the least and the lost. When the world waters down we add substance – always taking the highest road toward the highest standard to represent God with grace, peace, joy, and unconditional love.

I John 4:1-9 puts it like this, "Beloved, believe not every spirit, but try the spirits whether they are of God: because many false prophets are gone out into the world. 2 Hereby know ye the Spirit of God: Every spirit that confesseth that Jesus Christ is come in the flesh is of God: 3 And every spirit that confesseth not that Jesus Christ is come in the flesh is not of God: and this is that spirit of antichrist, whereof ye have heard that it should come; and even now already is it in the world. 4 Ye are of God, little children, and have overcome them: because greater is he that is in you, than he that is in the world. 5 They are of the world: therefore speak they of the world, and the world heareth them. 6 We are of God: he that knoweth God heareth us; he that is not of God heareth not us. Hereby know we the spirit of truth, and the spirit of error. 7 Beloved, let us love one another: for love is of God; and every one that loveth is born of God, and knoweth God. 8 He that loveth not knoweth not God; for God is love. 9 In this was manifested the love of God toward us, because that God sent his only begotten Son into the world, that we might live through him." The church doesn't follow the world order, we follow God's order.

Look now at John 2:11 is says, "This beginning of miracles did Jesus in Cana of Galilee, and manifested forth his glory; and his disciples believed on him." The church needs water so that **the disciples believe** – as our faith grows strong while in the presence of God. The more we watch God, experiencing divine actions, looking into the face of love increases our belief.

We are prepared for the journey; we gain greater witness when we spend time embracing the miraculous way of God. Expecting the miraculous, expecting water to turn to wine, the impossible becoming possible, creating a way out of no way.

Defying doctors, lawyers, debt collectors – knowing that God works when we bring our water faith, our water faith – small faith, mustard seed faith, knowing that God knows we don't have much, but with just a little God will work out the rest. I dare you to take a step, because you'll see God make many more, dare you to just step out on faith with some water faith, base model, flavorless, nothing to celebrate here – watch God turn your trial and temptation to triumph. They thought the celebration was just about over, the wine was running low – hmmm, I wonder is there anybody here that just stopped enjoying life. Worried because your wine has run out, worried because it seems your celebration is over, party ended, seemingly nothing to be happy about.

Well I stopped by to tell you that all you need is a little faith, some water faith – Oh, don't you know that God can and will keep us, love us, bless us, just walking in the presence of God. Your wine is low, but God! You been depressed, but God, sad – but God. Yes, God preforms miracles.

I know God does, and if God never turned water into wine again – that thing God did on Calvary is enough. Jesus, God the Son died and shed blood to redeem us – now we celebrate with the wine of Communion, knowing that God transformed our sin and sorrow to eternal joy and life.

Is there anybody here ready to present your water to God, bringing what you have with faith that God will transform your situation? Oh, out on the Hill, God sacrificed God to save us, to love us – yes when love appeared the world order crucified, but God lifted.

Jesus bled, suffered, died, and was buried. Maybe some thought the wine had run out and celebration was over – yet early on the third day, Christ rose from the grave with power and life. You don't need much – just a little faith, just a step, water will work, simple faith works with God, as God will work out the rest if we give what we have, just simple faith, simply come to the cross and embrace the emptiness knowing that Christ is risen. That Christ is risen – anybody know that Christ is risen?

As Christopher M. Rice penned:

Weak and wounded sinner
Lost and left to die
O, raise your head, for love is passing by
Come to Jesus
Come to Jesus
Come to Jesus and live!

Now your burden's lifted
And carried far away
And precious blood has washed away the stain, so
Sing to Jesus
Sing to Jesus
Sing to Jesus and live!

And like a newborn baby
Don't be afraid to crawl
And remember when you walk
Sometimes we fall, so
Fall on Jesus
Fall on Jesus
Fall on Jesus and live!

Sometimes the way is lonely
And steep and filled with pain
So if your sky is dark and pours the rain, then
Cry to Jesus
Cry to Jesus
Cry to Jesus and live!

O, and when the love spills over
And music fills the night
And when you can't contain your joy inside, then
Dance for Jesus
Dance for Jesus
Dance for Jesus and live!

And with your final heartbeat
Kiss the world goodbye

Then go in peace, and laugh on Glory's side, and
Fly to Jesus
Fly to Jesus
Fly to Jesus and live!

THE POWER OF PREACHING

SCRIPTURE

Luke 4:14-21 And Jesus returned in the power of the Spirit into Galilee: and there went out a fame of him through all the region round about. 15 And he taught in their synagogues, being glorified of all. 16 And he came to Nazareth, where he had been brought up: and, as his custom was, he went into the synagogue on the sabbath day, and stood up for to read. 17 And there was delivered unto him the book of the prophet Esaias. And when he had opened the book, he found the place where it was written, 18 The Spirit of the Lord is upon me, because he hath anointed me to preach the gospel to the poor; he hath sent me to heal the brokenhearted, to preach deliverance to the captives, and recovering of sight to the blind, to set at liberty them that are bruised, 19 To preach the acceptable year of the Lord. 20 And he closed the book, and he gave it again to the minister, and sat down. And the eyes of all them that were in the synagogue were fastened on him. 21 And he began to say unto them, This day is this scripture fulfilled in your ears.

OUTLINE

1. Preaching Heals v18
2. Preaching Delivers v18
3. Preaching Recovers v18
4. Preaching Liberates v18
5. Preaching Glorifies the Gospel v18

MESSAGE

According to current research and surveys church attendance is down, as membership declines around the country. There are a number of people that have abandoned the church for alternatives to include simply sleeping in on Sunday.

I would contend that the decline is directly connected with the state of humanity and our community – as there are several benefits to attending church. If for no other reason, the Bible admonishes us to attend.

Hebrews 10:22-25 says, "Let us draw near with a true heart in full assurance of faith, having our hearts sprinkled from an evil conscience, and our bodies washed with pure water. 23 Let us hold fast the profession of our faith without wavering; 24 And let us consider one another to provoke unto love and to good works: 25 Not forsaking the assembling of ourselves together, as the manner of some is; but exhorting one another: and so much the more, as ye see the day approaching."

Among the number of benefits received through attending church is the power of preaching. When we come to church, we are able to join with other believers as we help each other in the knowledge of faith in God, through the power of Father, Son, and Holy Spirit. Primarily central to all benefits is the sermon – as there is power in preaching. Let's focus on the benefit of preaching, the power of preaching.

Look with me at Luke 4:18, it reads, "The Spirit of the Lord is upon me, because he hath anointed me to preach the gospel to the poor; he hath sent me to heal the brokenhearted, to preach deliverance to the captives, and recovering of sight to the blind, to set at liberty them that are bruised,"

Preaching heals, as we continually need a remedy for the disease of transgression and the bacteria of sin. In Luke chapter 5 Jesus allows us to embrace the wisdom that those of us who are sick need a physician, we need the saving power of Christ to redeem us through the power of repentance.

The way and will of God are that we be made whole, that we secure health both physically and spiritually. Yes, we should seek holistic health which begins from the inside out. When God's word indwells our heart, mind, and soul we may embrace healing through the restorative power of God with God's word.

The Bible says in Hebrews 4:11-12, "Let us labour therefore to enter into that rest, lest any man fall after the same example of unbelief. 12 For the word of God is quick, and powerful, and sharper than any twoedged sword, piercing even to the dividing asunder of soul and spirit, and of the joints and marrow, and is a discerner of the thoughts and intents of the heart."

The power of preaching brings healing, as the word of God has the power of surgical precision. Although we often seek immediate gratification – there are times when suffering is necessary to wellness, we must know Christ in the fellowship of His suffering in order to fully embrace Jesus in the power of His resurrection. Sometime the pain of surgery is necessary for healing, God's word is sharper than any two-edged sword, piercing even to the dividing asunder of soul and spirit, and of the joints and marrow, and is a discerner of the thoughts and intents of the heart. Unlike humans, God can discern or prognosticate and diagnose even our thoughts and intents.

Yes, God's word - sharp as a surgeon's scalpel, cutting through everything, whether doubt or defense, laying us open to listen and obey. Nothing and no one is impervious to God's word. We can't get away from it — no matter what. God's word – the power of preaching brings healing to a sin sick world.
Focus again with me on verse 18, as it says,

"The Spirit of the Lord is upon me, because he hath anointed me to preach the gospel to the poor; he hath sent me to heal the brokenhearted, to preach deliverance to the captives, and recovering of sight to the blind, to set at liberty them that are bruised,"

Preaching delivers, the word deliverance and in this passage the word deliverance in the original Greek is "aphesis" – which is also an English word that means to release an unstressed vowel at the beginning of a word like transforming the word around to round. Rudimentarily connoting a release or to let go. In the original text this word that comes to us as deliverance means to forgive and let go, to release from bondage or imprisonment. God delivers – forgives, pardons our sin – letting them go as if they had never been committed, remitted from penalty.

Think of all the stuff you've ever done, now think if it was all still on your record. All the stuff some people may know and all the bad things that only God knows – now praise God for deliverance. Aren't you happy that God delivers, that the power of preaching confirms our deliverance? God loves us so much that the Bible puts it like this in Micah 7:18-19, "Who is a God like unto thee, that pardoneth iniquity, and passeth by the transgression of the remnant of his heritage? he retaineth not his anger for ever, because he delighteth in mercy. 19 He will turn again, he will have compassion upon us; he will subdue our iniquities; and thou wilt cast all their sins into the depths of the sea."

The power of preaching delivers through the word manifested in the presence of God the Holy Spirit. Somebody ought to say amen in this church followed by hallelujah toward God – we've been delivered. Examine again Luke 4:18, "The Spirit of the Lord is upon me, because he hath anointed me to preach the gospel to the poor; he hath sent me to heal the brokenhearted, to preach deliverance to the captives, and recovering of sight to the blind, to set at liberty them that are bruised,"

Preaching recovers, as that which was dead can live again just as God's presence recovered dry bones in

Ezekiel chapter 37, just as God raised Jesus from the dead. The text leads us to understand that those who were blind can recover sight through the power of God.

God's word is a lamp to our feet and a light to our path according to Psalm 119. We so desperately need God's word to see our way in life. Personal Bible study is essential to the Christian lifestyle. Walking with God's word while guided and enriched through God the Holy Spirit. We need the power of preaching to turn on the light that we might see the way of Christ.

Amazing Grace, How sweet the sound
That saved a wretch like me
I once was lost, but now am found
T'was blind but now I see

When your way is dark and dreary, seek the light of the Gospel, the way of Jesus – there is great light in the word of God. Challenged yet prepared for the journey through the direction of scripture, knowing that the Bible is right.

I wish we had some witnesses here today! Embracing God for dear life – understanding that we need God, faith in God to know that Jesus is risen. We must fellowship through the church as a testimony to God's work through faith – realizing that Jesus heals the blind, bringing recovery to our deepest darkest place!

Joyful, all you nations, rise.

Jesus, the light of the world.
Join the triumph of the skies.
Jesus, the light of the world.

Hail, the heaven-born Prince of Peace!
Jesus, the light of the world.
Hail, the Sun of Righteousness!
Jesus, the light of the world.

We'll walk in the light, beautiful light.
Come where the dewdrops of mercy shine bright.
O, shine all around us by day and by night.
Jesus, the light of the world.

Andrae Crouch wrote the theme song for the 1980's television show *Amen*, a song entitled *Shine on Me* – I certainly hope that the Lord will answer the petition melodically set to music.

Turn on the lights from heaven, Lord Shine on me, turn on the lights from heaven, Lord, shine on me. Turn on the lights and put me on the right road, help me find my way. Lord, turn on the lights from heaven. Lord, shine on me, shine on me. The power of preaching leads us to recovery, yes God recovers our sight.

Focus again on Luke 4:18 as it says, "The Spirit of the Lord is upon me, because he hath anointed me to preach the gospel to the poor; he hath sent me to heal the brokenhearted, to preach deliverance to the captives, and recovering of sight to the blind, to set at liberty them that are bruised,"

Preaching liberates, the power of preaching liberates the bruised – we need God's power to liberate us after our lives have been bruised, crushed, shattered by trials and tribulations. There are times when we feel like motherless children, when the storms are raging and we're wrecked by the angry seas of time.

Life got you down, gloom and despair on every hand – sick, sad, betrayed, almost destroyed, and crushed by obstacles? Well, God liberates us to breathe again – even when crushed, even after disaster, we can breathe again. Bruised but not trapped, crushed but not without relief, devastated but not destroyed.

God brings liberty even in the midst of our trials – we must learn to lean and depend on Jesus, we must trust God when we cannot trace God with faith to know that everything will be alright. Liberated prisoners to the word of God, wrapped, tied, tangled, swaddled in God's unconditionally sweet love. Glory to God! Glory to God! Glory to God!
The power of preaching: Preaching heals, preaching delivers, preaching recovers, and preaching liberates.

Lest I hold you too long in the shadow of noon focus again on Luke 4:18, "The Spirit of the Lord is upon me, because he hath anointed me to preach the gospel to the poor; he hath sent me to heal the brokenhearted, to preach deliverance to the captives, and recovering of sight to the blind, to set at liberty them that are bruised,"

Preaching glorifies the Gospel, the Good News about Jesus – Judah's Lion, the strength of Israel, Deliverer, Strong Tower, Miraculous, Mighty Healer, Way Maker, Liberator – somebody ought to just call His name, Jesus! Anybody love Jesus? There is good news for the sick, captive, chained, poor, brokenhearted, blind, and bruised – Jesus paid the price for our redemption.

God the Son makes it possible for us to fall and get back up again. Preaching is solely possible because of God's sacrifice for us, God's love for us – isn't that good news, Gospel to the perishing.

Christ surrendered life upon the cross to save us – good news, the Gospel. Jesus bled, suffered, and died to justify us forever – good news. Nevertheless, there is better news, Christ was buried, was buried, was buried – but got up from the grave with victory over sin, death, and the grave! Good News, the Gospel – aren't you glad for Jesus?

How many know that if God never does anything else, God is worthy of all our praise. God alone is worthy – you ought to thank and praise God right now! But there is ever better news – someday the sky shall part as Jesus returns to collect us that we may live with God forever!

Recorded in John chapter 14, Jesus said, "Let not your heart be troubled: ye believe in God, believe also in me. 2 In my Father's house are many mansions: if it were not so, I would have told you. I go to prepare a place for you. 3 And if I go and prepare a place for you, I will come again, and receive you unto myself; that where I am, there ye may be also."

Anybody here excited about the Gospel, excited about the Good News, excited that Jesus is coming back again?

How to reach the masses, men of every birth,
For an answer, Jesus gave the key:
"And I, if I be lifted up from the earth,
Will draw all men unto Me."
Oh! the world is hungry for the Living Bread,
Lift the Savior up for them to see;
Trust Him, and do not doubt the words that He said, "I'll draw all men unto Me."

Don't exalt the preacher, don't exalt the pew,
Preach the Gospel simple, full, and free;
Prove Him and you will find that promise is true, "I'll draw all men unto Me."

Lift Him up by living as a Christian ought,
Let the world in you the Savior see;
Then men will gladly follow Him Who once taught,
"I'll draw all men unto Me."
Lift Him up, lift Him up;
Still He speaks from eternity:
"And I, if I be lifted up from the earth,
Will draw all men unto Me."

PLANNED PARENTHOOD

SCRIPTURE

Jeremiah 1:4-10 Then the word of the LORD came unto me, saying, 5 Before I formed thee in the belly I knew thee; and before thou camest forth out of the womb I sanctified thee, and I ordained thee a prophet unto the nations. 6 Then said I, Ah, Lord GOD! behold, I cannot speak: for I am a child. 7 But the LORD said unto me, Say not, I am a child: for thou shalt go to all that I shall send thee, and whatsoever I command thee thou shalt speak. 8 Be not afraid of their faces: for I am with thee to deliver thee, saith the LORD. 9 Then the LORD put forth his hand, and touched my mouth. And the LORD said unto me, Behold, I have put my words in thy mouth. 10 See, I have this day set thee over the nations and over the kingdoms, to root out, and to pull down, and to destroy, and to throw down, to build, and to plant.

OUTLINE

1. God Made Us v5
2. God Separates Us v5
3. God Approves Us v5.

MESSAGE

Unfortunately, nearly a million abortions took place within the United States last year and nearly one million suicides globally.

People are hurting, humanity is in pain. The diseases of depression, utter sadness, and stress seem to envelope our society like stank on a skunk – as we seem marked by malodourous negative emotions.
Amidst the casualties of suicide and abortion, teenagers are extremely vulnerable members of our population. We are challenged to embrace solutions to these final actions used to solve temporary issues, with faith and hope while embracing our planned purpose. We were not created haphazardly without thought, as God planned us with great purpose – planned parenthood.

It seems that one of the greatest antidotes to suicide and abortion is the reality of purpose, embracing that God created us for a reason, God lovingly has sustained us that we may realize, materialize, and maximize our purpose.

We surely find a great example of God's process in the prophecy of Jeremiah. The Book opens with a biography allowing us to peep into the history of Jeremiah to the extent that we may enjoy God at work during our formation, before birth and womb – as the writer acknowledges the hand of God in life even before birth.

God has a plan for us even before we utter our first crying breath. God is a great parent, the ultimate provider, protector, and eternal planner. Let us focus on the scripture this morning as we gain inspiration, motivation, and hope for life through purpose.

Focus with me on Jeremiah 1:1-9 as it reads, "The words of Jeremiah the son of Hilkiah, of the priests that were in Anathoth in the land of Benjamin: 2 To whom the word of the LORD came in the days of Josiah the son of Amon king of Judah, in the thirteenth year of his reign. 3 It came also in the days of Jehoiakim the son of Josiah king of Judah, unto the end of the eleventh year of Zedekiah the son of Josiah king of Judah, unto the carrying away of Jerusalem captive in the fifth month. 4 Then the word of the LORD came unto me, saying, 5 Before I formed thee in the belly I knew thee; and before thou camest forth out of the womb I sanctified thee, and I ordained thee a prophet unto the nations. 6 Then said I, Ah, Lord GOD! behold, I cannot speak: for I am a child. 7 But the LORD said unto me, Say not, I am a child: for thou shalt go to all that I shall send thee, and whatsoever I command thee thou shalt speak. 8 Be not afraid of their faces: for I am with thee to deliver thee, saith the LORD. 9 Then the LORD put forth his hand, and touched my mouth. And the LORD said unto me, Behold, I have put my words in thy mouth."

God made us, as the Psalmist says in Psalms 139:13-14 "For thou hast possessed my reins: thou hast covered me in my mother's womb. 14 I will praise thee; for I am fearfully and wonderfully made: marvellous are thy works; and that my soul knoweth right well."

We are wonderfully and marvelously made by God our creator, the great architect of all ages. God stepped from behind the drape of nowhere, onto the platform of nothing, in the midst of a place called no place – and before there was a when or a where God miraculously made something out of nothing, made the world out of nowhere – parting waters from land.

Turned on the sun and moon to light the Earth before flame or electricity formed in the mind of humanity. Sprinkled the night sky with stars while completing the day with pillows of white clouds, God sprinkled the Earth with green grass and trees pointing toward heavens greatness. God, our God – made the butterflies glide and the grasshoppers lunge from grassy fields. God directed fish to defy oxygen and swim through chilly waters – God is a way maker, God created something out of nothing all to support the dust that the Lord created to walk and breathe through great architectural vision, power, and authority.

God created us, God fashioned us after God's image, talk about a plan! Planned Parenthood, you didn't get here by accident, we were planned on purpose, and we get to stay here because God loves us!

We must remain committed to the God that is within us to reach for hope, to spark the faith to keep on keeping on. As the song writer penned – sometimes you have to encourage yourself – stirring up the gift that is within you, allowing God the Holy Spirit to motivate your heart, soul, and mind toward the joy that only God can give.

Trusting God is the only way - Sometimes you have to encourage yourself. Donald Lawrence wrote,

"Sometimes you have to speak victory during the test, and no matter how you feel speak the word and you will be healed - speak over yourself, encourage yourself in the Lord. Sometimes you have to speak the word over yourself."

The pressure is all around but God is a present help. The enemy created walls but remember giants, they do fall - speak over yourself, encourage yourself in the Lord.

Life can hurt you so 'til you feel there's nothing left, no matter how you feel.

Speak over yourself and be encouraged!
Speak over yourself and encourage yourself in the Lord! You should take a moment right now just to say, "I'm encouraged!" Praise the Lord we are made by God – for that we should be thankful, with grace, hope, and Holy Ghost power to move on beyond our stress, pain, and depression.

Faith to know that we can do all that God says we can do. Faith to keep on living beyond suicidal feelings, faith to believe that we can take care of our babies if God blesses us with the gift of children – if God gives, then God provides! God made us, God will sustain us, God will take care of us – we are products of planned parenthood, the Lord planned us!

I don't know about you, but I'm running for my life, understanding like Jerimiah that God planned me before

I was formed in my mother's belly. If anybody asks you, tell them for me that I'm running for my life – still here because of God's grace, God's mercy, yes, the Lord made me and I'm still here because God has kept me. Praise God, worthy is the name, worthy to be praised, hallelujah for the Lamb, hallelujah for life.

God not only made us, God knows us – the scripture tells us that God formed us and God knows us! God knows both your joys and concerns – all our complaints and praise reports have been registered with the home office. God knows us! If God's eye is on the sparrow, then surely God watches after us. You are not alone, you are not without a friend, confidante, comforter, and eternal love.

God knows us, down to the number of hairs on our head – when you think you're having a bad hair day, just remember that God knows how many hairs are out of place and God still loves you. God knows all about us and still there is not one thing that can separate us from the love of God! The Lord's eye is on the sparrow and I know God surely watches after us.

Look again with me at Jeremiah 1:5, "Before I formed thee in the belly I knew thee; and before thou camest forth out of the womb I sanctified thee, and I ordained thee a prophet unto the nations."

God separates us, just as Jerimiah was sanctified, separated even before he came out the womb. Sanctified, separated into the family of God. We are wonderfully made by God and we are sanctified for service, set aside, made holy, consecrated with purpose.

I Peter 1:13-20 says, "Wherefore gird up the loins of your mind, be sober, and hope to the end for the grace that is to be brought unto you at the revelation of Jesus Christ; 14 As obedient children, not fashioning yourselves according to the former lusts in your ignorance: 15 But as he which hath called you is holy, so be ye holy in all manner of conversation; 16 Because it is written, Be ye holy; for I am holy. 17 And if ye call on the Father, who without respect of persons judgeth according to every man's work, pass the time of your sojourning here in fear: 18 Forasmuch as ye know that ye were not redeemed with corruptible things, as silver and gold, from your vain conversation received by tradition from your fathers; 19 But with the precious blood of Christ, as of a lamb without blemish and without spot: 20 Who verily was foreordained before the foundation of the world, but was manifest in these last times for you,"

Jesus died. God sacrificed God to bring us into the Holy Family – separating us to be holy as our Heavenly parent is holy. Calvary, activates our heavenly birth certificate and makes us citizens of the Kingdom of God, but more than just residents, we are members of the King's family, members of the royal priesthood. According to I Peter 2:9 we are a chosen generation, a royal priesthood, a holy nation, a peculiar people. It goes on to admonish that we should praise God who has called us out of darkness into his marvelous light!

The price that God paid through the blood of Christ is too great for us to end our purpose, terminate our contract through suicide, or destroy the opportunity of new life through abortion.

God paid for your life, shed blood to save us and give us purpose – sustaining us through an everlasting covenant, maintained through the presence of the Holy Spirit.

But it didn't just happen, God chose to make you family when you were formed and fashioned. We should be happy about that – glad to be passing from darkness to light. Often acting like adopted children, trying to get used to being in the family of God. Stumbling along the way, in trouble, and outside of the family custom – but every day is a better day, as the loving care of God continually brings us closer to Christ.

We should be glad for Jesus, glad that God has separated us through sacrifice and love. We're not worthy, we're favored, chosen by God through the power of love. I wonder is there anybody here that knows we are separated to be like Christ through the example and humility of God the Son – you don't know like I know what He's done for me!

The Lord has done too much for us to push away purpose, to end it all in one final stroke – we must push on, keep on keeping on, God created you for a reason!

Hebrews 2:10-17 says it like this, "For it became him, for whom are all things, and by whom are all things, in bringing many sons unto glory, to make the captain of their salvation perfect through sufferings. 11 For both he that sanctifieth and they who are sanctified are all of one: for which cause he is not ashamed to call them brethren, 12 Saying, I will declare thy name unto my brethren, in the midst of the church will I sing praise unto thee. 13 And again, I will put my trust in him. And again, Behold I and the children which God hath given me. 14 Forasmuch then as the children are partakers of flesh and blood, he also himself likewise took part of the same; that through death he might destroy him that had the power of death, that is, the devil; 15 And deliver them who through fear of death were all their lifetime subject to bondage. 16 For verily he took not on him the nature of angels; but he took on him the seed of Abraham. 17 Wherefore in all things it behoved him to be made like unto his brethren, that he might be a merciful and faithful high priest in things pertaining to God, to make reconciliation for the sins of the people."

We didn't get in on the family our looks, money, abilities, gifts, talents, temperance, or any human movement – we here on Jesus' account! All of our righteousness is but filthy rags, yet Jesus calls us to be brothers and sisters, we are family with Jesus! Children of the King, life will always get better for us – I'm so glad trouble don't last always.

Alas! and did my Savior bleed
And did my Sov'reign die?

*Would He devote that sacred head
For such a worm as I?*

*Was it for crimes that I had done
He groaned upon the tree?
Amazing pity! grace unknown!
And love beyond degree!*

*Well might the sun in darkness hide
And shut his glories in,
When Christ, the mighty Maker died,
For man the creature's sin.*

*Thus might I hide my blushing face
While His dear cross appears,
Dissolve my heart in thankfulness,
And melt my eyes to tears.*

*But drops of grief can ne'er repay
The debt of love I owe:
Here, Lord, I give myself away,
'Tis all that I can do.*

At the cross, at the cross where I first saw the light, and the burden of my heart rolled away, it was there by faith I received my sight, and now I am happy all the day!

Look again with me at Jeremiah 1:5, "Before I formed thee in the belly I knew thee; and before thou camest forth out of the womb I sanctified thee, and I ordained thee a prophet unto the nations."

God made us, God separates us, and **God approves us**, we are ordained to do the work that we have been called to do. God indwells us through the Holy Spirit and gifts us with the power of the scriptures to empower us for the work of Christ.

2 Timothy 2:11-15 says, "It is a faithful saying: For if we be dead with him, we shall also live with him: 12 If we suffer, we shall also reign with him: if we deny him, he also will deny us: 13 If we believe not, yet he abideth faithful: he cannot deny himself. 14 Of these things put them in remembrance, charging them before the Lord that they strive not about words to no profit, but to the subverting of the hearers. 15 Study to shew thyself approved unto God, a workman that needeth not to be ashamed, rightly dividing the word of truth."

God approves us through the truth of God's word. We must be students of the word, students of the actions, will, and way of God. If we are in the family of God, then we've got to act like Jesus – God the Son leads us to life, leads us to love not suicide or abortion.

Even when others brought death, even when others wanted to kill – Jesus ushered in life. Yes, life for us all. They hung Him high and stretched Him wide, then buried Him low in the grave – yet life prevailed and Jesus arose from the grave.

I stopped by to encourage you today to keep on living in spite of humanity's hatred, support life and not death – God is a creator and sustainer of life, be holy as God is holy, come on in the family and follow our Heavenly Parent. We were planned, yes planned parenthood – life on purpose.

When sadness, depression, deception, and defeat get you down – hold firm to faith, knowing that if we hold on to Jesus, knowing Him in the fellowship of His sufferings, we shall also know Him in the power of His resurrection. Weeping may come for a night, but joy – yes joy comes in the morning. Don't end it all, give it all time, lean on God's grace, mercy, and everlasting love emitting peace filled with joy!

This Joy that I have the world didn't give to me
This Joy that I have the world didn't give to me
This Joy that I have the world didn't give to me
The world didn't give it the world can't take it away

This Love that I have the world didn't give to me. This Love that I have the world didn't give to me. This Love that I have the world didn't give to me. The world didn't give it the world can't take it away

The Holy Ghost that I have the world didn't give to me. The Holy Ghost that I have the world didn't give to me. The Holy Ghost that I have the world didn't give to me. The world didn't give it the world can't take it away

The life that we have the world didn't give to us. The life that we have the world didn't give to us. The life that we have the world didn't give to us. The world didn't give it the world can't take it away.

Don't give it away through suicide or abortion – but leap for joy, clap your hands, pat your feet, thank God for the victory!

SOME WAYS TO PRAISE AND WORSHIP

SCRIPTURE

Psalms 138:1-5 A Psalm of David. I will praise thee with my whole heart: before the gods will I sing praise unto thee. 2 I will worship toward thy holy temple, and praise thy name for thy lovingkindness and for thy truth: for thou hast magnified thy word above all thy name. 3 In the day when I cried thou answeredst me, and strengthenedst me with strength in my soul. 4 All the kings of the earth shall praise thee, O LORD, when they hear the words of thy mouth. 5 Yea, they shall sing in the ways of the LORD: for great is the glory of the LORD.

OUTLINE

1. Put Your Heart into It v1
2. Praise in the Face of Your Idols v1
3. Learn to Worship in God's Direction v2
4. Let the Word Emerge v2
5. Don't Be Exempt (All the Kings) v4

MESSAGE

Over many years of ministry and church life I have come to understand that churches are often unique in their style of worship, even though we are favored to worship the same God. Within many churches there are praise and worship teams which seem to me to separate us in our congregational necessity to praise and worship God.

The church should collectively praise and worship God, as the Lord hasn't selected to bless just a few members of a team — but all of us have been blessed by God, therefore we should all come with hearts lifted toward God in deep adoration.

Aside from my observations toward separate movements of praise and worship — there is the issue that some congregations are known to worship better than others, although most often it's based on musical differences. The beat of the drum along with other instruments and the tonal quality of singers.

I've heard people say things like "they have church over there," "they get their praise on," and "that's a dry church." Often emotionalism is confused for true praise and worship. We have to be careful to guard our praise and worship to avoid trading what God desires for nightclub like sensations directed by satan to distract us from true worship.

Although praise and worship are enhanced with the sound of instruments — there are greater elements necessary for worship. Dancing and good music are not the evidence of worship, if that were the case drunkards and night club patrons would please God on Friday nights.

If it were about music some people would still be shouting off of "I Believe I Can Fly," which has been practically banned from church — what a difference a day makes. In addition to that, many of the songs sung in church are not biblically congruent. Everything that sounds good for itching ears is not good. We are challenged to guard worship through the scope of God's word, will, and way. In fact, we should know more scripture than music.

I wish you would hear me in this church today – we should know more scripture than music. Our praise and worship should be deeply rooted within biblical parameters.

Psalm 138 gleans from King David's relationship with God leading toward insight toward genuine praise and worship maintained through unpolluted vain repetitions of feel good emotions void of focus upon God.

Look with me at Psalms 138:1 it reads, "I will praise thee with my whole heart: before the gods will I sing praise unto thee."

Put your heart into it in order to please God through praise. Adoration void of a heartfelt foundation cannot be genuine – as the very action of praise summons our hearts into the presence of God. Heart strings are the first instrument that must sound to tune all other instruments.

Your lips, feet, and hands are not primary to praise, your heart is. If your heart is tuned to worship God then everything else will follow. Your heart directs the movement, I'm not talking about looking like you love God – looking like we are full of praise and sanctified, we're talking about genuine, real, pure worship. We must start with our hearts.

If you've ever been in a band or attended a concert then you know that a single pitch is produced first to set the standard, the tune for all instruments – if everything isn't tuned together the sound will be off. If we think we can praise God without hearts tuned to God – we're fooling ourselves.

In the original Hebrew text, the idea of throwing one's heart to God can be visualized from the meaning. Praise starts with the understanding that we are not worthy – we can hardly stand in the presence of God, our heart directs profound humility – praise is not about us, we are not the center of our story. God is the *Sine qua non*, the only essential element in worship. Praise is not for our entertainment; praise is not feel-good juice used to make us feel good.

In fact, true praise is all about reducing ourselves as God is magnified. Is there anybody here that can take the focus off of yourself long enough to give your heart to God. You may have an iPhone but you can't have iPraise that promotes you and your feelings over and above God. We must put our heart into praise and worship.

Focus again with me on Psalms 138:1 as it says, "A Psalm of David. I will praise thee with my whole heart: before the gods will I sing praise unto thee."

Praise in the face of your idols, realizing that we cannot allow anything to come before or between our worship. We must worship God no matter what or who the rest of the world bows to.

We cannot worship God while distracted by our idols – cell phones, lunch time, people, game time, and other things that we give our attention to while pretending to worship, while adopting a fantasy praise and worship. Hands in the air while our hearts are on the floor. Feet stomping and pounding, while hearts have stopped beating to the tune of God.

We are too distracted with each other, holding conversations with each other while more interested in social media updates. Using your phone during a conversation is rude. Although it may seem unimportant – because everybody seems to do it, nevertheless the cross is both vertical and horizontal – we are challenged to notice each other to embrace ministry. We must learn to reach out to each other with love, attention, respect, and dignity as Christ has provided us with the greatest example – as Jesus stopped to minister to the cry of a blind man, the problems of the woman at the well, and all of us at Calvary.

Even greater, we have the necessity to reach up, to connect with God without distraction. We must learn to praise God in the face of other gods, in the face of our idols – some singer said "I can make you put your phone down." Hmmm, if you can put your phone down for other things and activities — can you put it down long enough to worship God?

I'm not talking about using your phone for scripture or sermon notes — you good and well know what I'm talking about! Your phone should be on airplane mode or put away during worship. Moses took off his shoes and lowered himself in the presence of God — it's called respect, it's called reverence. I shouldn't even have to remind us of that.

Others need to stop clock watching — game time watching, children's Sunday sports, Sunday club meetings, lunch reservations, and all of the stuff that we allow to occupy our head and heart space during worship in order for us to fully commit ourselves to God! I wish there was an amen in this hostile environment.

God has given you God's best, God's only, God has sacrificed God for you — and all we have is our raggedy hearts to give back, that's the least that we could do. God has been too good to us for us to focus on our idols in the midst of praise and worship.

There are campaigns across the country to end distracted driving. It's dangerous to everyone around, it puts your life in jeopardy, distracted driving is an uneducated practice that proves a lack of intelligence. Nevertheless, I wish somebody would launch a movement to end distracted worship! It puts your life in danger, hinders your connection with God, possibly distracts others, and it's demonic to personally reduce God in your life. Whatever you allow to distract you from praise and worship is greater than God in your life! We've reduced God beneath our phone, children, lunch, time, and whatever else that we give primary place over worship.

But let's move on, I'm not trying to make you mad – just trying like the late Aretha Franklin's two hit songs, to get you to think and have respect.

Look now at Psalms 138:2 it reads, "I will worship toward thy holy temple, and praise thy name for thy lovingkindness and for thy truth: for thou hast magnified thy word above all thy name."

1. Put your heart into it
2. Praise in the face of your idols

Learn to worship in God's direction, as the psalmist admonishes us to turn toward the temple. We must turn toward God, direct our attention toward God. The focus of praise and worship should always be on God.

We must learn to turn away from ourselves and selfish desires. We must learn not to exalt the preacher or the pew – worship is all about God. We must learn to turn away from our wickedness, hatred, and personal feelings, with our heart turned to the direction of God.

We must worship with scripture upon our heart and mind with God the Holy Spirit activated within. The Lord is our rock, strength, and refuge – we must turn toward God with the desire to give our all in worship. Guide me, O Thou great Jehovah!

I Chronicles 16:23-29 says, "Sing unto the LORD, all the earth; shew forth from day to day his salvation. 24 Declare his glory among the heathen; his marvellous works among all nations. 25 For great is the LORD, and greatly to be praised: he also is to be feared above all gods. 26 For all the gods of the people are idols: but the LORD made the heavens. 27 Glory and honour are in his presence; strength and gladness are in his place. 28 Give unto the LORD, ye kindreds of the people, give unto the LORD glory and strength. 29 Give unto the LORD the glory due unto his name: bring an offering, and come before him: worship the LORD in the beauty of holiness."

Praise and worship should always be directed toward God, we are admonished to fully focus on the God that has saved, delivered, liberated, revived, sustained, quickened, and loved us. When we think about God and all that has been done for us – praises should flow from our heart to God. I wonder is there anybody here that knows anything about God – knowing that God woke us up this morning and started us on our way. There is no god like our God, yes God alone is worthy!

Look again with me at Psalms 138:2, it reads, "I will worship toward thy holy temple, and praise thy name for thy lovingkindness and for thy truth: for thou hast magnified thy word above all thy name."

Let the word emerge, as God's word is essential to praise and worship. How do we know what worship is or who God is without the scriptures? The core of worship appreciates God's presence in our lives and refreshes our memory toward the greatness of God while simultaneously ushering the motivation to change us toward the example of Christ. Our love for God should increase our love for others, our appreciation for God's forgiveness should activate forgiveness in us, our peace with God increases peace in our lives overall.

When God's word is embraced, true worship emerges – it's impossible to truly know God and reject the scriptures, discarding the Bible is not an option for genuine worshipers, the Bible is essential. The Bible is the first and greatest hymn book, the guide book, words for every occasion and stage of life. No matter what you've been through or are going through, the Bible has a reason to praise, a reason to worship God.

If you're sick, then the Bible reminds us that by His stripes we are healed – we can praise God for that. If you're struggling with bondage, we're reminded that God made a way out of no way for Moses and the Children of Israel when the Red Sea was parted, if you're stuck in a lion's den or a fiery furnace, if you are put down, let down, cut down, or kept down – there is hope in the word of God, is there a praise in this house today?

The Bible is our praise book, our worship guide – God's word is central to our worship. There is a breakthrough in the word of God, there is joy, love, and eternal peace – all in the word of God. We must let God's word emerge in worship, it's all that really matters as we know that God's word is true!

1. Put your heart into it
2. Praise in the face of your idols
3. Learn to worship in God's direction
4. Let the word emerge

Lest I hold you too long, focus with me on Psalms 138:4 it says, "All the kings of the earth shall praise thee, O LORD, when they hear the words of thy mouth."

Don't be exempt, as the passage says that all the kings, and we know the people, follow the direction of the monarch. Not a few kings, but all the kings – don't be exempt from God, don't opt out of praise and worship. Don't just arrive at church for the sermon, come get it all. We need all that God has to offer - we must be in the number.

You will be in a number one way or another, God's number or satan's number. We might as well worship God today as one day everybody will bow and confess – agnostic, atheist, heathen, worshiper, hater, liars, thieves, cheaters, blasphemers, and people of praise.

Philippians 2:5-11 says, "Let this mind be in you, which was also in Christ Jesus: 6 Who, being in the form of

God, thought it not robbery to be equal with God: 7 But made himself of no reputation, and took upon him the form of a servant, and was made in the likeness of men: 8 And being found in fashion as a man, he humbled himself, and became obedient unto death, even the death of the cross. 9 Wherefore God also hath highly exalted him, and given him a name which is above every name: 10 That at the name of Jesus every knee should bow, of things in heaven, and things in earth, and things under the earth; 11 And that every tongue should confess that Jesus Christ is Lord, to the glory of God the Father."

Why do you wait, dear brother,
Oh, why do you tarry so long?
Your Savior is waiting to give you
A place in His sanctified throng.

Why not? why not?
Why not come to Him now?
Why not? why not?
Why not come to Him now?

Jesus was crucified for us, buried and arose on the third day with victory over death, sin, and satan – we can be thankful for that! We should be filled with praise for that alone.

I heard the voice of Jesus say,
"Come unto Me and rest;
Lay down, thou weary one, lay down,
Thy head upon My breast."

I came to Jesus as I was,
Weary and worn and sad;
I found in Him a resting-place,
And He has made me glad.

When you think about the greatness of God and all that has been done for us – we should be filled with praise! We've got a reason to praise God, a reason to be thankful. We've been forgiven, God has saved and delivered us, there ought to be a praise in this house for God! Hallelujah, hallelujah, praise God!

SOME WAYS TO STAY BLESSED

SCRIPTURE

Jeremiah 17:5-7 Thus saith the LORD; Cursed be the man that trusteth in man, and maketh flesh his arm, and whose heart departeth from the LORD. 6 For he shall be like the heath in the desert, and shall not see when good cometh; but shall inhabit the parched places in the wilderness, in a salt land and not inhabited. 7 Blessed is the man that trusteth in the LORD, and whose hope the LORD is. 8 For he shall be as a tree planted by the waters, and that spreadeth out her roots by the river, and shall not see when heat cometh, but her leaf shall be green; and shall not be careful in the year of drought, neither shall cease from yielding fruit.

OUTLINE

1. Don't Trust People v5
2. Don't Dry Out v6
3. Trust God v7
a. Resource Rich v8
b. Promotes Growth
c. Mitigates Drought
d. Positions Productivity

MESSAGE

Throughout life it seems that we live in a continuation of change ushering us on a journey of ups and downs. We could say that we sometimes feel the curse of Adam and at other times we feel the blessing of Jesus.

Life takes us through the valleys and over the mountains.

The Bible seems to give us clues and examples leading toward blessings as we reject the curse of sin, transgression, and disease. Therefore, it seems essential that we embrace the scriptures to reach toward the great blessing that God has for us. According to Malachi chapter 3, our actions summon a curse or a blessing into our lives.

Malachi 3:8-12, "Will a man rob God? Yet ye have robbed me. But ye say, Wherein have we robbed thee? In tithes and offerings. 9 Ye are cursed with a curse: for ye have robbed me, even this whole nation. 10 Bring ye all the tithes into the storehouse, that there may be meat in mine house, and prove me now herewith, saith the LORD of hosts, if I will not open you the windows of heaven, and pour you out a blessing, that there shall not be room enough to receive it. 11 And I will rebuke the devourer for your sakes, and he shall not destroy the fruits of your ground; neither shall your vine cast her fruit before the time in the field, saith the LORD of hosts. 12 And all nations shall call you blessed: for ye shall be a delightsome land, saith the LORD of hosts."

The portion of scripture we pontificate this morning leads us to a season of history whereby the nation of Israel was going through tough times and as a result of their fears some favored making a deal with Egypt.

The very people that once enslaved them were now embraced as reliable. It's interesting how fear can often lead us into the arms of our enemies, drawing us away from faith in God – moving us away from blessed life. We need the word of God, the scriptures, the Bible to lead us to stay blessed.

Look with me at Jeremiah 17:5, "Thus saith the LORD; Cursed be the man that trusteth in man, and maketh flesh his arm, and whose heart departeth from the LORD."

Don't trust people, as our trust of people, often if not always, creates barriers and obstacles between us and faith. Hebrews 11:6 says, "Without faith it is impossible to please him: for he that cometh to God must believe that he is, and that he is a rewarder of them that diligently seek him."

Factually we know that we cannot stay blessed without faith as we cannot please God without faith, therefore we cannot place our faith in man.

It is almost unfathomable to think that people in the nation of Israel would ever think about creating any alliance, deal, bargain, or covenant with the Egyptians, the land of Egypt where they had been enslaved for centuries.

I wonder if we can identify with them, realizing that we have often allowed fear to motivate our actions toward trust in people, while rejecting faith in God. We've embraced false traditions, secularism, pluralism, political movements, and a number of other mundane fantasies moving us away from the truth of God's word.

"And the Word was made flesh, and dwelt among us, (and we beheld his glory, the glory as of the only begotten of the Father,) full of grace and truth. 15 John bare witness of him, and cried, saying, This was he of whom I spake, He that cometh after me is preferred before me: for he was before me. 16 And of his fulness have all we received, and grace for grace. 17 For the law was given by Moses, but grace and truth came by Jesus Christ." (John 1:14-17)

We must seek our blessings through the truth, through Christ, through the word of God. We must strive to stay in the presence of God, because the true blessing is in God's presence. The Lord is my Shephard, I shall not want – our blessing, our lack of want is all because of our Shepard, we never have to trust in man as long as we're walking in the favor of God.

Focus now with me on Jeremiah 17:6, "For he shall be like the heath in the desert, and shall not see when good cometh; but shall inhabit the parched places in the wilderness, in a salt land and not inhabited."

Don't dry out, as the Nation of Israel was pandering toward Egyptian demise – they were willing to align themselves with people that not only enslaved them in the past, the Egyptians were in worse shape than the Israelites in many ways. They were willing to misalign themselves as the passage reminds us that man makes bad decisions. Man often misses the blessings, just doesn't see the path that God presents, man ultimately dries out when left alone.

We need God to keep us alive, keep us from drying out.

Psalms 1:1-3 says, "Blessed is the man that walketh not in the counsel of the ungodly, nor standeth in the way of sinners, nor sitteth in the seat of the scornful. 2 But his delight is in the law of the LORD; and in his law doth he meditate day and night. 3 And he shall be like a tree planted by the rivers of water, that bringeth forth his fruit in his season; his leaf also shall not wither; and whatsoever he doeth shall prosper."

We cannot afford to dry out especially while standing within the great opportunity to follow Jesus – O, to follow Jesus! We will never dry out as long as we learn to follow Jesus. When we delight in the law of the lord, the law of Christ, the law to love God and each other will never dry you out.

When we walk with God, when we meditate in God's law both day and night – we will stand as trees by the rivers of water. We will never dry out while nourished by the law of God, by the word of God – thank God for the powerful rivers of great God's eternal word giving life to love.

Look with me now at Jeremiah 17:7, "Blessed is the man that trusteth in the LORD, and whose hope the LORD is."

Don't trust people
Don't dry out, and

Trust God, not man – if we really want to stay blessed, we must trust God. Yes, we must trust God – let's share four reasons to trust God and bring this sermon to conclusion

Focus on Jeremiah 17:8, "For he shall be as a tree planted by the waters, and that spreadeth out her roots by the river, and shall not see when heat cometh, but her leaf shall be green; and shall not be careful in the year of drought, neither shall cease from yielding fruit."

God is:

a. Resource Rich

b. Promotes Growth

c. Mitigates Drought
d. Positions Productivity

When we trust God, we become as a tree planted by waters, as God is resource rich. God never runs out, and is always able to provide for us, sustaining us from age to age through all of eternity. God is resource rich; God promotes growth as the passage says that the tree spreads roots at the river – stay blessed in the presence of God, trust in the Lord.

Proverbs 3:5-7 says, "Trust in the LORD with all thine heart; and lean not unto thine own understanding. 6 In all thy ways acknowledge him, and he shall direct thy paths. 7 Be not wise in thine own eyes: fear the LORD, and depart from evil."

We must trust God to embrace rich resources and growth. Then the verse says your leaf will stay green, the heat will not affect your growth. The fiery darts of satan will not take you out, your enemies will stumble and fall. Staying blessed by God! Hallelujah!

God is resource rich, promotes growth, and mitigates drought as the scripture goes on to say the tree by the waters doesn't have to cut back in times of drought – I wonder if anybody here knows that God will mitigate drought.

When others are having to cut back their joy, peace, love, and joy – when the rest are starving, God's people are full, fat, and fed – enough to live and enough to give.

David said that he had never seen the righteous forsaken or God's seed begging for bread. God is resource rich, promotes growth, mitigates drought, and lastly **Positions Productivity.** Verse 8 brings hope and motivates faith as we can find solace in knowing that the fruit does not fail to yield.

Isaiah 55:9-12, "For as the heavens are higher than the earth, so are my ways higher than your ways, and my thoughts than your thoughts. 10 For as the rain cometh down, and the snow from heaven, and returneth not thither, but watereth the earth, and maketh it bring forth and bud, that it may give seed to the sower, and bread to the eater: 11 So shall my word be that goeth forth out of my mouth: it shall not return unto me void, but it shall accomplish that which I please, and it shall prosper in the thing whereto I sent it. 12 For ye shall go out with joy, and be led forth with peace: the mountains and the hills shall break forth before you into singing, and all the trees of the field shall clap their hands."

Somebody ought to be glad in this church, knowing that you can walk in favor in season and out of season. Jesus bled, suffered, died, and got up from the grave that we might have victory with Him. We can stay blessed if we keep trusting God. Trusting when things don't go our way, trusting when things don't happen when we want them to, trusting when people say otherwise, believing God with all and in all that we have. Like Job, trusting even when we feel slighted, bruised, and confined.
Yes, stay blessed! Don't trust people, don't dry up – but stay on the Lord's side. Trust God! Who is on the Lord's side, is there anybody here on the Lord's side – stay blessed on the Lord's side!

HOW TO HANDLE WHAT YOU DISH OUT

SCRIPTURE

Luke 6:35-38 But love ye your enemies, and do good, and lend, hoping for nothing again; and your reward shall be great, and ye shall be the children of the Highest: for he is kind unto the unthankful and to the evil. 36 Be ye therefore merciful, as your Father also is merciful. 37 Judge not, and ye shall not be judged: condemn not, and ye shall not be condemned: forgive, and ye shall be forgiven: 38 Give, and it shall be given unto you; good measure, pressed down, and shaken together, and running over, shall men give into your bosom. For with the same measure that ye mete withal it shall be measured to you again.

OUTLINE

1. Approach Life with Love v35
2. Be Merciful v36
3. Resist Becoming Judgmental v37
4. Give v38

MESSAGE

Over the course of my life I've had the opportunity to dine in a number of restaurants and one of them stands out above all the others, not long after grad school – there was money in my pocket therefore better restaurants were available for my delight. In my opinion the best restaurant in Columbus was the now closed Strada International Cuisine – everything was delicious.

There were times when I wondered how they made everything taste so good. One of the things that made it a great restaurant was the fact that the head chef and owner required that the entire staff taste every dish.

In fact, I became so accustomed to asking about listings on the menu that it saddens me when in other restaurants – servers seem to nearly gleefully proclaim a lack of interest and taste for the food they serve. So much so that I've often said that restaurateurs should not hire people refusing to try the food they serve.

It only seems right that you become familiar with the product, the flavors, temperatures, spices, textures, and portions that contribute to the food served. How can one provide informed dialogue without having tried the food – I want you to try it before you serve it to me.

Thinking about the church it seems that we can apply the same principle. Psalms 34:8 says, "O taste and see that the LORD is good: blessed is the man that trusteth in him."

How can we honestly testify, tell others about the goodness of God – if we've never personally experienced the Lord's presence in our lives. Far too often we are dishing out what we have never had, along with dishing out that which we can't handle.

There are a number of people that will tell you about yourself, they will tell you what you need to do with God, but when the tables are turned, they can't handle criticism, correction, edit, or reproach. They can't handle what they dish out – becoming judge and jury in your life – but void of the ability to receive in return. Luke 6:42 says, "Either how canst thou say to thy brother, Brother, let me pull out the mote that is in thine eye, when thou thyself beholdest not the beam that is in thine own eye? Thou hypocrite, cast out first the beam out of thine own eye, and then shalt thou see clearly to pull out the mote that is in thy brother's eye."

Most, and I really think all of us, have some personal matters to tend to before delving into other people's business. We need to learn how to handle what we dish out; we should know the menu before we attempt to serve it. Check your self, check your wreck before you show up at somebody else's crime scene. We need to learn how to handle what we dish out.

The words of Christ in Luke chapter 6 most adequately lead us to handle what we dish out in a discourse with His disciples after having been ridiculed by some religious leaders for doing good while they were sinisterly seeking to get Jesus, to destroy and convict Jesus.

While Christ was doing good, they were both judgmental and condemning. The religious leaders were mad because Jesus allowed His followers to eat corn out of the field on one Sabbath and Jesus healed a man on another Sabbath. Because Christ didn't do things like they did things – they got mad, Jesus ask them is it better to do good or evil on the Sabbath day.

Essentially, when does our judgment and finger pointing become evil – when we leave our sins behind to go check somebody else, our sin increases the more. We are challenged to clean up what we've messed up, before messing around in the mess of others – and I guarantee you that there will never be unemployment with regards to disaster relief in your life, you will not run out of personal correction, you get to retire working on you, never having time to meddle with others. How to handle what you dish out.

Focus with me on Luke 6:35 it reads, "But love ye your enemies, and do good, and lend, hoping for nothing again; and your reward shall be great, and ye shall be the children of the Highest: for he is kind unto the unthankful and to the evil."

How to handle what you dish out – **approach life with love**, if you season life with love, embracing compassion toward others you will find that the return will not be bitter when applied as Christ prescribes in this verse.

In Professor Leo Buscaglia's book simply titled "Love," he says, "Love is always bestowed as a gift - freely, willingly and without expectation. We don't love to be loved; we love to love."

The verse says, "But love ye your enemies, and do good, and lend, hoping for nothing again." Jesus admonishes us to love our enemies, do good for them, and expect nothing in return. Love often gets a bad rap because we fail to follow the instructions that come with love – one of the primary directives that we often miss, is the necessity to love without expectation.

Love only hurts when you expect something back, when you want a return on investment. We get upset when we don't get the results we want – for someone to respond to our love, when if we gave love without expectation the greatest transformation will emerge from within, fostering a divine joy swaddled in peace.

We can handle what we dish out if we serve each other through the profound power of liberated love – given without strings, addendums, conditions, and expectations. Approach life with love.

Look now with me at Luke 6:36 it says, "Be ye therefore merciful, as your Father also is merciful."

How to handle what you dish out, **be merciful** - realizing that none of us would be here without God's mercy. We've been spared through the flood, cared for while careless, and loved while lost.

Sometimes people seem to forget where they came from – we haven't always been where we are today. Our history is sprinkled with questionable decisions and actions, don't sit there acting like you've always been saved, sanctified, praying and praising – mercy saved you, mercy kept and keeps you. Some of the bones hid in our closets still got some meat on them – that stuff you did that even you've been trying to forget, with all of our mistakes, how dare we try to pin somebody down to their mess.

What if you were tied to your past, your past substance abuse, past promiscuity, hatred, lies, confinement, theft, cheating, what if God held you to all you've ever done. Hmmm, what if God pinned you to what you're doing now, we still have stuff we're working on. So, if you've been given mercy, don't you think you should be merciful in return. Glory, glory hallelujah, God is, yes God is merciful. In 2 Samuel chapter 24 King David said, "Let us fall now into the hand of the LORD; for his mercies are great: and let me not fall into the hand of man."

I'm so glad that we don't have to depend on the mercy of man – God is merciful, I love to praise the Lord based on God's grace and mercy alone. The Psalmist said to "Make a joyful noise unto the LORD, all ye lands. 2 Serve the LORD with gladness: come before his presence with singing. 3 Know ye that the LORD he is God: it is he that hath made us, and not we ourselves; we are his people, and the sheep of his pasture. 4 Enter into his gates with thanksgiving, and into his courts with praise: be thankful unto him, and bless his name. 5 For the LORD is good; his mercy is everlasting; and his truth endureth to all generations." Anybody glad for mercy?

Focus now on Luke 6:37 it says, "Judge not, and ye shall not be judged: condemn not, and ye shall not be condemned: forgive, and ye shall be forgiven:"

Resist becoming judgmental, as we should never forget that we must reap what we sow – what goes around comes around. Our thoughts are not like God's thoughts, our ways are not like God's ways. While you are looking at the surface God knows the deep structure of our situations, God sees and weighs the heart, the intention of humanity. We will always misjudge using our little ignorant minds, we don't know what God knows, and we don't have enough smarts or information to adequately judge.

We lack the genuine grace and mercy to even begin to properly be the judge, so you best be careful trying to judge somebody else, because your judgment on them will result in the same measure and type of judgment passed on you.

If the tables are turned can you handle what you dish out? Do you want God to look beyond your fault to minister to your need or would you prefer to be cut down without a full measure of God's merciful understanding?

Reality doesn't set in until disaster knocks on your door – we tend to be more compassionate in matters concerning ourselves and our children. When their child does it, "Shame on them" – when our child does it, "Lord have mercy".

Don't be so quick to judge, like a boomerang your careless thoughts will return. All you can afford to throw is marshmallows when you live in a glass house and all of us live in the weakest structures of reality often feeling protected by false fleeting foundations fortified by fantasy. You're not protected any more than the next human, all of our righteousness is but filth.

Alas! and did my Savior bleed
And did my Sov'reign die?
Would He devote that sacred head
For such a worm as I?

Was it for crimes that I had done
He groaned upon the tree?
Amazing pity! grace unknown!
And love beyond degree!

I'm so glad that man's judgment did not meet me when in need – but my heart rejoices because it was down at the cross where love and mercy found me. Thank God for God, thank God for Jesus our great propitiation, atonement for eternal generations, love eternal from everlasting to everlasting.

Approach life with love,
Be merciful, and
Resist becoming judgmental.

Finally, look at Luke 6:38 it says, "Give, and it shall be given unto you; good measure, pressed down, and shaken together, and running over, shall men give into your bosom. For with the same measure that ye mete withal it shall be measured to you again."

We must learn to **give,** yes, we must learn how to give love, give mercy, give forgiveness. This whole chapter is about our attitude to do good and not evil. Christ brings love to our enemies through the power of our personal ministry to do good for our enemies, to resist judgement with and through the power of merciful love – that tells us how to give of our mercy, forgiveness, and love.

We must love in abundance, get a big heap of mercy, forgiveness, and love – press it down, shake it, get the air out. We have to learn to heap love on our enemies - that love covering a multitude of faults, that type of love sparking mercy, igniting forgiveness – abundant love given with no expectations, wanting nothing in return. Christ promises that we won't lose anything by it, as God will provide the return – whatever you dish out, God will dish out more!

In order to handle what we dish out we need to
1. Approach life with love
2. Be merciful
3. Resist becoming judgmental
4. Give

God has done too much for us, too much to save us from our wickedness, too much to bring us thus far on the way. We must let our actions display our gratitude, merciful because God showed me mercy, loving because God gave me love out at Calvary, when God sacrificed God for us. Forgiving because we've been forgiven.

We must learn to give beyond our feelings, give without expecting others to give us back. Our only expectation must be toward God, we must place all our trust in God who will not leave nor forsake us. Christ promises that when we forgive, we will be forgiven as we forgive, we will be judged like we judged. If we give, we'll get it back – but don't look to people look to God!

You can't beat God's giving, no matter how you try. And just as sure as you are living and the Lord is in heaven on high. The more you give, the more He gives to you, but keep on giving because it's really true that you can't beat God's giving, no matter how you try.

HOW TO REJECT BEING MYSTERIOUS

SCRIPTURE

2 Corinthians 3:12-14 Seeing then that we have such hope, we use great plainness of speech: 13 And not as Moses, which put a vail over his face, that the children of Israel could not stedfastly look to the end of that which is abolished: 14 But their minds were blinded: for until this day remaineth the same vail untaken away in the reading of the old testament; which vail is done away in Christ.

OUTLINE

1. Speak Plain v12
2. Embrace Transparency v13
3. Know What Christ Does v14

MESSAGE

Sometimes churches are very mysterious places, windows covered, people speaking in ancient languages, choirs singing seemingly secret songs, dress codes, and unofficial seating charts. Churches have special ceremonies, traditions, and cues sometimes specifically unique to certain regions, denominations, or individual churches.

The church can be a very mysterious place. Let's not even talk about church goers, church people and all of their eccentricities, there are times when church folks seem like a weird ball of crazy wearing good clothes. I know I'm preaching to the wrong crowd, but if there are some people at home or at breakfast right now that would attend church, but at some point, it got too strange and mysterious.

We watch the news and the church has accusations that seem stacked against it on many fronts. From church scandals involving pedophilia to money laundering and human trafficking – not to mention churches where the members are hateful, arrogant, and exclusionary.

Sometimes people look toward the church and it all seems too mysterious - what should we believe, where should we go, as unprepared preachers deliver misleading sermons steeped in mystery. There have been times when you could solve the case for Columbo, Sherlock Holmes, or Agatha Christie long before you'll unravel some mysterious sermons. For many the mysterious is simply motivation to stand clear of the church.

The church must continually examine itself to remain relevantly loyal to God as we embrace the Gospel, the Good News about Christ as central to thought, word, and action.

The church should reject being mysterious in order to effectively garner change throughout the world with the message of Christ that liberates with love, hope, and peace. The mystery has been revealed through the death, burial, and resurrection of Jesus the Christ.

The portion of scripture that we are focused on today – 2 Corinthians chapter 3 reminds us that the Old Testament is both mysterious and impossible to live by without Christ as the key to revelation through the Gospel of the New Testament.

The Old Testament tabernacle, temple, place of worship, or church if you will – had a curtain up that divided the place into sections and full access was not granted to everyone. Ultimately the High Priest was the only one permitted to walk beyond the final curtain or veil. Matthew 27:50-51 says, "Jesus, when he had cried again with a loud voice, yielded up the ghost. 51 And, behold, the veil of the temple was rent in twain from the top to the bottom; and the earth did quake, and the rocks rent;"

Because of Jesus there is no mystery – the veil has been torn, the curtain has come down, the covers are off and all of us have personal unlimited access to God. The church should seek to follow Christ in order to bring revelation to the people, testifying of the greatness of God simple, full, and free – void of mysterious talk or behavior.

Paul pens this second letter to the Church at Corinth believing that his first letter had not been completely effective. Chapter 3 reminds us that Jesus is the testator that brings the Biblical testament to full manifestation. The people of the Old Testament lived under a law of sin and death – standing individually outside of the curtain while represented collectively by the priest.

Jesus came to fulfill the law, not to destroy it but to fulfill it. Therefore, we live under a law of love whereby we all have full access and we become a family of priests as we are adopted into the family of God.

The law has been perfectly summarized to capsulize 613 laws into 2 commands that Christ issues, recorded in Matthew 22:36-40, "Master, which is the great commandment in the law? 37 Jesus said unto him, Thou shalt love the Lord thy God with all thy heart, and with all thy soul, and with all thy mind. 38 This is the first and great commandment. 39 And the second is like unto it, Thou shalt love thy neighbour as thyself. 40 On these two commandments hang all the law and the prophets."

When we embrace the way of Christ the church is no longer mysterious – all are welcome to live as Christ in the family of God under the law of love. We must remain divinely relevant, following the example of Jesus. People should know that we all have access to God. The church should seek to meet the needs of humanity with love. There is no longer mystery, but victory through Jesus. How to reject being mysterious.

Focus with me now at 2 Corinthians 3:12, "Seeing then that we have such hope, we use great plainness of speech:"

Reject being mysterious, **speak plain** without convoluted or confusing concepts or ideas. Don't over complicate God to try to make yourself look more biblically astute, theologically deep while spiritually shallow. Sometimes people want to act like God's bouncers – checking ID, carding, and choosing who stays and who goes from the celebration. However, I am glad that God the Holy Spirit directs and leads us through all truth inviting us to the celebration. Christ died that we might celebrate – it's so simple for us nevertheless it was sacrifice for God.

God sacrificed God to liberate us - to simplify the path for us. It's as simple as knowing that none of us came here special, we all came short of God's glory, but the blood, Oh, the blood – God has forgiven us and all of us needed God's forgiveness. Admit our transgression, believe on Christ, and commit your life to God's way. It's simple, accept God the Son as our example, choose God the Holy Spirit as our continual guide to love God with our heart, mind, and soul – and love each other as we love ourselves. It's not mysterious, repent, believe, be baptized, live like Jesus! Learn to love. The church must talk plain, what good is testimony if no one understands it?

Look at 2 Corinthians 3:13, "And not as Moses, which put a vail over his face, that the children of Israel could not stedfastly look to the end of that which is abolished:"

Embrace transparency, the Message Bible says it like this, "With that kind of hope to excite us, nothing holds us back. Unlike Moses, we have nothing to hide. Everything is out in the open with us. He wore a veil so the children of Israel wouldn't notice that the glory was fading away - and they didn't notice. They didn't notice it then and they don't notice it now, don't notice that there's nothing left behind that veil. Even today when the proclamations of that old, bankrupt government are read out, they can't see through it. Only Christ can get rid of the veil so they can see for themselves that there's nothing there"

The church should have nothing to hide, but everything to share. Don't hide the light under a bush – but let your light shine – everywhere you go! We must let our light shine! The mysterious has become demystified through the power of God. There is no monopoly, it's not about how good we sing, pray, or read – not about who preaches, ushers, or drums. We are all God's children, loved by our Heavenly Parent – we never have to cover up where we came from or what we've been through, there is glory in the story of what God has done, is doing, and will do for us!

It is no mystery what God can do – I know God has worked a way out of no way for me over, and over, and over again. My soul cries out hallelujah for the Lamb. What God has done for others I know God will do for you. Moses didn't want them to see that his face was growing dull – the glory that had been on him was beginning to fade, so he put on a veil to mask the change. Some of us do the same, start covering up to hide our weaknesses and imperfections – but I stopped by to tell you this morning, don't focus on me, don't look too closely because they don't have a veil big enough and dark enough to hide all my imperfections – but if we focus on God, I know what will.

I Peter 4:7-11 says it like this in the New International Version, "The end of all things is near. Therefore be alert and of sober mind so that you may pray. 8 Above all, love each other deeply, because love covers over a multitude of sins. 9 Offer hospitality to one another without grumbling. 10 Each of you should use whatever gift you have received to serve others, as faithful stewards of God's grace in its various forms. 11 If anyone speaks, they should do so as one who speaks the very words of God. If anyone serves, they should do so with the strength God provides, so that in all things God may be praised through Jesus Christ. To him be the glory and the power for ever and ever."

I'm glad that the Lord looked beyond our faults and saw our needs. Gossip won't cover our faults, hatred, finger pointing, unforgiveness, lies, and backbiting won't cover us – but love will. Love will cover the big bad wolf, love will change Cruella de Ville, rearrange Pluto, Tom, Yosemite Sam, Freddie Kruger, and that old lying thief Goldilocks – love will cover, love will change, love will take a bad situation and turn it around, Oh God's love! But before I lose my mind to praise in here – let's move on to the next verse.

Focus on verse 14, however I want you to hear 2 Corinthians 3:14-18 as it reads, "But their minds were blinded: for until this day remaineth the same vail untaken away in the reading of the old testament; which vail is done away in Christ. 15 But even unto this day, when Moses is read, the vail is upon their heart. 16 Nevertheless when it shall turn to the Lord, the vail shall be taken away. 17 Now the Lord is that Spirit: and where the Spirit of the Lord is, there is liberty. 18 But we all, with open face beholding as in a glass the glory of the Lord, are changed into the same image from glory to glory, even as by the Spirit of the Lord."

In order to reject being mysterious we need to Speak plain, embrace transparency, and **know what Christ does**, we cannot tell and do that which we do not know. Every member of the Body of Christ, every church member, every Christian should know how to tell the story, knowing what Christ did – we should be able to tell it simple, transparent, and plain.

There was a time when we couldn't get to God, our sin separated us – but Jesus, God the Son came and sacrificed Himself for us. The testimony is so simple, He died as a sacrifice for us, we deserved to die as punishment for our sin, but Christ stepped in and took our punishment – He died, was buried, but God raised Christ from the dead and now we have victory with Him over sin and death.

It's so simple Jesus took our punishment, had our charges dropped and as the scripture says there is liberty in the Lord's presence, Jesus got us in, then Jesus got us in the family. It's all about Jesus. Now in return we must follow the law of Christ, the command of Christ to love God with all of our heart, mind, and soul

- to love others like we love ourselves. Stop being so mysterious, there's nothing special about us without Jesus.

It's really not a Big Mac without special sauce – without the sacrifice, without the power of Christ's shed blood, you've got to have some special sauce. Nothing mysterious – just hold on to Jesus as we learn how to love. We are living the Bible together through education, missions, and ministry – nothing mysterious. God's word and love.

Brother Barney the purple dinosaur did not have to go to seminary and become a great theologian to simply sing:

I love you. You love me we're a happy family with a great big hug and a kiss from me to you, won't you say you love me too?

HOW TO AVOID A SETBACK

SCRIPTURE

Matthew 18:23-35 Therefore is the kingdom of heaven likened unto a certain king, which would take account of his servants. 24 And when he had begun to reckon, one was brought unto him, which owed him ten thousand talents. 25 But forasmuch as he had not to pay, his lord commanded him to be sold, and his wife, and children, and all that he had, and payment to be made. 26 The servant therefore fell down, and worshipped him, saying, Lord, have patience with me, and I will pay thee all. 27 Then the lord of that servant was moved with compassion, and loosed him, and forgave him the debt. 28 But the same servant went out, and found one of his fellowservants, which owed him an hundred pence: and he laid hands on him, and took him by the throat, saying, Pay me that thou owest. 29 And his fellowservant fell down at his feet, and besought him, saying, Have patience with me, and I will pay thee all. 30 And he would not: but went and cast him into prison, till he should pay the debt. 31 So when his fellowservants saw what was done, they were very sorry, and came and told unto their lord all that was done. 32 Then his lord, after that he had called him, said unto him, O thou wicked servant, I forgave thee all that debt, because thou desiredst me: 33 Shouldest not thou also have had compassion on thy fellowservant, even as I had pity on thee? 34 And his lord was wroth, and delivered him to the tormentors, till he should pay all that was due unto him. 35 So likewise shall my heavenly Father do also unto you, if ye from your hearts forgive not every one his brother their trespasses.

OUTLINE

1. Remember the Kingdom of Heaven v23
2. Remember Your Inabilities (Not Able) v25-26
3. Remember Payback v34-35

MESSAGE

Far too often we forget where we come from, what we've come through. Some of us have moved to the suburbs, forgetting our days in the hood – eating noodles for breakfast, lunch, and dinner. Country poor folk eating sugar or tomato or banana sandwiches. Stretching eggs with more milk than egg.

Your daddy sold moonshine and your momma sold tail, but somehow you forgot where you came from. Noses in the air, feeling yourself, looking down on the pill poppers and opioid abusers – and your nose has had more powder than a box of powdered donuts in a police station. We soon forget where we come from.

Some people know all the dimensions of a backseat – having been promiscuously inclined from backseats to bathrooms, yet judgmental about the sexual indiscretion of others. It's easy to forget where you come from.

We have to be careful operating in a seat of judgment because it is more than true that what comes around goes around – the Bible puts it like this in Galatians 6:7-8, "Be not deceived; God is not mocked: for whatsoever a man soweth, that shall he also reap. 8 For he that soweth to his flesh shall of the flesh reap corruption; but he that soweth to the Spirit shall of the Spirit reap life everlasting."

Don't forget where you've come from, don't forget that God forgives us as we forgive others. We are challenged to follow the law of Christ – the law to love one another with the same measure that we love ourselves.

Our focal scripture this morning recorded in the 18th chapter of Matthew we find a simile posed by Christ to bring visualization to forgiveness and the Kingdom of Heaven – in response to a question presented by Peter.

The disciple questioned Jesus as to the number of times we are required to forgive – in response Jesus tells him seventy times seven, followed by a narrative comparing the Kingdom of Heaven to a king and servants.

Jesus tells a story of a king who decided to call in and collect debts from servants that owed him money. One servant came forward and did not have the money to pay up. In today's currency it's thought that the servant owed around $100,000, but couldn't pay up. So, the king basically ordered the man, along with his wife, children, and goods, to be auctioned off at the slave market.

The poor servant begged the king for mercy and more time. The king was moved with compassion and erased the servant's debt.

Not long after the servant was forgiven of his debt to the king – the servant sought to collect from someone that owed him what we believe to be about $10 in modern currency.

The man begged for mercy and time to pay – but the servant had him thrown in jail. The king heard about the servant and called him evil! The king told the servant, "I forgave you of your debt when you begged for mercy. Shouldn't you be merciful to your fellow servant who asked for mercy?" The king was angered, reinstated the servant's entire debt having him tormented until he paid the money he originally owed. The king basically put the servant in escalated collections to demand the original debt. Jesus declares the same thing will be done to us by God if we fail to forgive others.

The servant had been forgiven – but his actions caused him to suffer a setback, his debt had been dismissed, but his unforgiveness, his lack of mercy put him back in the captivity of debt. He forgot where he came from, he was strained to handle what he dished out – setting him back. We need to avoid a setback.

Look with me at Matthew 18:23 as it reads, "Therefore is the kingdom of heaven likened unto a certain king, which would take account of his servants."

Remember the Kingdom of Heaven, as Jesus taught us to pray "Our Father which art in heaven, Hallowed be thy name. Thy kingdom come, Thy will be done in earth, as it is in heaven." We should seek the kingdom, living on earth under the reality of the kingdom. The family of God must continually remember the kingdom – understanding that we are citizens of the kingdom, expected to follow the way, will, rule, command, and law of the kingdom.

The rule and reign of God is the only eternal government; therefore, we are challenged to embrace the way of the kingdom now to avoid exile into everlasting punishment conflicting with the opportunity to live forever in a utopia of joy within the Kingdom of God.

The servant in the scripture today did not understand and/or embrace the kingdom. The servant neglected to realize that we must reap what we sow as a divine law. God said in Genesis 8:22 that, "While the earth remaineth, seedtime and harvest, and cold and heat, and summer and winter, and day and night shall not cease." We will reap what we sow as Galatians chapter six reminds us.

Kingdom law hinges upon the command of God to love neighbor as self – we must love each other, which will in turn manifest forgiveness, appreciation, and mercy. We become merciful as we realize and appreciate the great mercy that God has shown toward us all.

It's easy to suffer a setback when you forget your place, where you belong, your purpose to serve God with gladness. When we forget the kingdom, we become susceptible to the ways of the temporary world, rejecting the joys of the kingdom eternal. In order to avoid a setback, remember the Kingdom of God – the will and way of God to love one another.

Focus now with me on Matthew 18:25-26 the passage reads, "But forasmuch as he had not to pay, his lord commanded him to be sold, and his wife, and children, and all that he had, and payment to be made. 26 The servant therefore fell down, and worshipped him, saying, Lord, have patience with me, and I will pay thee all."

Remember your inabilities, the servant in the passage was unable to pay – he had an inability yet was unforgiving toward the next fellow's inability. We want mercy shown toward ourselves while remaining unmerciful toward others. We have greatly received the gifts of forgiveness and love, how can we be so unappreciative that we fail to give what we've been given. God's abundance keeps us in overflow, as I can guarantee that we can't beat God giving – we have been forgiven more than we are asked to forgive. The servant is believed to have owed around $100,000 in modern currency and he was unforgiving toward somebody that's believed to have only owed him $10.

Oh, but before we judge the servant's evil actions – we should examine our own. It's so easy to end up blinded to our own ways as the Bible says in Proverbs 21:1-2, "The king's heart is in the hand of the LORD, as the rivers of water: he turneth it whithersoever he will. 2 Every way of a man is right in his own eyes: but the LORD pondereth the hearts." We need to realize that all of us are flawed without God's presence. We cannot boast of any innate goodness within us – we are here today, better today, struggling through the storms because the power of God sustains and keeps us through trial and tribulation. Don't laugh at the struggles of others, reject unforgiveness and the tendency to stray away from love and compassion.

If you hold your neighbor's feet to the fire long enough, your feet will get hot – what goes around comes around! Be careful how you treat others while forgetting that we are all in this together. The strong should help the weak, hold them up where they're torn down – the Bible says it like this in Romans 15:1-5, "We then that are strong ought to bear the infirmities of the weak, and not to please ourselves. 2 Let every one of us please his neighbour for his good to edification. 3 For even Christ pleased not himself; but, as it is written, The reproaches of them that reproached thee fell on me. 4 For whatsoever things were written aforetime were written for our learning, that we through patience and comfort of the scriptures might have hope. 5 Now the God of patience and consolation grant you to be likeminded one toward another according to Christ Jesus:" Glory to God, we must continually be aware of our duty to help others through their struggles –

following Christ mandates that the strong bear the maladies of the frail.

The German philosopher Georg Wilhelm Friedrich Hegel known best for absolute idealism said, "To be aware of limitations is already to be beyond them." It seems that when we fail to love and have mercy toward others – we reveal additional weaknesses within ourselves.

Although the evil people often appear powerful upon the Earth, the truth is that in the sum of eternity, *sub specie aeternitatis* – they are the weakest as the day will come whereby the first shall be last and the last shall be first. The captives will be set free, those in bondage shall gain liberty – those persecuted for righteousness will gain the Kingdom of Heaven.

Perhaps there are those who viewed the cross as weakness, the grave as weakness – however Christ created a path to life eternal through the graveyard!

There is no greater testimony than when the odds are stacked against you, doubters all around, the underdog, the unexpected king! Jesus, ridiculed but righteous – anybody know that God can take the weak and make them strong or take the powerful and make them weak. Avoid a setback, don't cause God to set you back because of your hateful behavior – remember the Kingdom of God and remember your inabilities.

Look at verses 34-35, Matthew 18:34-35 says, "And his lord was wroth, and delivered him to the tormentors, till he should pay all that was due unto him. 35 So likewise shall my heavenly Father do also unto you, if ye from your hearts forgive not every one his brother their trespasses."

Remember payback, whatever you sow – you will reap. It's coming back, plant good stuff in the life of others, pass blessings along and watch God multiply favor in your life. We can't afford to hold grudges, unforgiveness, malice and such – God has been too good to us. Grace and mercy have been on our side, justice would have taken us out a long time ago - but thank God for mercy. Grateful that God the Son took our place, glad that Jesus the Son of God stands in for us as God the Holy Spirit stretches out in us! Hallelujah for the Lamb – God loves us and we never have to suffer a self-inflicted setback if we continue to follow God's way of love.

We must remember that there are consequences to our actions. Isaac Newton said, "For every action, there is an equal and opposite reaction." Someday we will be judged by God, separated like a shepherd separates sheep from goats according to Matthew chapter 25. We will be judged and separated based on what we did for Christ through our actions toward the least of us.

We are called to love one another, to feed the hungry, give relief to the thirsty, take in the stranger, clothe the naked, visit the sick and imprisoned. Our actions toward those in need classify us into the Kingdom of God — don't get setback through your actions, through your foolishness, but walk in the favor of God.

But, wait — I don't want you to leave here with the wrong impression, as if we will never suffer setbacks. Let me be clear — I don't want you to leave setback because of stuff you've been doing to get setback. But that doesn't mean you will never suffer a setback. In fact, as you learn to love and stop defeating yourself, or rejecting your relationship with God — the more you learn to love the more you may feel like you're being set back, love made a fool out of me. But don't worry about that kind of setback. Jesus said the first shall be last and the last shall be first. Jesus said that those persecuted for riotousness sake will gain the Kingdom of God. Then I know you know that Jesus seemed to have a setback over in Rome — but see there are times when a setback is just a setup for a comeback.

Jesus was crucified, suffered, bled, and died — was buried, a setback if you will. But they didn't realize He was the seed of David — they planted a seed, that seed was Jesus — the first fruit of humanity as up from the grave He arose, Calvary was just a setup for a comeback. Jesus arose with all power in Heaven and on Earth — we have victory in Jesus, knowing Him in the fellowship of His sufferings and the power of His resurrection. Glory to God, and Jesus is coming back for you — love God and love one another until He returns.

Take my life, and let it be
Consecrated, Lord, to Thee;
Take my moments and my days,
Let them flow in ceaseless praise,

Take my hands, and let them move
At the impulse of Thy love;
Take my feet and let them be
Swift and beautiful for Thee,

Take my voice, and let me sing
Always, only, for my King;
Take my lips, and let them be
Filled with messages from Thee,

Take my silver and my gold;
Not a mite would I withhold;
Take my intellect, and use
Every power as Thou shalt choose,

Take my will, and make it Thine;
It shall be no longer mine.
Take my heart; it is Thine own;
It shall be Thy royal throne,

Take my love; my Lord, I pour
At Thy feet its treasure-store.
Take myself, and I will be
Ever, only, all for Thee,

HOW TO AVOID A SELLOUT CHURCH

SCRIPTURE

Amos 7:10-17 Then Amaziah the priest of Bethel sent to Jeroboam king of Israel, saying, Amos hath conspired against thee in the midst of the house of Israel: the land is not able to bear all his words. 11 For thus Amos saith, Jeroboam shall die by the sword, and Israel shall surely be led away captive out of their own land. 12 Also Amaziah said unto Amos, O thou seer, go, flee thee away into the land of Judah, and there eat bread, and prophesy there: 13 But prophesy not again any more at Bethel: for it is the king's chapel, and it is the king's court. 14 Then answered Amos, and said to Amaziah, I was no prophet, neither was I a prophet's son; but I was an herdman, and a gatherer of sycomore fruit: 15 And the LORD took me as I followed the flock, and the LORD said unto me, Go, prophesy unto my people Israel. 16 Now therefore hear thou the word of the LORD: Thou sayest, Prophesy not against Israel, and drop not thy word against the house of Isaac. 17 Therefore thus saith the LORD; Thy wife shall be an harlot in the city, and thy sons and thy daughters shall fall by the sword, and thy land shall be divided by line; and thou shalt die in a polluted land: and Israel shall surely go into captivity forth of his land.

OUTLINE

1. Don't Limit God's Word v15
2. Speak Truth to Power v13-16
3. Know the Diagnosis, Prognosis and Prescription v17

MESSAGE

Somebody sold us out. It's easy to get support for that statement from most African-Americans as it is reasonable to understand that throughout the history of America, people of African origin have been sold and sold out within the American system.

Sympathy seems to arise from compassion without experience, however empathy arises from personal experience weaved with compassion born through the human expedition called life. People of color, minorities, women, and other disfranchised groups should be able to empathize with the sold out, underprivileged, enslaved, raped, maimed, and socially reduced.

Although slavery is purported to have ended in America with the signing of the Emancipation Proclamation, and discrimination with the Civil Rights acts passed in the 1960s, we are far from complete freedom and liberation for all.

In the book "From Good to Great" authored by Jim Collins – he writes that, "good is the enemy to great," idealizing that when things are good enough we will compromise or forfeit the desire to be great. When conditions are good enough, maybe even simply favorable, we tend to release great as an option.

Simplified, many of us are okay with leaving the loaf of bread as long as we can get a few slices – even if the whole loaf was ours in the first place. We planted the grain, milled it, prepared the flour, and created the bread – yet willing to give up the loaf for a few slices. Think about it, the Emancipation Proclamation without reparations is just a few slices. Free labor sustained the wealth of so many families, companies, and governments – yet slaves were never humanely compensated. But a small level of freedom was good enough to subvert optimal arrangements.

Furthermore, it seems that when people enjoy a level of freedom, they forget to reach for others in bondage. We have a moral responsibility to care for other persecuted peoples.

We have the responsibility like Harriet Tubman, perhaps the most well-known former slave, who over a ten-year span made 19 trips into the United States South and escorted over 300 slaves to freedom. And, as she once proudly pointed out to Frederick Douglass, in all of her journeys she, "Never lost a single passenger."

There are still discriminatory practices and issues spread throughout the country, especially in the Southern United States, whereby many Hispanic farm workers are working through slave like treatment. In some cases, human trafficking has presented actual slave conditions, environments, and systems.

Specifically, the tomato farm workers in Florida were so poorly treated that they began to cry out to food retailers for fair treatment. Women were especially mistreated and often sexually abused. Therefore, the workers organized to create the Fair Food Program to institute policies that protect workers from abuse.

The program helps to discourage abuse, create proper restrooms, gain fair wages, and maintain an independent review process. Many companies like McDonald's, Wal-Mart, Subway, Chipotle, Trader Joe's, and Burger King pay $0.01 per pound to participate in this empowering program.

On the other hand, Wendy's refuses to participate. So much so that the corporation discontinued purchasing tomatoes from Florida where over 90% of tomatoes are produced within the United States – choosing to purchase from Mexico where conditions seemingly remain deplorably slave like, all for cheaper tomatoes at the cost of morality.

I have carefully stood upon the sidelines of this issue, realizing that Wendy's has been a great supporter of this ministry – therefore, we did not want to rush to a decision.

Nevertheless, the time has come for us to join the struggle as Wendy's has started purchasing U.S. produce again – but fails to participate in the Fair Food Program. We cannot be a sellout church! Just because a company contributes to ministry – we cannot overlook or support immoral treatment of people anywhere. Got to let their tomatoes and burgers go.

The prophet Amos lived during a time period whereby the people around his community and neighbors mistreated the poor. God challenged Amos to speak out against wickedness and as the prophet spoke out, another religious leader asked him to either stop speaking out or move. In fact, the religious leader would later come to be instrumental in having Amos exiled, thrown out of town for speaking truth to power.

Focus now with me on Amos 7:15 the passage reads, "And the LORD took me as I followed the flock, and the LORD said unto me, Go, prophesy unto my people Israel."

In order to avoid a sellout church, we **don't limit God's word**, as what God commands us to do – we must do. Jesus commands us in Matthew chapter 22 to love God and love our neighbor – then Matthew chapter 25 admonishes us to feed the hungry, give relief to the thirsty, clothe the naked, take in the stranger, visit the sick and imprisoned.

God's word calls us to love, to morality, to humanity – we are called to the work of Social Justice as Christ has led the way to love the least of us. The work and life of Christ calls us to liberating love. We are purposed to care for others, we must focus on the stranger, the foreigners.

We can never reduce God's word or suppress God's word when it is convenient for us. Grants, gifts, governments, aid, reductions, and favors can never be allowed to block out love or subvert our commitment to the word and way of God.

We can't limit God's word, as God has been too good and true — I wonder does anybody know that we made it thus far by faith. We've come this far by faith — God has smiled on us, using others to help us along the way.

Challenging change through word and will — God has brought us to liberation. Just as the hand of God used Moses to lead others across the Red Sea to freedom, we have been purposed just the same to support liberation, justice, and freedom.

Amos 5:18-24 says, "Woe unto you that desire the day of the LORD! to what end is it for you? the day of the LORD is darkness, and not light. 19 As if a man did flee from a lion, and a bear met him; or went into the house, and leaned his hand on the wall, and a serpent bit him. 20 Shall not the day of the LORD be darkness, and not light? even very dark, and no brightness in it? 21 I hate, I despise your feast days, and I will not smell in your solemn assemblies. 22 Though ye offer me burnt offerings and your meat offerings, I will not accept them: neither will I regard the peace offerings of your fat beasts. 23 Take thou away from me the noise of thy songs; for I will not hear the melody of thy viols. 24 But let judgment run down as waters, and righteousness as a mighty stream."

We must let judgment run down as waters and righteousness as a mighty stream! We cannot afford to support wickedness against humanity anywhere, as God's word beckons us to the stream of righteousness.

You don't have to be academically astute or a great litigator to support righteousness, as the Bible tells us that Amos left the field, the passage says that the Lord took him as he followed the flock – he was shepherding sheep. We have no excuse, with God the Holy Spirit within you.

We are empowered to do the work of God the Son. Sometimes we have to step away from the flock – take some time off from our routine for the cause of Christ. Step away from a hamburger, sacrifice our appetite to help somebody else. Is there a witness, is there an amen in the house today?

Look with me at Amos 7:13-16 it says, "But prophesy not again any more at Bethel: for it is the king's chapel, and it is the king's court. 14 Then answered Amos, and said to Amaziah, I was no prophet, neither was I a prophet's son; but I was an herdman, and a gatherer of sycomore fruit: 15 And the LORD took me as I followed the flock, and the LORD said unto me, Go, prophesy unto my people Israel. 16 Now therefore hear thou the word of the LORD: Thou sayest, Prophesy not against Israel, and drop not thy word against the house of Isaac."

Speak truth to power, speak through word and deed – let your actions ring out the tenets of love. Let your actions cry out for the least of us, support your neighbor through love compassion, empathy, care, and justice.

Dr. Cornell West says that justice is what love looks like in public. We should not knowingly support companies, governments, and systems that mistreat our neighbors or strangers, foreigners from far off lands.

Amos was speaking out against idolatry and the mistreatment of the poor. The prophet says in Amos 5:8-14, "Seek him that maketh the seven stars and Orion, and turneth the shadow of death into the morning, and maketh the day dark with night: that calleth for the waters of the sea, and poureth them out upon the face of the earth: The LORD is his name: 9 That strengtheneth the spoiled against the strong, so that the spoiled shall come against the fortress. 10 They hate him that rebuketh in the gate, and they abhor him that speaketh uprightly. 11 Forasmuch therefore as your treading is upon the poor, and ye take from him burdens of wheat: ye have built houses of hewn stone, but ye shall not dwell in them; ye have planted pleasant vineyards, but ye shall not drink wine of them. 12 For I know your manifold transgressions and your mighty sins: they afflict the just, they take a bribe, and they turn aside the poor in the gate from their right. 13 Therefore the prudent shall keep silence in that time; for it is an evil time. 14 Seek good, and not evil, that ye may live: and so the LORD, the God of hosts, shall be with you, as ye have spoken."

Amos was disliked for speaking out, in fact the priest came and admonished him not to speak out in Bethel because it was the king's chapel, the king's city. Don't speak against the rich and powerful, don't challenge the government – stay silent in times of trouble, don't make waves.

Amos replied with continued vitality declaring that he had not been a prophet, Amos proclaimed that he had not been a voice for change, a prophet – but God called him! Amos wasn't acting on his own, he was acting on the authority and call of God. Amos kept on speaking until they put him out of town. We have been summoned to the same moral table, to speak truth to power in word and deed – to optimally let love manifest through our daily life.

Remember Jesus served the least, Jesus loved the least, Jesus was crucified for righteousness – we are liberated because of Christ. In order to follow Jesus – we must become liberators. We are challenged to take up the cross and follow Jesus. We are purposed to teach love to all nations, challenged to love all nations, challenged to speak truth to power – appreciating God's word.

People are struggling across the globe, yet we cannot let the number of global issues discourage us, suppress us, or stop us from working toward change – toward mercy, justice, morality, kindness, and lingering love.

We must speak truth to power, get the word out as a watchman upon the wall – sound the alarm for righteousness!

Dr. Martin Luther King Jr. said, "Injustice anywhere is a threat to justice everywhere. We are caught in an inescapable network of mutuality, tied in a single garment of destiny. Whatever affects one directly, affects all indirectly."

Even if your heart isn't big enough to grasp love unselfishly – then perhaps as we are commanded to love our neighbors as we love ourselves, you must start selfishly which seems to be a component of that empathy that I've been talking about today.
Maybe you need to selfishly realize that it's them today and you tomorrow. If we support injustice against others, the injustice will ultimately come home to roost like chickens in the twilight. What goes around comes around, demons will always turn on you – the wicked will knock at their door today and yours tomorrow. We must continually serve God and each other for the cause of Christ, the way of love! We have work to do!

Focus with me on Amos 7:17 it reads, "Therefore thus saith the LORD; Thy wife shall be an harlot in the city, and thy sons and thy daughters shall fall by the sword, and thy land shall be divided by line; and thou shalt die in a polluted land: and Israel shall surely go into captivity forth of his land."

How to avoid a sellout church, don't limit God's word, speak truth to power, and **know the diagnosis, prognosis, and prescription** – Amos knew that there was moral decay as the poor were being charged more for less, as people ignored God while embracing powerless idol gods.

We tend to lose focus on God while focusing on our idol gods – fantasies of freedom as we somehow feel privileged to live paycheck to paycheck while our children are being legally murdered in the streets and disproportionately incarcerated if they should survive the system outside of the institutionalized for-profit prison system.

We are often underemployed, denied adequate education, and systematically disfranchised from wealth – but don't be deceived it's not just African-Americans. While some poor European-Americans remained silent toward the mistreatment of others, the oppressors came for them. America's poor are getting poorer no matter your race, the income gap widens and the middle class are disappearing like Bison from the American plains.

I wonder is there anybody here that knows the middle class are becoming extinct and should be placed on the endangered species list. The cost of health care is rising, pollution is out of control, and political access is barricaded amidst deregulation, greed, and corruption.

The diagnosis is bleak, the condition of our country is nearly at life support status while few are calling for a code blue or even intensive care. The doctors have sold out for self-preservation – churches silent as a result of fear or a sellout leader/pastor/bishop exchanging people for photo shoots with politicians, personal privilege, chump change grants, or a modicum of prominence.

Just turn on your television, watch the so called Christian broadcasting stations and listen for the prophetic voices that resemble Amos, Isaiah, or Jeremiah. Where is the church? The diagnosis is bleak at best.

Amos knew the prognosis, God revealed that destruction, bondage, and gloom were on the horizon as punishment for sins against the poor and idol worship. God said, "Your feasts are disgusting to me, I will have nothing to do with them; I will take no delight in your holy meetings. Even if you give me your burned offerings and your meal offerings, I will not take pleasure in them: I will have nothing to do with the peace-offerings of your fat beasts. Take away from me the noise of your songs; my ears are shut to the melody of your instruments."

God lets us know that our worship, our celebration is not pleasing – music and offerings unaccepted when our actions don't match our heart, our service. How can you love God who you haven't seen and hate your brother? How can we follow Christ without compassion? I don't want my praise to go unappreciated by God, I wonder is there a witness – we don't want to praise and worship in vain.

We cannot expect God to bless us or take our worship seriously when we fail to love as Christ, God the Son has commanded. God is love, God is merciful, God is compassionate – we are called to be holy as God is holy, love is the only way.

Nevertheless, the wages of sin is death and our refusal to follow the law of Christ to act in love – refusal to embrace the way of God will ultimately end in destruction fused with punishment. God says, I will cut you off. We cannot be a sellout church.

Thank God, Amos embraced the prescription as we find a great example of hope and faith toward the last chapter of the prophecy.

Amos 9:10-15 says, "All those sinners among my people will be put to the sword who say, Evil will not overtake us or come face to face with us. 11 In that day I will put up the tent of David which has come down, and make good its broken places; and I will put up again his damaged walls, building it up as in the past; 12 So that the rest of Edom may be their heritage, and all the nations who have been named by my name, says the Lord, who is doing this. 13 See, the days will come, says the Lord, when the ploughman will overtake him who is cutting the grain, and the crusher of the grapes him who is planting seed; and sweet wine will be dropping from the mountains, and the hills will be turned into streams of wine. 14 And I will let the fate of my people Israel be changed, and they will be building up again the waste towns and living in them; they will again be planting vine-gardens and taking the wine for their drink; and they will make gardens and get the fruit of them. 15 And I will have them planted in their land, and never again will they be uprooted from their land which I have given them, says the Lord your God."

We must turn from our wicked ways, from our silence toward evil, from our hatred, from our lack of service and compassion. We are connected through the sacrifice of God. We hold the faith that change will come as we embrace faith under the tent. The passage indicates that God will put up the tent of David which and make good its broken places; and put up again damaged walls, bringing restoration.

Well, I'm glad that the tent is up – Jesus is the seed of David. Jesus is the great representative from the house of David. The tent was pitched at Calvary as God sacrificed God to save us, to motivate us toward love, grace, mercy, and compassion – to motivate us to be like Jesus.

We are blessed because Jesus walked in the favor of God's word, spoke truth to power, and Jesus is the prescription for us all. Love has made a way as Jesus commands us to love one another.

We cannot be a sellout church, the sacrifice of God at Calvary, the blood of Christ is too precious for us to sell out. Even greater is the testimony of Christ resurrection — we know that if we remain faithful to God, liberating change will come. Take up the cross and follow Christ. Don't sell out, but buy in — put your all in the way of God, invest your time, talent, and treasure into the Kingdom of God. Let us love the least as Christ did.

Reverend Dr. Carl Daw, Jr. the former executive director of the Hymn Society wrote:

Till all the jails are empty and all the bellies filled; till no one hurts or steals or lies, and no more blood is spilled; till age and race and gender no longer separate; till pulpit, press, and politics are free of greed and hate: God has work for us to do.

In tenement and mansion, in factory, farm, and mill, in boardroom and in billiard-hall, in wards where time stands still, in classroom, church, and office, in shops or on the street; in ev'ry place where people thrive or starve or hide or meet: God has work for us to do.
By sitting at a bedside to hold pale trembling hands, by speaking for the powerless against unjust demands, by praying through our doing and singing though we fear, by trusting that the seed we sow will bring God's harvest near: God has work for us to do.

Pragmatically, I am asking you to do three things today. 1. Pray for the strength of our sisters and brothers that labor for the fair treatment of others. 2. Ban Wendy's in your budget until they decide to be morally responsible and join the Fair Food Program. 3. Go to poorpeoplescampaign.org and donate $5. Feel free to join also – this is a movement originally started in part by Dr. Martin King, Jr. The resurgence of this movement brings joy to my heart and justice to our nation.

NEVER SETTLE FOR LESS THAN GOD'S PROMISE

SCRIPTURE

Amos 7:10-17 Genesis 15:1-4 After these things the word of the LORD came unto Abram in a vision, saying, Fear not, Abram: I am thy shield, and thy exceeding great reward. 2 And Abram said, Lord GOD, what wilt thou give me, seeing I go childless, and the steward of my house is this Eliezer of Damascus? 3 And Abram said, Behold, to me thou hast given no seed: and, lo, one born in my house is mine heir. 4 And, behold, the word of the LORD came unto him, saying, This shall not be thine heir; but he that shall come forth out of thine own bowels shall be thine heir.

OUTLINE

1. Reflect with God (After These Things) v1
2. Trust God to Protect and Provide v1
3. Don't Let Your Situation Overshadow God v2-3
4. Expect to be Personal (Your Bowels) v4

MESSAGE

Abraham is one of the more central personalities within the Bible, perhaps one of the most central characters of three major world religions – Christianity, Judaism, and Islam. God blessed Abraham to be father of many nations. Our connection with each other is deeply rooted within the biblical narrative as God's creation is finalized with one blood, one people, and one family.

Interestingly, Abraham's early life did not seem fruitful, it did not start off promising in terms of offspring – Abraham did not have children before he was 75, it's believed his first son was born when Abraham was 86 and his second son was conceived when he was 100 years old.

Early on it seemed like Abraham was going to die, the last of his seed, the last of his lineage – it did not look like He was going to be the father of anybody, must less of many nations. Have you ever examined your life and disapproved of your own conclusions – wondering why things didn't turn out differently?

There are times when it seems that all of our hopes and dreams have become fading fantasies parading as reminders of reality.

Langston Hughes, questioned, "What happens to a dream deferred? Does it dry up like a raisin in the sun? Or fester like a sore — And then run?
Does it stink like rotten meat? Or crust and sugar over — like a syrupy sweet? Maybe it just sags like a heavy load. Or does it explode?"

We look back over our life, think things over, and all we can do is weep and moan – what have I done, what have I produced, what have I contributed to the world, God's children, and the Kingdom?

If I understand human nature it must have been difficult for Abraham to know what God had promised in the face of a reality that seemed like fiction and not fact. God said one thing, yet for over eight decades – Abraham remained without proof of God's manifested promise. Could you imagine having to wait 80-100 years for anything – in this instant age, we don't have enough patience to wait for a cell phone to reboot or a movie to load, a few seconds becomes a lifetime for many of us.

Genesis 12:1-2 says, "Now the LORD had said unto Abram, Get thee out of thy country, and from thy kindred, and from thy father's house, unto a land that I will shew thee: 2 And I will make of thee a great nation, and I will bless thee, and make thy name great; and thou shalt be a blessing:" God invites Abraham to leave his home, community, and family – to follow God to fatherhood, to wealth, prosperity, and history. The Lord made Abraham a delicious offer – but the journey seemed sour. I wonder if anybody here has ever had to take the bitter and sweet road of life - from the sour to the savory, every step is hard, every mountain higher and valley lower, the way is tough!

Abraham walked in the promise of God, yet at many times during his life he seemed to feel left out of the favor of God. In the fifteenth chapter of Genesis we find Abraham not long after he had been through the struggles of war – although he was ultimately victorious, the aftermath of strife comes with the strain of recuperation. Abraham experiences a voice of assurance and comfort from God, nevertheless Abraham seems distraught just the same. But let's not judge Abraham – most of us have disagreed with God's assurance from time to time.

Abraham in essence says, Lord, I hear you – but where is my future? I got it God, but I don't see it God – time is running out. I don't see my getting what you said Lord – so tell me what I'll have to settle for. It seems that the father of nations deal is off and what next – what now, what could change things now? Seems I'll have to settle for sadness, settle to hand my prosperity over to my servant, settle for what I've been through in vain, but God do you have a plan?

Perhaps, like Abraham you've been trusting God – but your faith is fading, overshadowed by facts. You're ready to throw in the towel, checkmate, Uno, checker flag, bell – times up on the dream, now I guess I'll take what I can get. I'm here to tell you this morning that we should never settle for less than God's promise. You don't need a plan "B" with God!

Focus with me on Genesis 15:1 it says, "After these things the word of the LORD came unto Abram in a vision, saying, Fear not, Abram: I am thy shield, and thy exceeding great reward."

Reflect with God, always remembering what the Lord has done. After the issues of the war were settled, after Abraham rescued his nephew, after having travelled through the desert, Abraham pauses and listens to God, to have a little talk with God. I wish I had some folks that know the worth of prayer – the hymn writer said that just a little talk with Jesus makes it right, you ought to know that the Lord hears our faintest cry and will answer by and by.

Sometime we've got to reflect with God, humble ourselves in prayer and lean upon God's wisdom. We cannot afford to trust our own mind and assessment, can't trust what other people think about us – we've got to take our life to God and embrace God's assessment, holding firm to the Lord's promises, whatever God says is true. Never settle for less than God's promises.

Look again with me at Genesis 15:1, "After these things the word of the LORD came unto Abram in a vision, saying, Fear not, Abram: I am thy shield, and thy exceeding great reward."

Trust God to protect and provide, as far too often we want to trust God wants to bless us – but we reject how God wants to bless us. We want God to bless us and take care of us, however we want God to do it our way, follow our direction. God's complete way will always be superior to our ways.

Isaiah 55:8-9 says, "For my thoughts are not your thoughts, neither are your ways my ways, saith the LORD. 9 For as the heavens are higher than the earth, so are my ways higher than your ways, and my thoughts than your thoughts."

You never have to settle if you learn to trust, learn to have faith – as according to Hebrews chapter 11, faith is the substance of tings hoped for with the evidence of things unseen. When we trust God to protect and provide, to be as the passage said, our shield and reward.

If you truly know God you can be a witness while you wait, embracing a testimony in the midst of trials and tribulations. Walter Hawkins said, "Don't wait 'till the battle is over to shout now, you know in the end, you're gonna win".

Sometime we're so focused on what we don't have that we miss the blessings that we do have. Abraham was so focused on the future that he failed to celebrate the encouraging presence of God, he seemed to ungratefully ask God for more, asking God for the next blessing when God is blessing real good right now.

Sometime we're too busy trying to plan dinner before we finish lunch - be thankful for the bologna sandwich in your hand before begging up pot roast for dinner. Learn to trust God minute by minute, day by day – never settling for less than God's promise, trust in the Lord!

Look with me at Genesis 15:2-3 the passage reads, "And Abram said, Lord GOD, what wilt thou give me, seeing I go childless, and the steward of my house is this Eliezer of Damascus? 3 And Abram said, Behold, to me thou hast given no seed: and, lo, one born in my house is mine heir."

Don't let your situation overshadow God, as God's words of reassurance, comfort, and encouragement seemed merely a speed bump in Abraham's conversation with the Lord. Abraham wanted to know what God was going to give him – Abraham said I go childless, I have no seed, no heir – He's bothered, concerned, and dismissive. Abraham let's his situation overshadow God.

There are times when we neglect to praise God, worship God for being so good to us, because we're too focused on our situation. Going through too much to talk to God, worried away from worship, bad attitude – weary, wounded, and sad. We cannot afford to waste time while drained of joy, peace, and love founded within unmovable faith.

It's so easy to allow the strains of life, work, school, people, and family distracting us – leading us to settle for fair over favor, settling for good in exchange for great. Lead away from satisfaction by continued focus on situations.

We must embrace the way of God to experience the promise of God – although things may not appear as you think you want them, we must continue to rely on God, we can celebrate when our faith is complete. Although there are times when it seems that our faith is slipping away, we must hold on to God all the more.

The hymnist Robert Robinson penned:
Oh, to grace how great a debtor

Daily I'm constrained to be
Let that goodness like a fetter
Bind my wandering heart to Thee
Prone to wander, Lord, I feel it
Prone to leave the God I love
Here's my heart, oh, take and seal it
Seal it for Thy courts above
Here's my heart, oh, take and seal it
Seal it for Thy courts above

Never settle for less than God has promised – reflect with God, trust God, and don't let your situations overshadow God. All that you never had, you never will have if God says no, yet antithetically – can't nothing and nobody keep you away from God's promise! God will never ever let you down, whatever God says that you can believe – we can trust God even when we can't trace God. Don't let your situations, your problems overshadow God, in fact as the psalmist says we should come and magnify the Lord together. God is greater that any problem or situation that you may have. God is great and greatly to be praise.

Focus with me on Genesis 15:4 it reads, "And, behold, the word of the LORD came unto him, saying, This shall not be thine heir; but he that shall come forth out of thine own bowels shall be thine heir."

Expect to be personal, knowing that the Lord provides for us all – nevertheless, there are unique blessings that God bestows upon us individually. God cares about us as a collective and God cares about you individually, cares about me individually. God knows, sees, and cares about you.

There may be times when you feel all alone, maybe feeling like nobody cares – but you need to know that God cares, God hears, God sees, and God loves you! So much so that whatever God has promised us will become reality. Trust God and give it time – whatever God promised will manifest – the Lord is not a promise breaker.

We never have to settle for less than God's promise. God will take care of you. Jesus paid the price for the promise on the old rugged cross of Calvary, God the Son was crucified, buried, and arose with victory – an eternal testimony, defeating death and the grave you never have to settle for less than God's promise.

My hope is built on nothing less
Than Jesus' blood and righteousness;
I dare not trust the sweetest frame,
But wholly lean on Jesus' name.

When darkness veils His lovely face,
I rest on His unchanging grace;
In every high and stormy gale,
My anchor holds within the veil.

His oath, His covenant, His blood
Support me in the whelming flood;
When all around my soul gives way,
He then is all my hope and stay.

When He shall come with trumpet sound,
Oh, may I then in Him be found;
Dressed in His righteousness alone,
Faultless to stand before the throne.

On Christ, the solid Rock, I stand;
All other ground is sinking sand,
All other ground is sinking sand.

RESURRECTION WORK

SCRIPTURE

Nehemiah 5:1-5 And there was a great cry of the people and of their wives against their brethren the Jews. 2 For there were that said, We, our sons, and our daughters, are many: therefore we take up corn for them, that we may eat, and live. 3 Some also there were that said, We have mortgaged our lands, vineyards, and houses, that we might buy corn, because of the dearth. 4 There were also that said, We have borrowed money for the king's tribute, and that upon our lands and vineyards. 5 Yet now our flesh is as the flesh of our brethren, our children as their children: and, lo, we bring into bondage our sons and our daughters to be servants, and some of our daughters are brought unto bondage already: neither is it in our power to redeem them; for other men have our lands and vineyards.

OUTLINE

1. It May Compromise Many v1-2
2. It Puts Resources at Risk v3
3. It Puts Future Generations at Risk v5

MESSAGE

Rebuilding is often hard work. The struggle of restoration is often harder than building from scratch. When rebuilding, there is most often a previous structure that must be partially or completely removed in order for reconstruction. Assessments must be made, and generally the old structure or purpose must be evaluated to embrace the integrity of the original structure.

Construction can be stressful, brick by brick – architecturally preserving history into longevity through the manipulation and organization of space.

During the fifth and sixth centuries the city of Jerusalem had fallen to ruin after invasion from the Syrians – the temple and city needed resurrecting. If you've experienced the news media recently – war torn nations have been reduced to rubble. Iraq, parts of Syria, Yemen, and other places dealing with unrest have been reduced. Here in America entire towns have been devastatingly wiped away through wild fires, storms, and various natural disasters.

Roofs flattened, trees bent, commercial centers closed – buildings destroyed, which for many the loss of buildings, places of worship, centers of government, security, along with the marketplace become the central issue. It's easy to sometimes focus on the devastation of property as a result of war or natural disaster, but what about the people – what about the community. Far too often we value property over people.

Many preachers and Bible scholars present the prophesies of Ezra and Nehemiah as narratives centered around the rebuilding of the temple and the city of Jerusalem, especially with regards to the wall – border security. Nevertheless, I contend that amidst the resurrection work there is a third equally, if not more important, element essential to the prophecies, we must not forget the necessity to resurrect the Jerusalem community.

Within the fifth chapter of Nehemiah we may realize that the community, the socio-relational ecology needed rebuilding along with the temple and city. What good are buildings or fortifying walls without people to use and maintain them?

Nehemiah struggled to resurrect the city walls and the community, as we should be motivated by the movement of God's love to restore community, relationships, family, and human connectivity. We need to understand that nations cannot become great or great again without the restorative fortification of community. One blood, one people, one family. Nations and communities all around the globe need revitalizing resurrection work.

Look with me at Nehemiah 5:1-2 it reads, "And there was a great cry of the people and of their wives against their brethren the Jews. 2 For there were that said, We, our sons, and our daughters, are many: therefore we take up corn for them, that we may eat, and live."

It may compromise many, as the world can be dog eat dog, as greed, domination, and separatism often create social earthquakes destroying relational connectivity. Nehemiah had to deal with a fractured community of people. Divided by the usual divisive elements of class, experience, and political power.

The poor were being mistreated, drained from the comforts of life – barely getting by, struggling to make ends meet as the haves were exploiting the have-nots. We should be able to identify with such a society whereby the poor are neglected while profit and property eclipse people.

The people in the text today cried out for help, insisting that they were struggling to live without compromising the necessities of life and their children. Matthew 9:37 reminds us that the harvest is plentiful, yet the workers are few – God has work for us to do as Christ commands in Matthew chapter 22 that we love our neighbor, Romans 15:1 reminds us that we should bear the infirmities of the weak. We are challenged to care for those who are compromised by society.

We must know Christ in the power of His resurrection – realizing that the testimony of Christ should call us to take up the cross for the cause of Christ and that cause is love. We must embrace divine power and social justice for change as Christ loved, cared for, fed, and liberated humanity.

We must use our levels of influence to spread the Gospel, we must let the love of Christ manifest into action to bring restoration to our community. Big church buildings and meeting halls are worthless without people – we must care for the community. We must embrace resurrection work!

Life must be lived with purpose, for a purpose, and on purpose – the world truly is hungry for the Living Bread, we must bring love to meet the need of the compromised, misused, poor, underprivileged people – rejecting nationalistic separation to embrace all of humanity as God has created, sustained, and loved us. Let's care for the trafficked, pimped, starving, homeless, poor, neglected – care for the compromised.

Focus with me on Nehemiah 5:3 it reads, "Some also there were that said, We have mortgaged our lands, vineyards, and houses, that we might buy corn, because of the dearth."

It puts resources at risk and we are often so spiritual that our only answer is prayer – when prayer is a part of the process and solution, but not the only element. Faith without works is dead – yes, we must pray, but that's not all. We must pray, study our Bibles, and be led into action by God the Holy Spirit. Resources are at risk, people are of greater value than things, possessions, and resources – however that does not say that we don't need resources.

The point here is that we must prioritize, understanding that we should be concerned about one another's quality of life. Jesus admonished us to love others like we love ourselves. Do you like things, do you like living comfortably with food, shelter, and protection? We should be concerned. We should embrace resurrection work to facilitate resources for our community and our neighbors.

Over the last few months and through this year we are challenged to give, to support people reentering society outside of prison. Each month we have the opportunity to fulfill the command of Christ to focus on the prisoner. When each of us does our little part – together it becomes a big deal. We can help farm workers by focusing our attention on those companies that treat workers fairly. We can withhold our resources from companies like Wendy's, as we selflessly manage our resources to maximize the resources of others.

1 Timothy 5:18 indicates that a worker deserves to be paid – we care through our pockets. Where your heart is, your treasure is also. Show me your bank statement and I'll show you what you care about. We must learn to love our neighbors as we love ourselves – we must learn to love them with our resources as we love ourselves. Resurrection work must recognize the needs of others.

Lest I hold you too long look with me at Nehemiah 5:5 the passage reads, "Yet now our flesh is as the flesh of our brethren, our children as their children: and, lo, we bring into bondage our sons and our daughters to be servants, and some of our daughters are brought unto bondage already: neither is it in our power to redeem them; for other men have our lands and vineyards."

It puts future generations at risk if we fail to take action. The people cried to the Prophet Nehemiah, overly mortgaged, or in receivership/reposition, in bondage to credit and financial mistreatment – also realizing that their children are at risk.
The Harvard scholar Dr. Carter G. Woodson said, "If the Negro in the ghetto must eternally be fed by the hand that pushes him into the ghetto, he will never become strong enough to get out of the ghetto." And "If a race has no history, if it has no worthwhile tradition, it becomes a negligible factor in the thought of the world, and it stands in danger of being exterminated."

He knew just as the people of Nehemiah's day – that without a sustained commitment to community future generations are at risk. We must continually walk in the light of the Gospel – realizing that we must tell the story, we must continue to demand justice through love and faith. We are biblically allowed to become angry as long as we reject sin according to Ephesians 4:26. There are times when we should be angry – nevertheless there is a right way and a wrong way to handle matters.

We cannot adopt hatred, hatefulness, vengeance, and retribution – antithetically our anger should fuel us to pray, seeking divine solutions that foster lingering love. Our future is at risk – future generations need us to do as Nehemiah did, we must negotiate change.

The prophet called a meeting and spoke truth to power, he shared his heart, shared the situation and fostered social justice for the poor disfranchised people in Jerusalem. We must learn to seek solutions for others even when the issue may not directly affect us. We must do resurrection work for others and not for our glory. Our work must be done to the glory of God, serving others as if we are serving Christ – serving the least as if we are serving Christ.

I'm glad that God has not called us to take up the cross and follow Christ without an example. I Peter 2:21 reminds us that Christ is our example. Yes, to follow Christ we must be concerned about those at risk – hearing, praying, and serving the crying, hurting, destitute, the least of our society.
Christ shared our human condition, lived as one of us, and expressed His divine love to all by teaching, preaching, healing, leading, guiding, dying and rising for us. He healed the sick, fed the hungry, and ate with sinners. He leads us to feed the hungry, relieve the thirsty, clothe the naked, care for the stranger, visit the sick, and imprisoned.

We must like Nehemiah be concerned with the strength of the city, but we must prioritize people – realizing the need to care for our community. We can write letters to leaders addressing important issues, from Congress to the Vatican, Valley Forge and beyond.

Write letters to prisoners, take greeting cards to nursing homes. Join the Poor Peoples Campaign, volunteer to serve through a charitable organization, start a charitable organization addressing the needs of others. Pray to live with purpose and lasting love. In about a year from now the U.S. Census will commence – we can make sure to take it seriously.

Make sure that you are counted, get the word out to family and friends. The count, the census affects our voting districts, education, school districts, government allocations, and a number of other things – don't get counted out, be counted on to help embrace change.

I'm so glad that out of three men hanging at Calvary – one of them was sacrificed for us all. Jesus! God sacrificed God to save us as resurrection work emerged supreme through our great propitiation – Jesus, Jesus, Jesus, our Messiah, Jesus the Christ.

When thinking about Nehemiah and the building of the wall, I think about this church as over seven decades ago a preacher had a vision. Our founding Pastor Rubin Banes McCrary organized this congregation and over the course of our history, the men of the church built walls for worship – but notice the walls have fallen, but the community of believers are still here.

Dr. Charles Booth the late pastor of the Mt. Olivet Baptist church who was laid to rest this past week, said, "That after the wall was completed, Ezra read the law and the people in Jerusalem rejoiced, because they understood that it was God that not only punished them but it was also God that brought them an empathetic leader and it was God that was producing individuals who were willing to take risk, and the walls stood the test of time. The Greeks came and destroyed the Medo-Persian Empire, Alexander the Great came with all of the might and majesty of his military machine, the Jews ruled for a while, and then the Romans came into power – but the walls built by 80 year old man in 52 days were still standing, generations passed and then one day a 12 year old boy came from a little place called Nazareth, he stood within those walls."

That boy was 12 as I was 12 when I started preaching in this church several decades ago – I'm still trying to be like that 12 year old boy that stood within those Jerusalem walls – that boy was Jesus, does anybody know Jesus. Yes, that boy was in those walls for His first bar mitzvah – He talked with the doctors and lawyers, then later proclaimed to His parents that He was about His Father's business.

Living the Bible through education, missions, and ministry Jesus taught, healed the sick, and led disciples within the walls that Nehemiah built – then outside the walls was hung on a cross at Calvary, bled, suffered, and died not for the walls, but for the community – for us.

Anybody here know that Jesus died for us, then was buried for us – but I am so glad that the story does not stop there, the story does not end at a wall, but Jesus arose on the third day not for a wall, but for us, for all of us, Jesus got up from the grave with power, victory, and testimony for us all.

Jesus ascended into Heaven leaving us with a comforter, grace, mercy, peace, love, and joy. Life is sweeter with the Lord and your best day down here will never surpass the time we're going to have once Jesus returns! Won't that be a time – the community will be healed, liberated forever!

Every day will be sweeter than the last, joy will not end, tears will cease – everyday will be without cloud or storm and the community will worship God forever without end.

As Michael Bleecker and Mark Hall wrote:
Living, He loved me.
Dying, He saved me.
Buried, He carried my sins far away.
Rising, He justified freely forever
One day He's coming back gloriously!
Take up the cross, embrace the work, the resurrecting work of Jesus! Amen.

FREEDOM: READY, SET, GO

SCRIPTURE

Acts 12:1-12 Now about that time Herod the king stretched forth his hands to vex certain of the church. 2 And he killed James the brother of John with the sword. 3 And because he saw it pleased the Jews, he proceeded further to take Peter also. (Then were the days of unleavened bread.) 4 And when he had apprehended him, he put him in prison, and delivered him to four quaternions of soldiers to keep him; intending after Easter to bring him forth to the people. 5 Peter therefore was kept in prison: but prayer was made without ceasing of the church unto God for him. 6 And when Herod would have brought him forth, the same night Peter was sleeping between two soldiers, bound with two chains: and the keepers before the door kept the prison. 7 And, behold, the angel of the Lord came upon him, and a light shined in the prison: and he smote Peter on the side, and raised him up, saying, Arise up quickly. And his chains fell off from his hands. 8 And the angel said unto him, Gird thyself, and bind on thy sandals. And so he did. And he saith unto him, Cast thy garment about thee, and follow me. 9 And he went out, and followed him; and wist not that it was true which was done by the angel; but thought he saw a vision. 10 When they were past the first and the second ward, they came unto the iron gate that leadeth unto the city; which opened to them of his own accord: and they went out, and passed on through one street; and forthwith the angel departed from him. 11 And when Peter was come to himself, he said, Now I know of a surety, that the Lord hath sent his angel, and hath delivered me out of the hand of Herod, and from all the expectation of the people of the Jews. 12 And when he had considered the thing, he came to the house of Mary the mother of John, whose surname was Mark; where many were gathered together praying.

OUTLINE

1. Get Up v7
2. Get Ready v8
3. Follow v9

MESSAGE

Our text this week takes us to Luke's second dissertation of our Savior Jesus the Christ. Formally referred to as the Acts of the Apostles, although it is truly the Acts of Jesus and the Holy Spirit – the Acts of God within the life of the church. Within the Gospel penned by Luke we find Christ and the foundation of the church through the prefiguration of the New Temple.

The Gospel provides us with the divine insight that a New Temple will emerge along with the reestablishment of God's law to love within the temple of the heart occupied by the presence of God the Holy Spirit. The New Temple will be formed through the Body of Christ, the New Temple, the place where God dwells – our mind, heart, and soul. The Gospel manifests each of us as the temple – the place where God the Holy Spirit will reside, a church without walls. The word of the Lord comes to assure us that we are a church without walls as Zechariah 2:1-5 reads, "I lifted up mine eyes again, and looked, and behold a man with a measuring line in his hand. 2 Then said I, Whither goest thou? And he said unto me, To measure Jerusalem, to see what is the breadth thereof, and what is the length thereof. 3 And, behold, the angel that talked with me went forth, and another angel went out to meet him, 4 And said unto him, Run, speak to this young man, saying, Jerusalem shall be inhabited as towns without walls for the multitude of men and cattle therein: 5 For I, saith the LORD, will be unto her a wall of fire round about, and will be the glory in the midst of her."

Just as Luke shares the Good News of Christ as He teaches toward the Kingdom, the New Temple, and the New Jerusalem – Acts brings us the manifestation of Christ's great teaching. The book of Acts begins with move in day, as we see the evidence of God the Holy Spirit developing residence within humanity as Christ's sacrifice executed real-estate acquisition – God sacrificed God to salvifically procure our mind, heart, and soul for the eternal indwelling of God the Holy Spirit.

The primary tension within Acts seems to surround the division between people who can't think outside of the brick walls of the old temple paradigm. The traditions of the brick are too alluring for some who becomes agitated at the thought of a New Temple, where love abides as the law of God. A New Temple where people are treated with equity, respect, and familial love.

Old temple people wanted everyone to be physically circumcised, wanted everyone to embrace a kosher diet, they wanted everyone to celebrate cultural traditions irrelevant to the practice of faith in Christ. The New Temple, the temple of human hearts motivated love beyond degree – admonishing mixed cultures homogenized around the work, will, and way of Jesus through the power of the Holy Spirit. Anybody here know it's not about bricks and buildings – but it's about people. We are the temple, we are the church – one blood, one people, and one family – preserved by God's love.

Christ admonished them to spread the movement of the Gospel from Jerusalem to Judea, from Judea to Samaria, and to all the world. While teaching in Jerusalem a murder takes place, as a man named Stephen was murdered, stoned to death for the cause of Christ. Not long after the murder greater unrest was fueled, ejecting many believers from Jerusalem into Judea – later creating a large following in a city called Antioch, where Paul was able to establish a great church without walls. As with any great movement there was continued opposition.

Paul was eventually arrested not long after James was executed for allegiance to Christ the King. Religious haters allied with corrupt government to diminish the work of believers. Paul was jailed in opposition to the movement of Christ, a movement to love, a movement to include all cultures into the family of God, a movement celebrating the work of Christ. Paul had work to do for God, yet the evil powers on Earth emerged to censure the movement.

Our text today brings us into the onramp of Paul's confinement. Have you ever felt hindered from your divine purpose - blocked from God's command in your life – halted by hatred and negative negotiators? Aren't you glad that God always has the upper hand – that God always has the keys to freedom? God can and will make a way out of no way.

Nearly in the middle of the book, Paul is stopped by jail, with so much work remaining for the apostle, he's locked up. Anybody ever been denied access, locked up in the middle of your story – in need of a liberating miracle – in need of freedom to do God's work?

Look with me at Acts 12:7 it reads, "And, behold, the angel of the Lord came upon him, and a light shined in the prison: and he smote Peter on the side, and raised him up, saying, Arise up quickly. And his chains fell off from his hands."

Get up and be free. Chapter 12 commences by recounting the death of James the brother of John and the political reasoning behind the arrest of Paul, as the Bible tells us that Herod had him jailed to gain political favor from the Jews. Have you ever had someone put you down based on the opinion of others? The American system of law says that you are innocent until proven guilty – but we should know that public opinion and prejudice often reverses the process making one guilty until proven innocent. Paul seemed to be in one of those situations, guilty until proven innocent.

Paul was confined and heavily guarded, to the extent that guards were both outside and inside his cell. Paul went to sleep between two Roman guards, seemingly captured within the inescapable bowels of a Roman jail. Full of purpose, ministry, and passion for the Gospel of Jesus – locked up while full of powerful potential to serve humanity for the great potentate of eternity. Separated from service while severed by soldiers, but I wonder is there anybody here that knows God can work a miracle for you?

Romans 8:28-31 says, "And we know that all things work together for good to them that love God, to them who are the called according to his purpose. 29 For whom he did foreknow, he also did predestinate to be conformed to the image of his Son, that he might be the firstborn among many brethren. 30 Moreover whom he did predestinate, them he also called: and whom he called, them he also justified: and whom he justified, them he also glorified. 31 What shall we then say to these things? If God be for us, who can be against us?"

When the Lord has work for you to do, when purpose is before you – all you need to do is be willing and present, God will work it out when it seems that all hope is lost. I know God will, I should have been dead – but the Lord keeps working miracles for me. I am a miracle; I know the Lord is still in the miracle working business — there is no situation too hard for God.

The Bible says that the church prayed without ceasing — then under the shadow of night an angel appeared, touched Paul and told him to get up, in fact get up quickly. Paul got up and the chains fell off — hallelujah for Jesus! Paul got up and the chains fell off — we need to learn to take action within the movement of God. The Lord will make a way! Sometimes the chains are ready to fall off, we just need to get up with faith and watch God move.

James 2:14-20 says, "What doth it profit, my brethren, though a man say he hath faith, and have not works? can faith save him? 15 If a brother or sister be naked, and destitute of daily food, 16 And one of you say unto them, Depart in peace, be ye warmed and filled; notwithstanding ye give them not those things which are needful to the body; what doth it profit? 17 Even so faith, if it hath not works, is dead, being alone. 18 Yea, a man may say, Thou hast faith, and I have works: shew me thy faith without thy works, and I will shew thee my faith by my works. 19 Thou believest that there is one God; thou doest well: the devils also believe, and tremble. 20 But wilt thou know, O vain man, that faith without works is dead?"

James chapter 2 reminds us that we need faith — but the work of Christ should be the fruit of our faith. There are times when we need to do as Paul and rest, call it a night, save your strength, get some sleep, be still through your situation, get quiet and wait on the Lord – but when the Lord says move, we must move. The angel said get up and do it quickly – some of us need to get up at the command of God. Get up, get up and go as we are directed by Christ in Matthew 28:19-20, directed to go and teach all nations, baptizing them in the name of the Father, and of the Son, and of the Holy Ghost: Teaching them to observe all things whatsoever Christ has commanded and Jesus has commanded us to love God and love each other.

God is calling us to get up, change our posture, rearrange our position, correct our attitude, get alert, and get up – let the chains fall. Yes, faith never fails – the church was praying, God was moving. Paul was arrested, but God led him to rise up from between two guards – somebody just saw that, you know God can raise you up when the world is trying to hold you down, hold you back, and count you out.

It seems to me that he was being held until they could execute him as they did with James the brother of John – but God's hand! Oh, the enemy would have destroyed Paul, the enemy would have snuffed us out a long time ago – but the hand of God!
God has work for us to do, we are here to be like Jesus – we're here to spread the Gospel of Jesus, the message is love. The way is love, the will is love, the work is love – you are here to go and teach all nations to love. Love through service, love the stranger, the hungry, thirsty, sick, imprisoned, and naked. If you truly

want to be free – get up and let God bless you! Get up and go for God.

Focus now with me at Acts 12:8 it reads, "And the angel said unto him, Gird thyself, and bind on thy sandals. And so he did. And he saith unto him, Cast thy garment about thee, and follow me."

Get up and then **get ready**, the passage said he was directed to get dressed, gird yourself – get your clothes fixed, put your shoes on, get your coat on, let's get on the move. You know that's what we tell our children – get your shoes and coat on, which means get ready, it's time to go. Just because the chains have fallen, there is no time to stand around – fix yourself, get ready and let's go!

Some of us gave our life to God, we joined the church, stood up long enough for the chains to fall but are still standing in stagnated situations. Still unready, unprepared, uncovered, under resourced – just glad the chains have fallen, not willing to gird up, tighten up, fix your resources, put shoes on and let's run on a little further. You ever had to escape? When released from bondage, you don't have time to stay – but pack your bags and be on the way. Sometime there is no time to pack too much – you got to just gather up and get on. Get up and get ready – God has work for us to do. You joined the church a while ago, got up and the chains fell – now what?

It's time to get ready, time to live the Bible together through education, missions, and ministry. It's time, we've rested long enough, stood long enough – now it's time to ready yourself. Freedom most often requires work and preparation – planning with sacrifice. Get up, and get ready.

Put your clothes on, put your shoes on, put your coat on – you need your resources. We need to put on the word of God, we need to put on love and truth. We need to walk in the garment of the Holy Spirit – spiritually covered by Heaven's haberdashery.

Ephesians 6:13-18 says it like this, "Wherefore take unto you the whole armour of God, that ye may be able to withstand in the evil day, and having done all, to stand. 14 Stand therefore, having your loins girt about with truth, and having on the breastplate of righteousness; 15 And your feet shod with the preparation of the gospel of peace; 16 Above all, taking the shield of faith, wherewith ye shall be able to quench all the fiery darts of the wicked. 17 And take the helmet of salvation, and the sword of the Spirit, which is the word of God: 18 Praying always with all prayer and supplication in the Spirit, and watching thereunto with all perseverance and supplication for all saints;"

We need to be dressed for freedom, prepared to do the work of Christ. Freedom: ready, set, go – get up and get ready.

Look with me at Acts 12:8-9 it reads, "And the angel said unto him, Gird thyself, and bind on thy sandals. And so he did. And he saith unto him, Cast thy garment about thee, and follow me. 9 And he went out, and followed him; and wist not that it was true which was done by the angel; but thought he saw a vision."

Get up, get ready, and **follow.** Matthew 16:24 reminds us that Christ said that we must take up the cross and follow Him, God knows the plans set for us both individually and collectively. God has plans to prosper you, plans to lead you through faith and favor. Without Jesus we are lost, we are in bondage, we are imprisoned – we become free from the curse of death through adoption into the family of God. Once we become family, we are admonished to emulate our great example Jesus – we must take up the cross and follow.

I am made to rejoice today as I can see the pattern of God, the hand of God working through the text – as Paul found himself resting between two Roman guards, the church was praying while the politicians seemed to be plotting.

It seemed that Paul's head was soon to come off just like James the brother of John. It seemed that all was over for him, but I wonder if anybody knows that the Lord is the author and finisher of our faith. Yes, God writes our story – God is the great author, as the Lord told Jeremiah, I know the plans I have for you.

Does anybody know that God has a plan! As Paul is awakened by the angel, I'm reminded that God is the same yesterday, today, and forever more – with great power to perform miracles. The Lord can free us, liberate us from the bondage of the enemy – is there anything too hard for God?

If we need a testimony to freedom, Jesus is free from the grave, sin, and death – I don't know how Paul felt that night, but he could have certainly been comforted in knowing that God allowed Jesus to hang between - two just as Paul was guarded by two – there's nothing too hard for God.

I'm remind that God sacrificed God as Jesus hung, suffered, bled, and died between two thieves – they laid Jesus to rest in a tomb. Some thought that the story ended there, but Christ got up from the grave to free us all!

We have been made free to live as Jesus lived, teach as Jesus taught, and love as Jesus loved. We are free to do the work of Christ, walk in the will and way of God as the Holy Spirit guides us through the scripture and life. Ready, Set, Go – yes, walk with the Lord and be hearers and doers of God's work. Free to live like Jesus!

Get up, get ready, and follow Jesus

I leave you with the words of Hebrews 12:1-3, "Wherefore seeing we also are compassed about with so great a cloud of witnesses, let us lay aside every weight, and the sin which doth so easily beset us, and let us run with patience the race that is set before us, 2 Looking unto Jesus the author and finisher of our faith; who for the joy that was set before him endured the cross, despising the shame, and is set down at the right hand of the throne of God. 3 For consider him that endured such contradiction of sinners against himself, lest ye be wearied and faint in your minds."

HOW TO GET PAST CRYING

SCRIPTURE

Habakkuk 1:1-4, 2:1-4 The burden which Habakkuk the prophet did see. 2 O LORD, how long shall I cry, and thou wilt not hear! even cry out unto thee of violence, and thou wilt not save! 3 Why dost thou shew me iniquity, and cause me to behold grievance? for spoiling and violence are before me: and there are that raise up strife and contention. 4 Therefore the law is slacked, and judgment doth never go forth: for the wicked doth compass about the righteous; therefore wrong judgment proceedeth. **Habakkuk 2:1-4** I will stand upon my watch, and set me upon the tower, and will watch to see what he will say unto me, and what I shall answer when I am reproved. 2 And the LORD answered me, and said, Write the vision, and make it plain upon tables, that he may run that readeth it. 3 For the vision is yet for an appointed time, but at the end it shall speak, and not lie: though it tarry, wait for it; because it will surely come, it will not tarry. 4 Behold, his soul which is lifted up is not upright in him: but the just shall live by his faith.

OUTLINE

1. Don't Try to Judge God v1:1-4
2. Seek God v2:1
3. Live by Faith (Be Patient) v2:2-4

MESSAGE

The poet Henry Wadsworth Longfellow organized these words into a poem entitled *Rainy Day*, as he penned:

The day is cold, and dark, and dreary;
It rains, and the wind is never weary;
The vine still clings to the mouldering wall,
But at every gust the dead leaves fall,
And the day is dark and dreary.

My life is cold, and dark, and dreary;
It rains, and the wind is never weary;
My thoughts still cling to the mouldering Past,
But the hopes of youth fall thick in the blast,
And the days are dark and dreary.

Be still, sad heart! and cease repining;
Behind the clouds is the sun still shining;
Thy fate is the common fate of all,
Into each life some rain must fall,
Some days must be dark and dreary.

Now I'm told that only the highest class of preacher in prestigious churches quotes Longfellow – and I don't want you to think of me as some highfaluting pontiff. So, let me quote a more down to Earth singer that allowed the concept of this song to flow melodically from her beautiful voice – as Ella Fitzgerald sang in 1944 with the Ink Spots:

Into each life some rain must fall
But too much is falling in mine
Into each heart some tears must fall
But some day the sun will shine
Some folks can lose the blues in their hearts
But when I think of you another shower starts
Into each life some rain must fall

It seems to me that these gloomy words that loom from Longfellow's pen and Fitzgerald's voice sum up the feelings of tragedy – they encase emotions that the human experience may universally embrace. I wonder if there is anybody here that has had to cry sometime? Anybody ever have to lay awake at night?

Yes, we've all had our rainy days – into every life some rain does fall. We've had moments when the forecast of our emotions called for extreme precipitation on our face. Tears rolled down like showers from a thunderous storm.

Don't you remember when the climate of your life was set to depression, heartache, and pain? Remember when your love left, remember the child that ran away, the sad prognosis from your doctor, laid off, broke, busted, and disgusted – hurt produced tears that lead you to crying! All of us have had some of those days and perhaps some of those seasons.

The climate of your life – just stuck on sad, like school age children your clip moved to red a long time ago.

You've been denied recess and forget about an afternoon snack - life is like that sometime.

The prophet Habakkuk went through a season of lamentation, crying while sadly irritated. Habakkuk is unique in his writing as he does not address Israel to warn impending doom or to admonish righteous living. Habakkuk has a conversation with God that in essence inquired as to why bad things happen to good people, he inquired as to how long Israel would be allowed to exist while facilitating the mistreatment of the poor, he wanted to know how long would power, creed, and hatefulness persist.

Once God so graciously answered (and you do know God does not have to answer us), projecting that the Babylonians would be used to bring correction to Israel through the bowels of captivity – Habakkuk remained unsatisfied. The prophet could not understand why God would use even worse people to bring judgment on struggling Israel.

I wonder if you know that God can make a way out of no way? You can trust God even when you cannot trace God. The prophet was crying over things out of his control and above his pay grade, needlessly worrying sadly as we often do. Worried about that over which we have no control – forgetting that God's love has already settled every problem both behind us and before us. The prophet needed to get beyond crying as we do.

Look now with me at Habakkuk chapter 1 verses 2-4 as it reads, "The burden which Habakkuk the prophet did see. 2 O LORD, how long shall I cry, and thou wilt not hear! even cry out unto thee of violence, and thou wilt not save! 3 Why dost thou shew me iniquity, and cause me to behold grievance? for spoiling and violence are before me: and there are that raise up strife and contention. 4 Therefore the law is slacked, and judgment doth never go forth: for the wicked doth compass about the righteous; therefore wrong judgment proceedeth."

To get past crying, **don't try to judge God**. We will never have the ability to judge God, to grade God's paper, power, or performance – and the very frustration of trying will always bring you to sadness. The Serenity prayer penned by the respected theologian Reinhold Niebuhr reminds us to be practically realistic as we pray:

God, grant me the serenity to accept the things I cannot change, the courage to change the things I can, and the wisdom to know the difference. Living one day at a time, enjoying one moment at a time; accepting hardship as a pathway to peace; taking, as Jesus did, this sinful world as it is, not as I would have it; trusting that You will make all things right if I surrender to Your will; so that I may be reasonably happy in this life and supremely happy with You forever in the next. Amen.

We must learn to embrace God's love in every season of our life – understanding that God's love will always present the best outcome for all of humanity. We are not wise enough to evaluate the process – we must wait until the finished product.

The scripture reminds us in 1 John 3:2, "Beloved, now are we the sons of God, and it doth not yet appear what we shall be: but we know that, when he shall appear, we shall be like him; for we shall see him as he is."

We are not God's board of directors, although God will hear us as the Lord heard and responded to Habakkuk's questions – God never has to reply. As the late Andrae Crouch wrote, whatever God says our response should simply be "Amen."

Judging God is a waste of time, that will produce nothing but frustrated tears. Anytime you feel like playing judge, throw out all your cases toward God and others – in order to work on the most important case of your life – your own.
Judge you against the example of Jesus the Christ. Judge you against God the Son and you will always have a case to work on. How to get past crying.

Look now with me at Habakkuk 2:1, "I will stand upon my watch, and set me upon the tower, and will watch to see what he will say unto me, and what I shall answer when I am reproved."

We must **seek God** to get past crying, far too often we see our problems and situations – we see questions and uncertainty, but we need to see God.

In fact, we need to follow the example of God – where would we be if God judged us on what we look like without the filter of love. Talk about a mess in the morning, you know how you look when you first wake up, breath still hot from sleep, hair in need of a comb, body needs a bath and some cocoa butter – well as bad as we look physically when we first wake up, we look worse spiritually under the influence of our sins both past, present, and perhaps those to come, nevertheless God loves us. God does not welcome or affirm our sin – but God both welcomes and loves us.

God sought and saved us while yet sinners – Jesus died for us; we need to learn to seek God as God has sought us. Look beyond yourself, beyond your situations, beyond your problems, beyond your depression, beyond your bank account, beyond any and everything that stands between you and God. When we seek God and give it to the Lord – love will move us beyond the pit of pain dug by the spade of sorrow and gift us with a well of joy springing forth with sweet water eternal.

When problems arise, we need to emulate the later actions of the prophet Habakkuk as he stood waiting to see what God would do.

Hmmm, when you can't understand, then just stand and wait on God. I don't understand why they treat me bad when I've presented good – just stand and wait on God.

Don't understand why government is the way it is, bigotry, racism, and tyranny seasoned with corruption – just stand and wait for God. From hospitals to court rooms – seek God!

We may not understand it now – we may not even understand how God did it later, but we can rest on God's eternal love to keep us eternally and that should be enough to keep us happy – like a baby's rattle or graham cracker cookie or like grandma's starlight peppermint candy carefully unwrapped on Sunday morning.

Is there anybody here seeking God? Well I'm here to tell you as Jesus said, "Seek and ye shall find, knock and the door shall be opened." Knock, knock – seeking God in every situation! Ain't God all right – I know God is alright!

But lest I hold you too long – although I know you know that when we talk about the goodness of God and all that has been done for us – something liable to get started in here! God is so good, naw, God is great and greatly to be praise – hmmm, naw, God is excellent, Oh, how excellent is God's name!

God is worthy, see when you start to praise God, tears of despair disappear for tears of joy. Seek God.

Look with me at Habakkuk chapter 2 verses 2-4 the passage reads, "And the LORD answered me, and said, Write the vision, and make it plain upon tables, that he may run that readeth it. 3 For the vision is yet for an appointed time, but at the end it shall speak, and not lie: though it tarry, wait for it; because it will surely come, it will not tarry. 4 Behold, his soul which is lifted up is not upright in him: but the just shall live by his faith."

Some ways to get past crying:

Don't try to judge God, seek God, and finally, we must **live by faith** – patiently waiting, seeking, and trusting God. Our English version of the Bible provides parenthetic summery as we are admonished in 2 Corinthians 5:7 that we walk by faith, not by sight.

Is there anybody here that would have lost their mind a long time ago if you lived by what you see. Like Habakkuk wondering why do bad things happen to good people?

Why are babies dying at the border or separated from family, why has the income gap continued to increase as the rich get richer and the poor get poorer? Why can't I find a partner to love and love me back? Why don't children come out perfect – can we come up with a baby that doesn't need feeding and changing, why, why, why?

Habakkuk records the vision, makes it plain – knows to wait, because the word of the Lord shall become

manifested. Embrace God even on the run – God said write it so it can be read even on the run.
Have you ever been on the run – life got you all twisted and confused? Sometimes crying and not even knowing why – timid at every turn, but when we study to show ourselves approved, and we embrace God's truth in our lives! Hallelujah, glory hallelujah – just wait on the Lord, just wait, the promise will come. Why and when are not important when we trust God! Why, why, why?

Well I can't tell you why – but in the words of the song composed by Clifton Jones:

Trouble in my way, I have to cry sometimes.
Trouble in my way, I have to cry sometimes.
I lay awake at night, but that's alright;
Jesus will fix it after while.
Stepped, stepped in the furnace a long time ago;
Shadrech, Meshach and Abendigo.
No, they were not worried, oh, this I know;
they knew that Jesus will fix it after while.
Trouble in my way, I have to cry sometimes.
Trouble in my way, I have to cry sometimes.
I lay awake at night, but that's alright;
Jesus will fix it after while.
Jesus, He will fix it.
Gonna be alright.
It's gonna be alright in the morning,
He's gonna make a way.

Anybody here glad – because Jesus fixed it out on Calvary? Glad because He captured the victory over sin, death, the grave, and every enemy? Glad because He arose with all power in Heaven and in Earth – glad that Jesus fixed it! Glad that trouble don't last always! Glad that Jesus fixed it! So glad!

Glad that Revelation 21:3-4 says, "And I heard a great voice out of heaven saying, Behold, the tabernacle of God is with men, and he will dwell with them, and they shall be his people, and God himself shall be with them, and be their God. 4 And God shall wipe away all tears from their eyes; and there shall be no more death, neither sorrow, nor crying, neither shall there be any more pain: for the former things are passed away."

And God shall wipe away our tears – how to get past crying, have faith in God.

LIVING THE BIBLE TOGETHER: THROUGH EDUCATION

SCRIPTURE

2 Timothy 3:14-4:5 But continue thou in the things which thou hast learned and hast been assured of, knowing of whom thou hast learned them; 15 And that from a child thou hast known the holy scriptures, which are able to make thee wise unto salvation through faith which is in Christ Jesus. 16 All scripture is given by inspiration of God, and is profitable for doctrine, for reproof, for correction, for instruction in righteousness: 17 That the man of God may be perfect, throughly furnished unto all good works.

4:1 I charge thee therefore before God, and the Lord Jesus Christ, who shall judge the quick and the dead at his appearing and his kingdom; 2 Preach the word; be instant in season, out of season; reprove, rebuke, exhort with all longsuffering and doctrine. 3 For the time will come when they will not endure sound doctrine; but after their own lusts shall they heap to themselves teachers, having itching ears; 4 And they shall turn away their ears from the truth, and shall be turned unto fables. 5 But watch thou in all things, endure afflictions, do the work of an evangelist, make full proof of thy ministry.

OUTLINE

1. Never Stop Learning (Continual) v14-15
2. Know the Product v16-17
3. Know the Stakes v4:3-5

MESSAGE

This week's scripture portion seemed mis-organized as we used the latter part of the text last week and this week it seems like we are reading in a time machine headed back to the past.

Nevertheless, I am gleeful that the scriptures have been presented this way. If you were not present last week, I will fill you in and if you were here – this will be a refresher. Last week our Assistant Pastor explained that the Apostle Paul was confined to a Roman jail – he requested that Timothy bring him a few items - via this letter that we are reading from today.

We gain access to Paul's lifestyle, character, and perhaps other physical behavioral aspects that formulated the Apostle's mind.

He wanted his cloak, parchments, and book. Two of the three things that he sent for required intellect to appreciate. He asked for his cloak or coat – because we later learn that winter is coming.

Paul is now approaching the sunset of life, as the final scenes of his life were swiftly approaching – very likely his last winter was on its way and Paul needed his coat.

But just when one would think that his next request would have been some delectable delight, a savory soup, or choice cut of meat – Paul says, bring my parchments and books. We are able to surmise that Paul valued study, he valued reading, and thinking.

Bring my coat to keep me warm and bring me something to read. In fact, bring my parchments so that I may study the scripture, bring my book so that I may dig deep into the word of God. Paul must have known that Jesus commissioned us to go teach – the summon to teach is repeated as our mission to spread Jesus to all the world.

Just as good readers make great writers, good learners, make great leaders. We must value education in order to truly live the Bible together.

Last week's understanding of Paul's request for his cloak, parchments, and books – grants us the benefit of knowing that Paul walks it like he talks it, lives it like he preaches it. In 2 Timothy, chapter 3 describes many factions of our society today - Paul says in the last days perilous times shall come, "...men shall be lovers of their own selves, covetous, boasters, proud, blasphemers, disobedient to parents, unthankful, unholy, 3 Without natural affection, trucebreakers, false accusers, incontinent, fierce, despisers of those that are good, 4 Traitors, heady, highminded, lovers of pleasures more than lovers of God; 5 Having a form of godliness, but denying the power thereof: from such turn away. 6 For of this sort are they which creep into houses, and lead captive silly women laden with sins, led away with divers lusts, 7 Ever learning, and never able to come to the knowledge of the truth. 8 Now as Jannes and Jambres withstood Moses, so do these also resist the truth: men of corrupt minds, reprobate concerning the faith. 9 But they shall proceed no further: for their folly shall be manifest unto all men, as theirs also was. 10 But thou hast fully known my doctrine, manner of life, purpose, faith, longsuffering, charity, patience, 11 Persecutions, afflictions, which came unto me at Antioch, at Iconium, at Lystra; what persecutions I endured: but out of them all the Lord delivered me. 12 Yea, and all that will live godly in Christ Jesus shall suffer persecution. 13 But evil men and seducers shall wax worse and worse, deceiving, and being deceived."

Wow! Sin plunges humanity beneath the ignorance of evil worsened by a lack of Biblical study under the guidance of God the Holy Spirit. The human condition is diseased by sin and consistently requires divine remedy.

Paul's letter to Timothy suggests that God's word, the scriptures, the Bible presents the best and only remedy for wickedness. 2 Timothy 2:15 says, "Study to shew thyself approved unto God, a workman that needeth not to be ashamed, rightly dividing the word of truth." We must live the Bible together through education.

Look with me at 2 Timothy 3:14-15 as it reads, "But continue thou in the things which thou hast learned and hast been assured of, knowing of whom thou hast learned them; 15 And that from a child thou hast known the holy scriptures, which are able to make thee wise unto salvation through faith which is in Christ Jesus."

In order to live the Bible together through education we should **never stop learning**. I would contend that practically every demonic situation and dilution becomes manageable toward maturity when we are committed to Bible learning.

We must continually seek the wisdom of the scriptures to embrace the will, way, and wisdom of God. The Bible has the solution to all of the world's ills, as we are made overcomers through the example of Christ – who overcame the world, defied the grave, and defeated death.

Nevertheless, many of us struggle powerlessly as we embrace Bible possession while rejecting Bible study – we own a Bible while neglecting to read it. Then there are times when we read but abandon meaningful study. James 1:22 reminds us that we must be hearers and doers of God's word.

In order to affectively, truly, and authentically be a Christian we must follow Christ. To be a follower of Christ, we must study the path of God the Son, Jesus the Christ. We cannot afford to allow our interest in God's word to become latent, dormant, or diminished – antithetically we must remain thirsty for God's Holy Word.

We must maintain quiet time with God, embracing an intimate connection with our Bible. Just as we set aside time for everything else – we must set aside intentional time for Bible learning as we educate ourselves to the way of God. You cannot holistically follow Jesus if you do not know Him.

Paul admonishes Timothy to remain committed to what he's learned while remembering the origin of your learning. Paul essentially encourages the young pastor to remain steadfast toward the faith.

Paul had been socially afflicted; he was on the no fly list if you will – enemy of the state and the people. Paul was old now and experiencing his last days confined to a cold Roman jail.

The Romans didn't care for him as they did not want any power to overshadow their own government, the Jews rejected his faithfulness to Jesus. Many of the converts, the church by and large, distanced Paul because his imprisonment seemed powerless seasoned with faithlessness, embarrassment possibly staining the collective of the early church.

Haven't you ever known people that will kick you when you're down? People that try to disqualify you for Heaven based on their limited analysis – more concerned about your situation than their own. Paul had some enemies, affiliates of the church that foolishly used his incarceration to disqualify him as a man of God.

I need you to know that we don't get to choose for God. Who God calls - whoever God chooses – God will justify. In the words that the Gospel artist James Cleveland used to sing:

Please be patient with me, God is not through with me yet.
If you should see me and I'm not walking right,
and if you should hear me and I'm not talking right;
Please remember what God has done for me,
when He gets through with me, I'll be what He wants me to be.
When God gets through with me, I shall come forth, I shall come forth like pure gold.

Paul reminds Timothy to live in the light of God's wisdom – rejecting unfounded opinionated judgmental rhetoric designed to divide, disrupt, and destroy God's tender children. We must learn to reject our mundane musings to embrace God's wisdom – we are living the Bible together through education.

Focus with me on 2 Timothy 3:16-17 as it reads, "All scripture is given by inspiration of God, and is profitable for doctrine, for reproof, for correction, for instruction in righteousness: 17 That the man of God may be perfect, throughly furnished unto all good works."

We should **know the product** of living the Bible together through education – as Biblical learning produces perfection through God's Holy Scriptures, Biblical learning produces perfection through God's word. Verse 16 exposes the profitability of scripture for doctrine, reproof, correction, and instruction in righteousness.

God's word produces the vehicular resource of perfection to transport us unto all good works – whereby we may fulfil the great command and mission of Christ.

Studying God's word produces wisdom while defusing ignorance. Prophecy emerges from God's word, as we gain inspiration and hope for things to come through the foundational paradigm spread throughout the Biblical narrative. God is preeminently perspicacious throughout all of eternity – as God's word makes us both individually and collectively optimal for purposeful service.

I wonder if anybody here can remember their "before Jesus and after Jesus" picture. How was your life before and how is it now? Where were you going, and how much greater the destination when God the Holy Spirit as your travel agent.

You can never go wrong with God. Paul essentially conveys to Timothy the world condition – yet provides the solution. When we embrace the scriptures, we get back correction, we become aware of our mistakes, our wrong, and our sins through Biblical teachings, training, guidance, and education. We will never get better without correction applied with love, forgiveness, mercy, and grace. You can never get right, if you don't know you're wrong.

God's word produces a better me, a better you, and a better us. If we spread the Gospel, tell the good news about Jesus and watch the world change - admonishing others to study while living through the power of God's word. We are made better through God's word as we live the Bible together through education.

Look with me at 2 Timothy 4:3-5 it reads, "For the time will come when they will not take the true teaching; but, moved by their desires, they will get for themselves a great number of teachers for the pleasure of hearing them; 4 And shutting their ears to what is true, will be turned away to belief in foolish stories. 5 But be self-controlled in all things, do without comfort, go on preaching the good news, completing the work which has been given you to do."

We should remain aware, we should **know the stakes** – learning now for later, stocking up on God's word to store within our heart, mind, and soul, as 2 Timothy chapter 4 is a postlude to this life. The text seems to warn us that a time will come when the truth will be in limited supply. Genuine Bible education will be nearly impossible to experience while false teachers dispense foolish stories.

I wonder is there anybody here that knows a shortage is on the way, in fact the truth seems to be polluted within many of the popular voices we hear, the talking heads don't seem to be talking right. Distorted, dissuaded, and deficient truth is best called a lie. When the truth is partnered with falsehoods, it's best to call it what it is, a lie.

The intention to deceive, when the truth is altered to destroy us or lead us away from God – we should automatically know that demonic droppings, impurities are as a fly in the ointment, poisonous to the whole. The enemy wants us to be deceived and divided from the truth, because God is truth and without truth – we're without God.

When we fail to embrace biblical learning, education, and study – we risk a future filled with lies. Unverifiable nuggets of illusion without the balance of the truth when the days of deception fully creep in as perilous times flood our world.

We need to educate ourselves now in the ways of God, as someday it may be too late. We must work while the day is yet with us, as the night cometh when no one will be able to work. We need to live the Bible together through education.

We must resist the foolish stories to embrace true belief in God, disjoined from fantasy – founded upon the truth approved through the guidance of God the Holy Spirit. Yes, we need to be biblically educated – we are living the Bible together through education.

Lest, I hold you too long – be reminded today that winter is on the way, just as it was for Paul residing as a prisoner in a Roman jail as he penned this letter.

Walking within the shadow of life, waiting for death as one could possibly see darkness picking up the pace to gain traction for transition. Paul was at death's door while jailed in Rome, with winter on the horizon – he clasps pen and paper to message Timothy before Instant Messaging and Snapchat.

Paul reminds the young pastor to stay in the faith, don't forget what you've learned. Now bring me my cloak, parchments, and books. This triad, these few - just one more than two – this little list reminds us to keep studying, keep learning to the end, never forget what you've learned. Don't forget the importance of Biblical education.

Well as we stand in the shadow of noon, it's time to get out of here, soon we will need to grab our coats to get out of here, as winter is coming – but like Paul, after we get warm enough – not luxurious, but condition-able, the BRING ME THE PARTCHMENTS AND THE BOOKS.

Hmmm, can I talk to you on my way to my seat – yeah, yeah bring me my coat, let me survive with the basics until the Lord returns, now that we got that out the way bring me my Bible and my books.

God speaks within the Holy Scriptures, every word given by God. Sixty-six books recorded by approximately forty writers – every book, every word, every dot brings joy, sweet everlasting joy. We live to study and study to live God's word, as the word of God is a well of life that will never run dry.

I wish I has somebody here glad about the Book! Bring the Book and Adam with Eve can testify that God is our creator, bring the Book as Noah floats through on the ark, bring the Book so that Abraham with Sarah knows that God doesn't break promises, bring the Book so Moses can illustrate how God's hand delivers, Oh, have you been in the Book? Daniel was protected in the lion's den and Shadrach, Meshach, and Abednego were cooled in the fiery hot furnace.

I feel like Paul this morning – bring the Book! Bring the word of God, the scriptures, bring me the Bible! Bring the Book, Jesus died on the old rugged cross, was buried, and arose from the grave!

Bring the Book so that we may live the Bible together through education, with value and thanksgiving forever understanding, not by power and not by might – but God. Bring the Book so we never forget what we've learned – He died, was buried, arose from the grave, and we know that someday Jesus shall return for us. Bring the Book and let's live the Bible together.

HOW TO BE GRATEFULLY CLEAN

SCRIPTURE

Luke 17:11-19 And it came about that when they were on the way to Jerusalem he went through Samaria and Galilee. 12 And when he went into a certain small town he came across ten men who were lepers, and they, keeping themselves at a distance, 13 Said, in loud voices, Jesus, Master, have mercy on us. 14 And when he saw them he said, Go, and let the priests see you. And, while they were going, they were made clean. 15 And one of them, when he saw that he was clean, turning back, gave praise to God in a loud voice; 16 And, falling down on his face at the feet of Jesus, he gave the credit to him; and he was a man of Samaria. 17 And Jesus said, Were there not ten men who were made clean? where are the nine? 18 Have not any of them come back to give glory to God, but only this one from a strange land? 19 And he said to him, Get up, and go on your way; your faith has made you well.

OUTLINE

1. See Your Healing v15
2. Be Willing to Turn Back v15
3. Acknowledge God v15
4. Be Humble v16

MESSAGE

Our scripture today, presents the encounter of ten diseased people and Jesus. Our great savior, Jesus was on the path to Jerusalem, traveling through Samaria and Galilee when He was summoned by ten leprous men.

They had leprosy, although we are not told the stage of their afflictions – we may infer that their symptoms can be paralleled to the usual conditions.

These men would have more than likely lived 5-20 years before they would have known their unhealthy fate. Leprosy often comes on gradually as skin becomes affected and infected eventually nerve damage may render sufferers completely anesthetized with the inability to feel pain. Now initially this may seem ideal, however – the inability to feel pain leads to undetected injury.

When you can't feel pain, you'll continue to injure yourself while remaining unaware. Hmmm, the lack of feeling brings us to ignore injury – when we can't feel pain, our bodies have shut us out of our physical cognition.

No pain felt will bring us to increased injuries experience. Just because you don't feel it – doesn't mean you're not experiencing it. Then to make matters worse, often the final stages brought on blindness and respiratory stress.

Ten afflicted men came to Jesus with leprosy – possibly void of the ability to feel pain, blind, and short of breath. Ten men with a degenerating disease.

Challenged by increased susceptibility to injury, blindness, and respiratory stress/shortness of breath.

It seems to me that our society is epidemically infected with spiritual leprosy. Think about it we seem to be psychologically fried, numb, and desensitized to tragic emotions. We suffer from some level of blindness as the truth pans from clear view and we become short of breath – denying, distorting, and diminishing the truth as voices against evil become silent.

Yes, it seems to me that we are infected with spiritual leprosy – violence unchecked because we lack the feelings to fully experience the pain of a mass shooting. Our lack of ability to feel the pain, causes the injuries to increase and intensify.

Many of us are comfortable as our children watch violence, participate digitally through video games that encourage physically detached violence while cognitively attached. We stab and shoot through games – blood, guts, and gloom have somehow become exciting – does that make sense? We have spiritual leprosy – we don't feel it, can't see it, and refuse to breathe or speak against it.

We're diseased, we've been soiled by the impurity of sin like harmful bacteria beckoning us from wellness to sickness. Just as ten leprous men came to Jesus – we need God the Son to cleanse and make us well again, restore our wellness. We need to feel, see, and breathe – we need the power of Jesus in our lives.

Well, the ten men cried out for mercy, they called out to Jesus – they gained the attention of Jesus and He told them to go show themselves to the priest, and as they went, they were healed.

Although there were ten men, only one gratefully returned to praise God – which seems to speak loudly as to the way of the world, the pattern of humanity as the entitled seem to outnumber the grateful.
They left diseased, they departed on the instruction of Christ – they were granted the mercy they requested, yet lacked the gratitude to turn and gain further access to Christ our great Savior. Oh, but one man was grateful, he turned and Jesus gave the healed man greater confirmation and affirmation as Jesus told the man that his faith had made him well. The longer we stay with Jesus, the stronger we get:

Blessed assurance, Jesus is mine
O what a foretaste of glory divine
Heir of salvation, purchase of God
Born of His Spirit, washed in His blood

We must learn to turn toward God at all times as reciprocally we gain the assurance of holistic wellness – grateful for Jesus. Gratefully clean, gratefully connected – grateful for love. How to be gratefully clean.

Look with me at Luke 17:15 it reads, "And one of them, when he saw that he was clean, turning back, gave praise to God in a loud voice;"

You need to **see your healing**, we need to see our healing, acknowledge wellness, acknowledge the power of God that sustains and keeps us. We must learn to see the many blessings that God has bestowed upon us. Far too often we suppress blessings while magnifying our sadness, lack, and deficiency – when we would be exponentially better if we embraced God on the bright side of life.

When upon life's billows you are tempest tossed,
When you are discouraged, thinking all is lost,
Count your many blessings, name them one by one,
And it will surprise you what the Lord hath done. Count your blessings, name them one by one; Count your blessings, see what God hath done; Count your blessings, name them one by one; Count your many blessings, see what God hath done.

Look with me again at Luke 17:15 it reads, "And one of them, when he saw that he was clean, turning back, gave praise to God in a loud voice;"

We must be willing to see our healing and we need to **be willing to turn back**. There are too many of us that come to God when we have issues and situations – but we get ghost when all seems well again, attempting to use God like an ATM machine.

Ten people healed, nine men went on their way – but one was grateful enough to turn and worship God. I wonder is there anybody here – that knows God has been too great in your life to just keep on going? We've got to turn and acknowledge our blessing, Thank you

Lord. Can anybody here turn for just a minute and tell the Lord thank you? Thank you, Lord, for all that you've done for us.

Thank You Lord, thank You Lord, thank You Lord
The greatful heart
With a greatful heart
With a song of praise
With an outstreched arm
I will bless Your name
Oh, thank You Lord, yes
I just wanna thank You Lord
Focus with me again on Luke 17:15 it reads, "And one of them, when he saw that he was clean, turning back, gave praise to God in a loud voice;"

We should see our healing, be willing to turn back, and **acknowledge God**. The other nine previously diseased men may have moved on – but one guy turned to praise God. Unashamedly loud praising God. Is there anybody here that said like the song writer?

I said I wasn't gonna tell nobody but I couldn't keep it to myself, what the Lord has done for me.

You ought to been there, when He saved my soul.
You ought to been there, when He put my name on the roll

Then I started walking, started talking, started singing, started shouting about what the Lord has done for me. what the Lord has done for me.

Focus with me on Luke 17:16 as it reads, "And, falling down on his face at the feet of Jesus, he gave the credit to him; and he was a man of Samaria."

We must see our healing, be willing to turn, acknowledge God, and **be humble**. Ten afflicted men were healed but one turned to praise and fell on his face at Jesus feet. We must humble ourselves to the way of Jesus – gratefully clean.

If the Lord has done anything for us, and God has done so much for us, we need to be humble, stop acting like we pulled ourselves up by our own bootstraps. Maybe you want to keep embracing lies, like you're all that – but I am humbly here to tell you that I can't live without the Lord. We should be so grateful – praising at Jesus feet like the gratefully healed leper.

Poet Karen Holland, penned the poem "At the Feet of Jesus:

Come, fall before the throne of grace,
At the feet of Jesus, seek His face.

His love so wide and long, so high, so deep,
His power and mercy so complete,
found before the throne, at Jesus' feet.

To the feet of Jesus bring all your fears,
At the feet of Jesus - He'll dry all your tears.

Come to the throne, come worship the One you adore, At His feet, sing with joy forevermore.

Focus with me again on Luke 17:16 as it reads, "And, falling down on his face at the feet of Jesus, he gave the credit to him; and he was a man of Samaria."

Jesus has made us clean to present us acceptable before the throne of God – we should be gratefully clean. We should see our healing, be willing to turn, acknowledge God, be humble, and know that you're not supposed to be here.

The returning man gratefully filled with praise for Jesus, giving Jesus the credit! I wonder do we give Jesus the credit as we should? The text says that he was of Samaria – the man was a Samaritan.

The man was a foreigner and stranger – in John 4:9 the woman of Samaria said to Jesus, "Why do you, a Jew, make a request for water to me, a woman of Samaria? She said this because Jews have nothing to do with the people of Samaria."

The leper that turned to praise was from Samaria – this guy was not an insider, he was an outsider not just by disease, he was an outsider by birth.

Anybody here ever been an outsider? Not based on what you've done, not based on meritocracy – just born on the wrong side of the tracks. Born poor, born to the wrong family, born the wrong color, born to the have nots?

The Samaritan leper wasn't supposed to be there, he was an outsider granted inside access. Although the ten lepers had collectively requested mercy – only the one that returned received personal attention from God the Son our great Messiah.

That's what grateful praise does for us, that's what humility does for us. We cannot afford to go to God embracing entitlement – we must humbly acknowledge our blessings and walk gratefully clean pointing to the Savior our great healer. The Samaritan wasn't likely to be there – but faith made him well.

Anybody here with enough faith to see what the Lord has done, faith to turn in praise, faith to acknowledge God, faith to know that we don't belong here, we are not worthy but faith to be glad that God has redeemed us. We should be willing to turn toward God – as we reap what we sow and with great expectation - I am looking forward to that day when Jesus shall return for us.

Jesus suffered, bled, and died – someday He will return for us and for that we should be grateful that we've been picked up, turned around, feet on solid ground, and awaiting our Savior's return.

O for a thousand tongues to sing
my great Redeemer's praise,

*the glories of my God and King,
the triumphs of his grace!*

*My gracious Master and my God,
assist me to proclaim,
to spread thro' all the earth abroad
the honors of your name.*

*Jesus! the name that charms our fears,
that bids our sorrows cease,
'tis music in the sinner's ears,
'tis life and health and peace.*

*He breaks the power of cancelled sin,
he sets the prisoner free;
his blood can make the foulest clean;
his blood availed for me.*

*To God all glory, praise, and love
be now and ever given
by saints below and saints above,
the Church in earth and heaven.*

HOW TO AVOID WORD BURN

SCRIPTURE

Jeremiah 5:11-14 For the house of Israel and the house of Judah have dealt very treacherously against me, saith the LORD. 12 They have belied the LORD, and said, It is not he; neither shall evil come upon us; neither shall we see sword nor famine: 13 And the prophets shall become wind, and the word is not in them: thus shall it be done unto them. 14 Wherefore thus saith the LORD God of hosts, Because ye speak this word, behold, I will make my words in thy mouth fire, and this people wood, and it shall devour them.

OUTLINE

1. Never Move Against God v11
2. Never Disregard God v12
3. Never Feel Untouchable v12
4. Never Trust a Windbag Preacher v13
5. Never Forget You Can't Survive v14

MESSAGE

Growing up I frequently heard the phrase "sticks and stones may hurt your bones, but words will never hurt you" – I question the integrity of these words as not long after learning this phrase, we were taught the metonymic adage, coined by English author Edward Bulwer-Lytton that "The pen is mightier than the sword."

Proverbs 18:21 says, "Death and life are in the power of the tongue: and they that love it shall eat the fruit thereof." There is power in the tongue, power in words – life and death.

Whoever came up with the idea that words could never hurt you – must have been isolated from conversation, void of both written and audible communication.

In fact, many of us have forgotten most of our physical fights, bludgeoning battles, and adverse altercations – but negative words are rehearsed continually within the metropolis of our mental movements. Words can hurt us long after physical wounds have disappeared into the pause of the past.

Hebrews 4:12 says, "For the word of God is quick, and powerful, and sharper than any twoedged sword, piercing even to the dividing asunder of soul and spirit, and of the joints and marrow, and is a discerner of the thoughts and intents of the heart."

God's word is divinely powerful, as we are guaranteed blessings through obedience to God or cursing/misfortune when disobedient to God's word. The righteous holiness of God's word will either testify for or against us – as the choice to embrace or reject the word rests individually upon each of us. Joshua 24:15 admonishes us to choose to serve God without hesitation.

Someday we will be divided by those who received or those who rejected God's word. For according to Romans chapter 6, the wages of sin is death, but the gift of God is eternal life – we will continually die in damnation or live in eternal abundance with God based on our response to God's word.

Biblically, the prophecy of Jeremiah seems to summon us toward the rich wisdom of God's word leading us from self-direction to divine guidance. Jeremiah was commissioned by God to proclaim the word of God – warning Israel with Judah that disregarding, disrespecting, and denying God will bring destruction.

Jeremiah was sent to tell the people that God would bring judgment against the disobedient, wicked, and idolatrous. The poor, less fortunate, and underprivileged were ill-treated through corruption.

Nevertheless, the primary issue emerged from fully or partially abandoning God – they had fully or partially walked away from God. Israel and Judah had walked away from the Creator, away from the one that had delivered them from Egypt, brought them from slavery, gave them a land, protected generation to generation – walked away from the great voice, walked away from the powerfully nurturing word of God.

Jeremiah came to deliver a word for God, a word of warning worthy of contemplation – a word that would preserve some and burn others.

In Jeremiah 5:14 God purports that God's words spoken through Jeremiah would become as fire burning people like wood, burning the disobedient, the wicked - like fire burns wood. What a mighty powerful word, the word will give you life or proclaim your death – the choice is yours. To burn or not to burn, that truly is the question.

In William Shakespeare's famous play Hamlet, the opening soliloquy uttered by King Hamlet, "To be, or not to be, that is the question: Whether 'tis nobler in the mind to suffer. The slings and arrows of outrageous fortune, Or to take arms against a sea of troubles."

We could certainly use part of that today – to burn or not to burn that is the question: whether it is alright to struggle through and suffer through the burn of being against God or be blessed in service for God.

I guarantee you - we will never win against God. In fact. God's very word will ultimately burn the unrighteous like fire burns wood. We must learn to reject the burn and embrace God's word. How to avoid word burn, how to avoid word burn.

Look with me at Jeremiah 5:11 as it reads, "For the house of Israel and the house of Judah have dealt very treacherously against me, saith the LORD."

In order to avoid word burn, in order to avoid eternal destruction, we must **never move against God**. Israel and Judah moved against God as they neglected

worship, forsaking God for the things and traditions of other people. They wanted to be like other people, support other ideologies, envious of the powerless while rejecting our supremely powerful God.
No matter how great we think we are we are still no match for God. Jeremiah reminds us that we will ultimately be held accountable for our response to God's word. Now, don't get me wrong - this isn't about perfection, God is merciful. The Lord allows us to make mistakes – but when we choose to make moves against God, we're making moves in the wrong direction.

James Weldon Johnson's novel, *The Autobiography of an Ex-Colored Man,* gives voice to a preacher named John Brown – literarily articulated and tuned Johnson writes, "He struck the attitude of a pugilist and thundered out, 'Young man, yo' arm's too short to box wid God!" I wonder is there anybody here that has the good mind to know that our arms are too short to box with God. We don't stand a chance against God! Never move against God.

In 1927 James Weldon Johnson goes on to pen pleading, poetic words in his book *God's Trombone,* articulating the call of homecoming he says:

"Young man—
Young man—
Your arm's too short to box with God.

But Jesus spake in a parable, and he said:
A certain man had two sons.

*Jesus didn't give this man a name,
But his name is God Almighty.
And Jesus didn't call these sons by name,
But ev'ry young man, Ev'rywhere,
Is one of these two sons.*

*Oh-o-oh, sinner,
When you're mingling with the crowd in Babylon—
Drinking the wine of Babylon—
Running with the women of Babylon—
You forget about God, and you laugh at Death.
Today you've got the strength of a bull in your neck*

*And the strength of a bear in your arms,
But some o' these days, some o' these days,
You'll have a hand-to-hand struggle with bony Death, And
Death is bound to win.*

*Young man, come away from Babylon,
That hell-border city of Babylon.
Leave the dancing and gambling of Babylon,
The wine and whiskey of Babylon,
The hot-mouthed women of Babylon;
Fall down on your knees,
And say in your heart: I will arise and go to my Father."*

Never move against God.

Look with me at Jeremiah 5:12 as it reads, "They have belied the LORD, and said, It is not he; neither shall evil come upon us; neither shall we see sword nor famine:"

We should never move against God and we should **never disregard God**. They denied God, acted like God hadn't delivered, protected, and preserved them. Humm, we can't be judgmental toward them – as we frequently disregard God through our words and deeds, yes often actions speak louder than words. They turned their backs on God as many of us have done in this present age.

But I'm here to tell you that we should never count God out, never disregard God, in close calls and last-minute situations – God still has plenty of time. God's ways, God's time, God's thoughts are not our way, time, or thoughts – God's ways are always beyond superior to any solution that we could ever come up with. God can when nobody else can.

I wish there was somebody here to testify that God can when nobody else can. Anybody here know that God can make a way where there is no way – into God's hand every sinner will die and every believer shall live – never disregard God.

Curtis Burrell composed the words that the singer James Cleveland made famous:
There will be mountains
That I will have to climb
And there will be battles
That I will have to fight
But victory or defeat
It's up to me to decide
But how can I expect to win

If I never try
I just can't give up now
I've come too far from where
I started from
Nobody told me
The road would be easy
And I don't believe He's brought me this far
To leave me.

Never count God out, don't disregard God.

Focus now on Jeremiah 5:12 it says, "They have belied the LORD, and said, It is not he; neither shall evil come upon us; neither shall we see sword nor famine:"

We should never move against God or disregard God, as we should **never feel untouchable**. They said that nothing would ever happen to them, no evil, they said they would never see the sword nor famine – untouchable. It was as if they were saying, "God, who?"

They spoke as if God could not or would not act against their transgressions, they didn't believe in the judgment of God – the consequence to actions. It almost seems like we're reliving the sentiments birthed through the ignorance of our biblically historic predecessors.

Our culture has given way to antagonistic movements against God, denying the salvific power of Jesus while feeling untouchably safe, coddled by an egotistical ontological assumption of superiority to God. Simply put, we are ignorant at our very core and the infantile darkness of our mind requires the light of God's word to abundantly mature.

We must walk in the light of God's word to realize that we are not worthy, we are not untouchable – God can pull the plug on any aspect of our life at any time. Never think that you are big and bad enough to get beyond God's reach. God can bring any part of your life to a halt – I wonder if there is a witness that God can shut it all down? Never think we're untouchable, in fact we should welcome the hand of God in our lives both for correction and celebration.

Isaiah chapter 64 resonates the contemplative stave, "But we are all as an unclean thing, and all our righteousnesses are as filthy rags; and we all do fade as a leaf; and our iniquities, like the wind, have taken us away. 7 And there is none that calleth upon thy name, that stirreth up himself to take hold of thee: for thou hast hid thy face from us, and hast consumed us, because of our iniquities. 8 But now, O LORD, thou art our father; we are the clay, and thou our potter; and we all are the work of thy hand."

Observe Jeremiah 5:13, it says, "And the prophets shall become wind, and the word is not in them: thus shall it be done unto them."

We should never move against God, never disregard God, never feel untouchable, and we should **never trust a windbag preacher**. Everything that sounds good sliding from a slithering silver tongue, in a three-piece suit, polished shoes - is not right. Every preacher taunting matriculation through prestigious academic institutions, while driving expensive luxury automobiles parked in exclusive driveways is not preaching the Gospel. You can't trust windbags winged, fly by the seat of your pants sermons based on cereal box religion and personal ideologies fueled by individual agendas.

Don't trust people just because they sound good, as the Russian proverb admonishes *Doveryai, no proveryai* - trust but verify!

I John 4:1-4 says, "Beloved, believe not every spirit, but try the spirits whether they are of God: because many false prophets are gone out into the world. 2 Hereby know ye the Spirit of God: Every spirit that confesseth that Jesus Christ is come in the flesh is of God: 3 And every spirit that confesseth not that Jesus Christ is come in the flesh is not of God: and this is that spirit of antichrist, whereof ye have heard that it should come; and even now already is it in the world. 4 Ye are of God, little children, and have overcome them: because greater is he that is in you, than he that is in the world."

Some of the entertainers calling themselves preachers on television and pulpits across the country are nothing more than charlatans filled with wind. Don't trust just anybody, but don't let your distrust lead you to disqualify everybody. We need preachers – Romans chapter 10 reminds us that we need preachers to help us increase our faith through the hearing of God's word. We need preachers – but we need those who are not ashamed of the Gospel of Jesus, we need preachers who understand the power of salvation, prepared preachers who have studied, unashamed workers correctly presenting the truth.

The sermon should not be your only contact with God's word. You must read, study, pray, and remain in continual connection with God. The preacher's job is to help you in your journey through confirmation of God's word in order to increase your faith. You should not become dependent, in contrast, we must mature under the light of God's word – we need more than wind. We need more than empty feel good sermons – we need the challenge of God's love as we are motivated to love God, self, and each other. We need a word! Oh, yes, we need the word of God – it is life, love, and lasting joy. We need God's word, no humanistic ideology will ever compare to the mighty word of God!

Thomas Anthony Whitfield penned the prayerful words:

We don't need another political uprising
We don't need another conqueror on the scene
What we need is a special word, that will bond within our hearts and give us direction from above. We need a word from the Lord.

Lord, we lack Thy wisdom and Thy understanding
Lord, we lack the very love You showed Your Son

Lord, we've altered in Thy ways and we stand so much to gain.

*So give us Your word Lord, speak Lord
We need a word from the Lord, A word from the Lord.*

*Just one word from the Lord
Will move all the doubts
And cause the sun to shine
And give peace of mind
Speak Lord, speak*

Finally focus with me on Jeremiah 5:14 it says, "Wherefore thus saith the LORD God of hosts, Because ye speak this word, behold, I will make my words in thy mouth fire, and this people wood, and it shall devour them."

Get blessed not burnt by God's word, never move against God, never disregard God, never feel untouchable, never trust a windbag preacher, and **never forget you can't survive**. We need God's word for survival – nevertheless we must choose to live or die by God's word, we must choose to allow the word of God to testify for us or against us. We will be cursed through disobedience or blessed through obedience to God's word. We can't live without the word of God.

Just as we need the power of God to save us – we need the word, as God and God's word are one. God's word is alive and indivisible. John 1:1-4 says, "In the beginning was the Word, and the Word was with God, and the Word was God. 2 The same was in the beginning with God. 3 All things were made by him; and without him was not any thing made that was made. 4 In him was life; and the life was the light of men."

Anybody here know that we cannot survive without God, the one that woke us up this morning? Kept blood running warm in our bodies all night long – tenderly woke us up with love eternal, granted a new day to get it right. To connect with God and fulfill the purpose that the word calls us to, the call to live and love – called to service by the word. Rejecting the burn to receive the blessing.

Blessed because of God's word! In the beginning was the word, and the word was with God, and the word was God! Anybody here know that there is power in God's word? We've been kept from creation to Calvary, by the power of God's word.

Anybody glad for the word? Oh, the word came – yet some refuse to receive and someday the consequence will be great, but we are called to be blessed, called to serve as Jesus did. Jesus the manifestation of truth – the word become flesh.

Jesus our Immanuel – He gave His life that we may live, the word was sacrificed and the word prevailed. The joy of Christ's resurrection released us at Calvary with victory forever through our great gift Jesus – happy for the word fortified by God's great grace. We need Gods word to bless us and not burn us, there is victory in the word of God. Oh, Jesus! We cannot live by bread and water alone – but we need every word that comes from God.

In 1887 John H. Sammis penned "Trust and Obey," one of over 300 hymns that he authored:

*When we walk with the Lord
in the light of his word,
what a glory he sheds on our way!
While we do his good will,
he abides with us still,
and with all who will trust and obey.*

*Not a burden we bear,
not a sorrow we share,
but our toil he doth richly repay;
not a grief or a loss,
not a frown or a cross,
but is blest if we trust and obey.*

*But we never can prove
the delights of his love
until all on the altar we lay;
for the favor he shows,
for the joy he bestows,
are for them who will trust and obey.*

*Then in fellowship sweet
we will sit at his feet,
or we'll walk by his side in the way;*

what he says we will do,
where he sends we will go;
never fear, only trust and obey.
Trust and obey, for there's no other way
to be happy in Jesus, but to trust and obey.

LIVING THE BIBLE TOGETHER: THROUGH MISSIONS

SCRIPTURE

2 Thessalonians 1:1-12 Paul, and Silvanus, and Timotheus, unto the church of the Thessalonians in God our Father and the Lord Jesus Christ: 2 Grace unto you, and peace, from God our Father and the Lord Jesus Christ. 3 We are bound to thank God always for you, brethren, as it is meet, because that your faith groweth exceedingly, and the charity of every one of you all toward each other aboundeth; 4 So that we ourselves glory in you in the churches of God for your patience and faith in all your persecutions and tribulations that ye endure: 5 Which is a manifest token of the righteous judgment of God, that ye may be counted worthy of the kingdom of God, for which ye also suffer: 6 Seeing it is a righteous thing with God to recompense tribulation to them that trouble you; 7 And to you who are troubled rest with us, when the Lord Jesus shall be revealed from heaven with his mighty angels, 8 In flaming fire taking vengeance on them that know not God, and that obey not the gospel of our Lord Jesus Christ: 9 Who shall be punished with everlasting destruction from the presence of the Lord, and from the glory of his power; 10 When he shall come to be glorified in his saints, and to be admired in all them that believe (because our testimony among you was believed) in that day. 11 Wherefore also we pray always for you, that our God would count you worthy of this calling, and fulfil all the good pleasure of his goodness, and the work of faith with power: 12 That the name of our Lord Jesus Christ may be glorified in you, and ye in him, according to the grace of our God and the Lord Jesus Christ.

OUTLINE

1. Share Christ (Spread to Thessalonians) v1
2. Embrace the Collective (Bowed) v3
3. Get Them Counted v5,11
4. Bring Encouragement v7
5. To the Glory of God v12

MESSAGE

The Lord led Paul to help organize the church at Thessalonica – gathering people that would ultimately suffer great persecution for their faith while Paul would reside from exile to incarceration.

The glorious mission of Christ was transferred through the Gospel, as the Thessalonian Christians stood strong against hatred and evil. There should be at least five people here that know sometime your mission is much greater than the moment.

Maybe you wanted to give up in the moment, you wanted to let them take you there – but you know we have to often suck it up, shake it off – get through the moment to fulfill the movement. Sometimes persecution may come in the moment – come for a season, but we must remain focused on the mission.

We are called, we are elected and then sent out with a mission. In John 17:18 Jesus prays for us pleading, "As thou hast sent me into the world, even so have I also sent them into the world."

Jesus has sent us into the world with a purposeful mission. Jesus said in Matthew 28:19-20, "Go ye therefore, and teach all nations, baptizing them in the name of the Father, and of the Son, and of the Holy Ghost: 20 Teaching them to observe all things whatsoever I have commanded you: and, lo, I am with you alway, even unto the end of the world. Amen."

Paul knows well the importance of embracing God's mission, God's way above any other. In 1 Thessalonians chapter 1 Paul gives God's praise and glory for the endurance of the young persecuted church. Hmmm, I feel like shouting for them right now – it's hard to find ride or die kind of folk in this age of photoshopped friends - fake, pretend, fantasy friends clicking the imaginary likes in our head.

I'm just glad to know that Paul knew some ride or die folks – a little struggle did not stop the Gospel movement. Hallelujah for the Lamb – our God is so good as the weak stand strong in God's hands. We must remain motivated toward the mission to teach and baptize as we journey through life with love for God and neighbor. We are living the Bible together: through missions just as the Thessalonian church did.

Look with me at 2 Thessalonians 1:1-2 as it reads, "Paul, and Silvanus, and Timotheus, unto the church of the Thessalonians in God our Father and the Lord Jesus

Christ: 2 Grace unto you, and peace, from God our Father and the Lord Jesus Christ."

In order to live the Bible together through missions we need to **share Christ**. The Apostle starts this letter to the Thessalonians in the name and power of Jesus – his greeting seems to emerge from the joy of the Gospel. Paul enters this literary lesson with Jesus, as the mission is impossible without Jesus.

In the words of the American Baptist hymnist Lydia Baxter:

Take the name of Jesus with you,
Child of sorrow and of woe.
It will joy and comfort give you,
Take it then where'er you go.

Take the name of Jesus ever
As protection ev'rywhere.
If temptations 'round you gather,
Breathe that holy name in prayer.

At the name of Jesus bowing,
When in heaven we shall meet,
King of kings, we'll gladly crown him
When our journey is complete.

Precious name, O how sweet!
Hope of earth and joy of heaven;
Precious name, O how sweet!
Hope of earth and joy of heaven.

The beauty of God's way never sends us alone – Jesus said in John 14:16-18, "And I will pray the Father, and he shall give you another Comforter, that he may abide with you for ever; 17 Even the Spirit of truth; whom the world cannot receive, because it seeth him not, neither knoweth him: but ye know him; for he dwelleth with you, and shall be in you. 18 I will not leave you comfortless: I will come to you."

Then he goes on to say in the last chapter, last two verses of Matthew, "Go ye therefore, and teach all nations, baptizing them in the name of the Father, and of the Son, and of the Holy Ghost: 20 Teaching them to observe all things whatsoever I have commanded you: and, lo, I am with you alway, even unto the end of the world. Amen."

We must share Jesus; we should always go with God – we never have to go alone! The Lord says go, then says I'll go with you and never leave you. We should be thankful to live the Bible together with God and each other as we allow the manifestation of Christ's mission to live within us all.
Focus now on 2 Thessalonians 1:3 as it says, "We are bound to thank God always for you, brethren, as it is meet, because that your faith groweth exceedingly, and the charity of every one of you all toward each other aboundeth;"

The mission requires that we **embrace the collective**, as we need each other to successfully complete the challenge to go under the guidance of the

Gospel. We cannot live the Bible together while attempting to do the mission while divided – we must embrace each other. Paul seems delighted as he remembers the Thessalonian's charity toward each other – they loved each other.

Our working together should be inspirationally refreshing to all who gaze upon God's love gloriously shining through our mission. We should have charity, love toward each other.

The world should look upon the church and see the great Gospel – overflowing with an abundance of love flowing from the sacrifice of Christ at Calvary. We must stand together upon God's word, fulfilling God's will – done God's way.

Love should guide us to peacefully work together as a testimony of who God is, as Jesus prays in John chapter 17 that we may become one in order to testify of God's existence. When we become one, when we get on one accord – the world can see a reflection of God: Father, Son, and Holy Spirit.

Look with me at 2 Thessalonians chapter 1 verses 5 and 11 as they read, "Which is a manifest token of the righteous judgment of God, that ye may be counted worthy of the kingdom of God, for which ye also suffer:" and verse 11 says, "Wherefore also we pray always for you, that our God would count you worthy of this calling, and fulfil all the good pleasure of his goodness, and the work of faith with power:"

We are living the Bible together through missions, we must share Christ, embrace the collective, and **get them counted**. Our faith is not about exclusion, antithetically our faith is about inclusion – our mission is to teach the Gospel to all nations. We should want everybody in the human family counted within the family of God.

Rescue the perishing, care for the dying,
snatch them in pity from sin and the grave;
weep o'er the erring one, lift up the fallen,
tell them of Jesus, the mighty to save.

Though they are slighting Him, still He is waiting, waiting the penitent child to receive;
plead with them earnestly, plead with them gently.
He will forgive if they only believe.

Down in the human heart, crushed by the tempter,
feelings lie buried that grace can restore;
touched by a loving heart, wakened by kindness,
chords that are broken will vibrate once more.

Rescue the perishing, duty demands it.
Strength for thy labor the Lord will provide;
back to the narrow way patiently win them,
tell the poor wanderer a Savior has died.

Rescue the perishing,
care for the dying;
Jesus is merciful,
Jesus will save.

We must compel the world to get counted, you must be in the number – get counted. Praying that our neighbors be found worthy of the Kingdom – essentially embracing Jesus, the only way to be found worthy.

We have a mission to go to the world, a mission to care and connect. What a mighty God we serve, I'm glad to be counted and I want the world to taste and see that the Lord is good, the Lord is great, and greatly to be praised!

Focus on 2 Thessalonians 1:7 as it states, "And to you who are troubled rest with us, when the Lord Jesus shall be revealed from heaven with his mighty angels,"

We have a mission to clasp as we share Christ, embrace the collective, get them counted, and **bring encouragement**. Paul says if you're troubled you can rest with us and you'll experience Jesus after a while. Yeah, Paul basically says – if you're going through something, just hold on. Hang tight, hold on with me, I'm yet holding on, so just hold on with me and we'll experience Jesus.

Jesus is revealed through our patient ability to rest in the midst of troubles along the way. Don't fret, don't give up – just hold on with Jesus.

Don't come with negative notions, slide on up out of my life if all you have is sad sayings, we don't need people keeping us down, always singing the blues, never happy about anything – we need encouragement. We need people praying with us and for us – we need a good yes you can, even better we need people willing to even love us when we can't.

Bring encouragement to the mission, be positive, have faith – believe! We are living the Bible together: through missions.

God has been too good to us for us to act as though life is worthlessly hopeless – we should joyfully proclaim the Gospel. The love of Jesus should be seen in us as we encourage the least and lost as God's grace lifts all life as the tide lifts all ships.
We should share Jesus, embrace the collective, get them counted, bring encouragement, and now focus with me on 2 Thessalonians 1:12 as the passage says, "That the name of our Lord Jesus Christ may be glorified in you, and ye in him, according to the grace of our God and the Lord Jesus Christ."

We must remember that the mission is **to the glory of God**. The mission is not about us; all of the glory is to God. When we understand that it's about God's glory - then everything else better falls into place. Once you truly enter into a relationship with God, once you get just a glimpse – a peek at the Savior is more than awesome, motivates our mission to tell everybody.

Makes you feel like the man in that old Williams Brother's song, *"I'm just a nobody trying to tell everybody, about somebody, who can save anybody."*

Jesus died to set us free, the good news, the Gospel – Jesus was sacrificed for us, loved us, died to atone for our sins, was raised from the dead with victory that we might know Him in the power of His resurrection, and when the final call is made upon His return we shall live in eternal peace. Our joy, our great joy should emerge from eternal gratitude for the one who calls us to go!

After Calvary, Jesus said, "All power is given unto me in heaven and in earth. 19 Go ye therefore, and teach all nations, baptizing them in the name of the Father, and of the Son, and of the Holy Ghost: 20 Teaching them to observe all things whatsoever I have commanded you: and, lo, I am with you alway, even unto the end of the world. Amen."

We have not been left alone, to seek after God's will in darkness, but have been blessed with the light of the scriptures. When the Lord Jesus ascended, He promised to be with us always, in the power of God's Word and Holy Spirit.

To God be the glory great things He has done
So loved He the world that He gave us His son
Who yielded His life an atonement for sin
And opened the life gate that all may go in

Praise the Lord, praise the Lord let the earth hear His voice
Praise the Lord, praise the Lord let the people rejoice

Come to the Father through Jesus the Son
Give Him the glory great things He has done

*O perfect redemption the purchase of blood
To every believer the promise of God
The vilest offender who truly believes
That moment from Jesus a pardon receives*

Great things He has taught us great things He has done

*And great our rejoicing through Jesus the Son
But purer and higher and greater will be
Our wonder our worship when Jesus we see.*

We are living the Bible together: through education, missions, and ministry.

GOD WILL ALWAYS PASS THE TEST

SCRIPTURE

Hebrews 12:18-29 For ye are not come unto the mount that might be touched, and that burned with fire, nor unto blackness, and darkness, and tempest, 19 And the sound of a trumpet, and the voice of words; which voice they that heard intreated that the word should not be spoken to them any more: 20 (For they could not endure that which was commanded, And if so much as a beast touch the mountain, it shall be stoned, or thrust through with a dart: 21 And so terrible was the sight, that Moses said, I exceedingly fear and quake:) 22 But ye are come unto mount Sion, and unto the city of the living God, the heavenly Jerusalem, and to an innumerable company of angels, 23 To the general assembly and church of the firstborn, which are written in heaven, and to God the Judge of all, and to the spirits of just men made perfect, 24 And to Jesus the mediator of the new covenant, and to the blood of sprinkling, that speaketh better things than that of Abel. 25 See that ye refuse not him that speaketh. For if they escaped not who refused him that spake on earth, much more shall not we escape, if we turn away from him that speaketh from heaven: 26 Whose voice then shook the earth: but now he hath promised, saying, Yet once more I shake not the earth only, but also heaven. 27 And this word, Yet once more, signifieth the removing of those things that are shaken, as of things that are made, that those things which cannot be shaken may remain. 28 Wherefore we receiving a kingdom which cannot be moved, let us have grace, whereby we may serve God acceptably with reverence and godly fear: 29 For our God is a consuming fire.

OUTLINE

1. Is it Better than Abel's? v24
2. Can it Be Shook Up? v26-27
3. Will it Burn? v29

MESSAGE

Tests often bring stress and anxiety, some of us are good at taking tests and some of us shiver in our boots at the thought of a test. Depending on the test many things could be at risk. People miss opportunities over failed tests.

Students are disqualified as manifested prerequisites often depend on test results – entire academic careers and scholarships have been determined by a test.

Let's not forget medical testing – life and death are judged by results. From EKG to MRI, from blood tests to throat cultures – tests can change one's prospective on the future. DNA tests come to prove or disprove blood ties to ancestry. Yes, a test can make or break perceptions of success.

Any teacher will tell you that examination is often essential to learning, doctors will embrace the methodology of examination to determine diagnosis, prognosis, and prescription. Tests are often important, requiring that we pass for one outcome or another.

We go into the process of examination hoping to pass, as the question emerges will God pass the test? Psalm 34:8 invites us to taste and see that the Lord is good – we are invited to examination, contemplation, and verification. Our God can stand the test, we should not mock or take God for granted – nevertheless we are invited to try God, as God countlessly invites us to lean in with words like "prove me now".

1 John 4:1-7 says, "Beloved, believe not every spirit, but try the spirits whether they are of God: because many false prophets are gone out into the world. 2 Hereby know ye the Spirit of God: Every spirit that confesseth that Jesus Christ is come in the flesh is of God: 3 And every spirit that confesseth not that Jesus Christ is come in the flesh is not of God: and this is that spirit of antichrist, whereof ye have heard that it should come; and even now already is it in the world. 4 Ye are of God, little children, and have overcome them: because greater is he that is in you, than he that is in the world. 5 They are of the world: therefore speak they of the world, and the world heareth them. 6 We are of God: he that knoweth God heareth us; he that is not of God heareth not us. Hereby know we the spirit of truth, and the spirit of error. 7 Beloved, let us love one another: for love is of God; and every one that loveth is born of God, and knoweth God."

The book of Hebrews seems to perfectly layout the pontification that Jesus always passes the test, as the first four sections of the book reveal the manifested reality of Christ against the backdrop of biblical history.

Chapters 1 & 2 remind us that the angels were early messengers as the Torah unfolds – Hebrews brings us to understand that if you think the angels were great messengers, just think about Jesus.

The angels brought a message, Jesus is the message. Oh, according to the Johannian preface – In the beginning was the word and the word was with God, and the word was God. Jesus is greater than the angels. Jesus passes examination, passes the test every time.

Chapters 3 & 4 remind us that Moses led the Children of Israel to the promised land, nevertheless Jesus is the chief cornerstone to the heavenly paradigm – with all power and access to the great city of Heaven.

Chapters 5-7 remind us of the priesthood as the priest would represent the people in the ritual of atonement and sacrifice – Jesus is the great Royal High Priest that has made us a family of priests. We can all have a talk with God, there is no veil – we can go to God in prayer.

Chapters 8-10 remind us of the Levitical system of sacrifice emerging from covenant – Jesus is the only sacrifice, we don't need any more goats, bulls, and doves. Jesus passes the test!

Hebrews celebrates the greatness of Jesus, the book magnifies the salvific work of Jesus, God the Son. The opening sections of this work lay out the case, then we are transitioned into an example of faith working through humanity in chapter 11 which then perfectly positions us toward the interrogative of every examination – will it pass the test, will we pass the test, most specifically does God: Father, Son, and Holy Spirit pass the test?

Look now with me at Hebrews 12:24 as it reads, "And to Jesus the mediator of the new covenant, and to the blood of sprinkling, that speaketh better things than that of Abel."

Will it pass the test, **is it better than Abel's**? In the first few chapters of the Bible in the book of Genesis, the children of Adam and Eve are become the characters within the narrative of the first biblically recorded murder. As Cain murders his brother Abel.

The Bible tells us in Genesis chapter 4 that Abel's blood cried out from the earth and seems to bring judgment against Cain. If you think that Abel's blood was special – I need you to know that the blood of Jesus, doesn't just cry out for one, but it cries out to set us all free, there is power in the blood.

The prolific inspirational song writer Andraé Crouch penned the beautiful exhortation:

The blood that Jesus shed for me
Way back on Calvary
The blood that gives me strength
From day to day
It will never lose its power

It reaches to the highest mountain
It flows to the lowest valley
The blood that gives me strength
From day to day
It will never lose its power

Yes, there is power in the blood of Jesus,

1 Peter 1:18-21 says, "Forasmuch as ye know that ye were not redeemed with corruptible things, as silver and gold, from your vain conversation received by tradition from your fathers; 19 But with the precious blood of Christ, as of a lamb without blemish and without spot: 20 Who verily was foreordained before the foundation of the world, but was manifest in these last times for you, 21 Who by him do believe in God, that raised him up from the dead, and gave him glory; that your faith and hope might be in God."

God loves us so much that we have been gifted with the presence of God. Romans 5:6-11 says, "For when we were yet without strength, in due time Christ died for the ungodly. 7 For scarcely for a righteous man will one die: yet peradventure for a good man some would even dare to die. 8 But God commendeth his love toward us, in that, while we were yet sinners, Christ died for us. 9 Much more then, being now justified by his blood, we shall be saved from wrath through him. 10 For if, when we were enemies, we were reconciled to God by the death of his Son, much more, being reconciled, we shall be saved by his life. 11 And not only so, but we also joy in God through our Lord Jesus

Christ, by whom we have now received the atonement."

There is power in Jesus, the Son of God always passes the test, the pattern of Christ's sacrifice provides salvation and guidance to all who believingly receive.

Focus with me on Hebrews 12:26-27 as it reads, "Whose voice then shook the earth: but now he hath promised, saying, Yet once more I shake not the earth only, but also heaven. 27 And this word, Yet once more, signifieth the removing of those things that are shaken, as of things that are made, that those things which cannot be shaken may remain."

Can it be shook up, will God pass the test, can Jesus be shook up? We need never forget that 1 John 4:4 says, "Ye are of God, little children, and have overcome them: because greater is he that is in you, than he that is in the world." Can't nobody shake Jesus! Ain't no power on Earth that could keep Him down.

We can always trust in God, John 2:17-22 says, "And his disciples remembered that it was written, The zeal of thine house hath eaten me up. 18 Then answered the Jews and said unto him, What sign shewest thou unto us, seeing that thou doest these things? 19 Jesus answered and said unto them, Destroy this temple, and in three days I will raise it up. 20 Then said the Jews, Forty and six years was this temple in building, and wilt thou rear it up in three days? 21 But he spake of the temple of his body. 22 When therefore he was risen from the dead, his disciples remembered that he had said this unto them; and they believed the scripture, and the word which Jesus had said."

Jesus has given us the example for life – keep building, keep maturing, keep progressing, stay on the path – but never let the world shake you! In fact, remember that God is the only real mover and shaker – Hebrews 12:26-27 reminds us that God's voice alone is powerful enough to shake Heaven and Earth. I'm so glad that our God has the victory! God is mighty in battle, a fortress, and a strong tower.

They can't shake us, can't scare us, can't kill us, and the world can't touch us without permission – and God's arms are protecting us through trial and tribulation. God will shake the Earth just to free us! God's word is powerful enough to lead us over the mountain and through the valleys – God can't be shook, God is the shaker! Is there a witness! Anybody trust that God can, when nobody else can?

Focus with me on Hebrews 12:29 as it reads, "For our God is a consuming fire."

God will always pass the test, Father, Son, and Holy Spirit. **Will it burn?** Our God is burning, but never burnt, God is a consuming fire. The Lord can burn away the impurities of the world, separating the good from the bad, and the usable from the unusable.

Job 23:9-10 says, "On the left hand, where he doth work, but I cannot behold him: he hideth himself on the right hand, that I cannot see him: 10 But he knoweth the way that I take: when he hath tried me, I shall come forth as gold."

Please be patient with us, God is not through with us yet – when God gets through with us, we shall come forth as pure gold.

Tried through the fire as God burns out the dross of guilt and sin through the power of God's word. We have been baptized in the water and the fire of God the Holy Spirit.

We're saved, sanctified, Holy Ghost filled, and fire baptized - Jesus on our mind and running for our life. Tried through the internal spiritual fire, kindled by the Holy Spirit – keeping the light of our heart shining with love. Our Founding Pastor Rubin McCrary used to say, "You better keep your light trimmed and burning – somebody down in the valley is trying to get home." When the light of the Holy Spirit is active in the believer, the light is a testimony to our maturing – not perfect, but perfecting, as the spiritual fires of the Holy Spirit burn out sin and illuminate our way as we are led by the Holy Spirit into all truth.

I'm so glad that Jesus saved us, I'm so glad that Jesus saved you – now we need to be ready when the Lord returns. We need to know that we know that we know God's way is the only way. God is much greater than

Abel, certainly better than Cain, but you best believe superior to all of humanity – God the Father, Son, and Holy Spirit is the only true God that will pass all the tests every time – creator, redeemer, savior. God is greater than Abel, greater than all of humanity.

God cannot be shook, I'm glad that we can't shake God – the Lord is truly most powerful!

No, you can't make me doubt Him in my heart,
doubt Him in my heart.

He's my friend, friend until the end
Hears me when I call
never lets me fall
that's why I know all about him
you can't make me doubt him!

I Got the Love of Jesus
I know too much about Him
I feel the fire burning as God is working on me burning transgressions while establishing love in my heart.

Oh, I need you to know that God passes all of the tests – the greatest victory for us commenced at Calvary. When God sacrificed God to save us all – there is power in Jesus! God so loved the world that we have been given Jesus – and that's worth shouting about. Christ was crucified so that we might be heirs with Him and pass the test also. In Adam we all died, in Christ we all live.

Because He did not stay on the cross, they entombed Him – yet He did not stay in the grave. Glad that Jesus arose from the grave with victory over sin and death – Jesus passed the test, providing hope for our future. Glad that God passes every test, every examination – any way you look at God all you see is good, great, and better.

I serve a risen Savior, He's in the world today
I know that He is living, whatever men may say
I see His hand of mercy,
I hear His voice of cheer and just the time I need Him He's always near

He lives (He lives), He lives (He lives), Christ Jesus lives today.
He walks with me and talks with me
Along life's narrow way
He lives, He lives salvation to impart
You ask me how I know He lives?
He lives within my heart.

God passes all the tests! Oh, taste and see that the Lord is good.

YOU CAN TAKE IT TO THE BANK

SCRIPTURE

Jeremiah 32:1-3, 6-15 The word that came to Jeremiah from the LORD in the tenth year of Zedekiah king of Judah, which was the eighteenth year of Nebuchadrezzar. 2 For then the king of Babylon's army besieged Jerusalem: and Jeremiah the prophet was shut up in the court of the prison, which was in the king of Judah's house. 3 For Zedekiah king of Judah had shut him up, saying, Wherefore dost thou prophesy, and say, Thus saith the LORD, Behold, I will give this city into the hand of the king of Babylon, and he shall take it; 6 And Jeremiah said, The word of the LORD came unto me, saying, 7 Behold, Hanameel the son of Shallum thine uncle shall come unto thee, saying, Buy thee my field that is in Anathoth: for the right of redemption is thine to buy it. 8 So Hanameel mine uncle's son came to me in the court of the prison according to the word of the LORD, and said unto me, Buy my field, I pray thee, that is in Anathoth, which is in the country of Benjamin: for the right of inheritance is thine, and the redemption is thine; buy it for thyself. Then I knew that this was the word of the LORD. 9 And I bought the field of Hanameel my uncle's son, that was in Anathoth, and weighed him the money, even seventeen shekels of silver. 10 And I subscribed the evidence, and sealed it, and took witnesses, and weighed him the money in the balances. 11 So I took the evidence of the purchase, both that which was sealed according to the law and custom, and that which was open: 12 And I gave the evidence of the purchase unto Baruch the son of Neriah, the son of Maaseiah, in the sight of Hanameel mine uncle's son, and in the presence of the witnesses that subscribed the book of the purchase, before all the Jews that sat in the court of the prison. 13 And I charged Baruch before them, saying, 14 Thus saith the LORD of hosts, the God of Israel; Take these evidences, this evidence of the purchase, both which is sealed, and this evidence which is open; and put them in an earthen vessel, that they may continue many days. 15 For thus saith the LORD of hosts, the God of Israel; Houses and fields and vineyards shall be possessed again in this land.

OUTLINE

1. We Can Trust God v1 & 6
2. We Are in the Family v6
3. The Process Leads to Possession v15

MESSAGE

Jeremiah prophesied from the darkness of a war pillaged land. The Assyrians brought utter destruction to the Northern Kingdom and God brought words of warning and hope through Jeremiah to the Southern Kingdom of Judah.

Houses had been burnt, confiscated, and vacated as the spoils of war soiled the peace of the land. Fields had been pillaged and trampled underfoot as armies occupied the city. Vineyards had been stripped and destroyed – future festivals folded into an abyss as the juice of celebrations to come dissipated into the devastation of forfeited fruits.

Disobedient backsliding blocked the bountiful blessings that God had bestowed upon Israel. Relational resources often rust like tin when we neglect to maintain a real relationship with God – we need God, as vibrant life is impossible without divine directions. They turned their backs on God – and God turned on them to prompt them to return to relationship.
The judgment of God manifested as the Children of Israel worshiped idols, embraced foreign traditions, and neglected righteousness/God's way. Nevertheless, God spoke through Jeremiah to say judgment will come, consequences will come, but ultimately another chance will arrive. Healing will arrive, forgiveness, restoration, and possession. I'm so glad that we serve a God that continues to open arms to restoration. God is gracious and merciful – you can take that to the bank. God will restore, God will forgive the repentant heart. We've all sinned and come short of the glory of God – all have needed the assurance of God's presence through the midst of our trials and temptations. Sometimes we fall, but God remains to help us back up again – you can take that to the bank.

Focus with me on Jeremiah 32:1-8 as it reads, "The word that came to Jeremiah from the LORD in the tenth year of Zedekiah king of Judah, which was the eighteenth year of Nebuchadrezzar. 2 For then the king of Babylon's army besieged Jerusalem: and Jeremiah the prophet was shut up in the court of the prison, which was in the king of Judah's house. 3 For Zedekiah king of Judah had shut him up, saying, Wherefore dost thou prophesy, and say, Thus saith the LORD, Behold, I will give this city into the hand of the king of Babylon, and he shall take it; 6 And Jeremiah said, The word of the LORD came unto me, saying, 7 Behold, Hanameel the son of Shallum thine uncle shall come unto thee, saying, Buy thee my field that is in Anathoth: for the right of redemption is thine to buy it. 8 So Hanameel mine uncle's son came to me in the court of the prison according to the word of the LORD, and said unto me, Buy my field, I pray thee, that is in Anathoth, which is in the country of Benjamin: for the right of inheritance is thine, and the redemption is thine; buy it for thyself. Then I knew that this was the word of the LORD."

Jeremiah chapter 32 commences with the word of God – revelation came to the prophet to prepare him for possession in the midst of devastation. Anybody here, know that God often works in unlikely times and ways? God can pronounce instructions for success in the whirlwind of failure. War torn, ravished land – sad citizens seized by depression while distant from the divine. Yet the man of God embraces a heavenly telegram, a word from God navigated the bleak mood to bring a word of relief and revelation.

No matter what you are going through – when God speaks, that's more than enough to make it through. God's word brings strength to the believer, celebration to the broken heart, life that lingers in love.

When God speaks – God spoke at the dawn of this civilization and water puddled away from land to divide into oceans. When God spoke, the green grass popped up from the brown earth as insects began to farm the land.

God's voice – fish swam through lazy streams and mighty rivers. God spoke – birds took flight to procure worms and seeds, fertilizing for future growth – yes, at God's voice trees stretched out, praising our Great God with outstretched branches uplifted toward the heavens adorned by sweet fruit to refresh us all. God's voice, God's word. When God speaks – you can take it to the bank.

Read with me now, Jeremiah 32:8, "So Hanameel mine uncle's son came to me in the court of the prison according to the word of the LORD, and said unto me, Buy my field, I pray thee, that is in Anathoth, which is in the country of Benjamin: for the right of inheritance is thine, and the redemption is thine; buy it for thyself. Then I knew that this was the word of the LORD."

We are in the family, as Jeremiah is reminded that he has the right of inheritance. Even though the land was under siege – he could lay claim to it before he could fully occupy it. Hmmm, in some ways it was kind of like when we were kids and felt the need to call dibs. God's word came to lead him into a blessing, even before he could enjoy it. He's able to make a claim now for later just because he's family. He can gain ownership without possession just because he's in the family.

Promised without possession – having to maintain patience through the process – but no worries, because family secures it all. I'm glad that we are family, the Bible says in Ephesians 1:10-12, "That in the dispensation of the fulness of times he might gather together in one all things in Christ, both which are in heaven, and which are on earth; even in him: 11 In whom also we have obtained an inheritance, being predestinated according to the purpose of him who worketh all things after the counsel of his own will: 12 That we should be to the praise of his glory, who first trusted in Christ."

We are family – you can take that to the bank because Jesus was sacrificed – God sacrificed God that we might be family. We are family, entitled by relationship. Entitled by birth – we can lay claim, call dibs because Jesus introduced us to the waters of Baptism, saved us through the sacrifice of the blood, and maintains us through the presence, the indwelling of God the Holy Spirit. We are family, we all rise in Jesus our great example, redeemer, and savior.

Jeremiah, signed the papers, sealed the scroll and gave instructions to preserve the documents in jars – their vaults. He basically took the deeds to the vault, to the bank – put them in the jars. Preserve the faith, hold on to hope!

You can take it to the bank:
God's word will never fail, we are in the family, and **the process leads to possession.**

Look at the text, Jeremiah 32:13-15 says, "And I charged Baruch before them, saying, 14 Thus saith the LORD of hosts, the God of Israel; Take these evidences, this evidence of the purchase, both which is sealed, and this evidence which is open; and put them in an earthen vessel, that they may continue many days. 15 For thus saith the LORD of hosts, the God of Israel; Houses and fields and vineyards shall be possessed again in this land."

Yes, the process leads to possession – there will be times when God speaks from the dust, from our troubled times. Jeremiah was in the mix of tough times – but God, the word of the Lord brought instruction, encouragement, hope, and motivated peace – we may be down and out for a season, but we will be restored!

Might be laid off, but work shall return, may be sick and can't get well but Jesus is on the mainline. You may feel maxed out, credit crippled – but we shall be the head and not the tale, the lender and not the borrower. You can take God to the bank!

Sign, sealed and delivered – cap the bottle, commit to God as God has committed to us. God committed at Calvary as we are beckoned to commit at the cross. Committed to service, committed to prayer, committed to love – take it to the bank!

In the melodic summons of the American Baptist minister William Herbert Brewster as he composed "The Old Landmark":

*Well let us all go back to that old landmark
Let us all go back to that old landmark*

*Well let us all go back to that old landmark
Let us stay in the service of the Lord*

*Well let us kneel and pray in the old time way
Let us kneel and pray in the old time way*

*Well let us kneel and pray in the old time way
He will hear us and be near us
We'll be given bread from Heaven
Tell the story of His glory
It will warn them, it will turn them
It will save this old world from sin and shame*

*Well
I want to see a big revival in the old time way
I want to see a big revival in the old time way
Sinner yearning, convert learning
Christian yearning, fire burning
He will hear us, and be near us
It will warn them, it will turn them*

*Come on down to the river in the old time way
Sons and daughters, parting waters
Comin' up shouting, nobody doubting
He will hear us and be near us
We'll be given bread from heaven*

*Tell the story of His glory
It will warn you, it will turn you*

Everybody shouting, nobody doubting
Everybody happy in the service of the Lord

Well let us all go back to the old landmark
Everybody happy, everybody happy, everybody happy
Everybody happy in the service of the Lord

You can take it to the bank!

HOW TO SERVE

SCRIPTURE

Psalms 100:1-5 A Psalm of praise. Make a joyful noise unto the LORD, all ye lands. 2 Serve the LORD with gladness: come before his presence with singing. 3 Know ye that the LORD he is God: it is he that hath made us, and not we ourselves; we are his people, and the sheep of his pasture. 4 Enter into his gates with thanksgiving, and into his courts with praise: be thankful unto him, and bless his name. 5 For the LORD is good; his mercy is everlasting; and his truth endureth to all generations.

OUTLINE

1. Joyful v1
2. Together (All Lands) v1
3. Focused on God v3
4. Thankful Before Benefit v4
5. Embrace the Generations v5

MESSAGE

Service is at the core of the Christian continuum as God the Son sets the standard of love incarnate – Jesus is the true embodiment of service, the ultimate manifestation of love in action. The life of Jesus the Christ brings example to Christian service, as Jesus taught, fed, healed, led, befriended, mentored, saved, and made disciples.

Jesus served, Jesus led others to serve as the Bible says in Luke 10:1-5, "After these things the Lord appointed other seventy also, and sent them two and two before his face into every city and place, whither he himself would come. 2 Therefore said he unto them, The harvest truly is great, but the labourers are few: pray ye therefore the Lord of the harvest, that he would send forth labourers into his harvest. 3 Go your ways: behold, I send you forth as lambs among wolves. 4 Carry neither purse, nor scrip, nor shoes: and salute no man by the way. 5 And into whatsoever house ye enter, first say, Peace be to this house."

Jesus served and He led others to serve – Jesus sent His empowered disciples to go forth and serve. The words of Matthew chapter 25 and 28 articulates Jesus as we are admonished to serve – feed the hungry, give relief to the thirsty, take in the stranger, clothe the naked, visit the sick and imprisoned as we go forth teaching and baptizing. Biblical church leadership is founded and rooted within principles of service, even the title deacon etymologically rises from the Ancient Greek language - deacon/ diakonos, correlating an icon of service.

I don't know about you, but I have been around churches and organizations where service was indoctrinated, yet hospitality was hauntingly hellish. Hmmm, have you ever known people that will hatefully help you? Some people are more sour than sweet, rough talking, mean mugging, vile, odious personalities that would rather bring persecution over peace. Christian service requires more than motions – it must be motivated through the movement of God the Holy

Spirit. Faith without works is dead, while works without faith are weak. We must learn to biblically serve, following the tenets of God's great standards.

Look with me at Psalm 100 as we think about how to serve – the first verse reads, "Make a joyful noise unto the LORD, all ye lands."

We should be **joyful,** as we are collectively admonished to make a joyful noise in praise. Far too often we are too distracted, disconnected, and distant from the truth of our blessings. We spend too much time complaining, when we should joyfully testify to the greatness of God and all that has been done for us.

We should be gladly motivated to pay it forward, glad to do for others as God is so good to us. We are too blessed to be stingy, mean, impolite, and rude. If you know like I know all that it has taken God, cost God to get us to this point – just thinking about God's love should send us running in the way of Christ prepared with the strength of the Gospel.

I've witnessed sad service in some churches – crazy church kitchen committees serving more hatefulness than ham – often served to grieving families not long after the finality of a funeral. 2 Corinthians 9:6-7 says, "But this I say, He which soweth sparingly shall reap also sparingly; and he which soweth bountifully shall reap also bountifully. 7 Every man according as he purposeth in his heart, so let him give; not grudgingly, or of necessity: for God loveth a cheerful giver."

We should give our time, talent, and treasure cheerfully – we should fulfil our purpose with love, walking after the manner of Christ. Serve with joy, serve like Jesus, serve with gladness.

We can grasp the joy that the 1907 composer Henry van Dyke pens to the melodic final movement of Ludwig van Beethoven's final symphony.

Joyful, joyful, we adore Thee
God of glory, Lord of love
Hearts unfold like flow'rs before Thee
Op'ning to the Sun above
Melt the clouds of sin and sadness
drive the dark of doubt away
Giver of immortal gladness
fill us with the light of day

All Thy works with joy surround Thee
Earth and heav'n reflect Thy rays
Stars and angels sing around Thee
center of unbroken praise

Field and forest, vale and mountain
Flow'ry meadow, flashing sea
chanting bird and flowing fountain
call us to rejoice in Thee

Thou art giving and forgiving
ever blessing, ever blest
well-spring of the joy of living
ocean-depth of happy rest

*Thou the Father, Christ our Brother—
all who live in love are Thine
Teach us how to love each other
lift us to the Joy Divine*

*Mortals join the mighty chorus
which the morning stars began*

*Father-love is reigning o'er us
brother-love binds man to man.
Ever singing, march we onward
victors in the midst of strife
joyful music lifts us sunward
in the triumph song of life.*

Look again at Psalm 100:1 – the passage beckons all nations to make a joyful noise, we should serve **joyfully**. Far too often we are grossly isolated – mentally suffering within the trauma of complete disconnection. God remedied the unhealthy mental condition of loneliness early on within the dispensation of the Creation Age.

We are not designed to do everything alone – somethings are best done with help, better with a partner, done in collaboration. The psalmist calls us to worship the Lord **together**, come let us worship the Lord together! Let us serve together.

The English metaphysical poet John Donne scribed the words: *No man is an island entire of itself; every man is a piece of the continent, a part of the main;*

if a clod be washed away by the sea, Europe is the less, as well as if a promontory were, as well as any manner of thy friends or of thine own were; any man's death diminishes me, because I am involved in mankind. And therefore never send to know for whom the bell tolls; it tolls for thee.

We are absolutely better together, when all God's children get together – what a time. We serve together to maximize our purpose. Ecclesiastes 4:9-12 says, "Two are better than one; because they have a good reward for their labour. 10 For if they fall, the one will lift up his fellow: but woe to him that is alone when he falleth; for he hath not another to help him up. 11 Again, if two lie together, then they have heat: but how can one be warm alone? 12 And if one prevail against him, two shall withstand him; and a threefold cord is not quickly broken."

We can serve together, joyfully and collectively praising God through our service. Look with me at Psalms 100:2-3 it says, "Serve the LORD with gladness: come before his presence with singing. 3 Know ye that the LORD he is God: it is he that hath made us, and not we ourselves; we are his people, and the sheep of his pasture."

We must stay **focused on God**, as Christian service is impossible without devotion to God. We learn to serve as God has served us. We must serve with love, grace, and mercy – never forgetting to forgive as we have been forgiven.

Watch God, walk with God – never lose sight of the one who is mighty in battle, yet the preserver of peace.

We must serve like God – our great creator and redeemer. God feeds the hungry through flourishing fields, relieves the thirsty through the showers of spring, God clothes the lilies of the valley while providing cover for me, there is enough medicine in the hem of God's garment to cure world disease, enough power in God's hand to set the prisoner free, and aren't you so glad that God takes the stranger into the Holy Family – Oh, look at you and me! Stay focused on God.

Look now with me at Psalms 100:4 as it reads, "Enter into his gates with thanksgiving, and into his courts with praise: be thankful unto him, and bless his name."

We should be **thankful before benefits,** as the text tells us to come in with thanksgiving – arrive with a spirit of appreciation. Don't come asking, don't come begging, don't come with you in the way – selfishly focused on you. Come with adoration – Oh, come let us adore Him, Oh, come let us adore Him, Oh, come let us adore Him Christ the King. Somebody, please say amen in this church.

We are not burdened to serve; we are privileged to serve – we are favored to serve. When we serve, we emulate the ways of Jesus, God the Son. When we take up the apron, towel, and water to wash the feet of another – we serve as Jesus served. When we support mercy over justice as Jesus did when He said, "Let anyone of you without sin, cast the first stone."

Hmmm, somebody ought to say amen. When we feed the hungry as Jesus fed thousands or when we stop for the hurting as Jesus stopped for the woman at the well and for the blind man Bartimaeus. We must learn to serve like Jesus – unselfishly grateful that Jesus has led the way. Realizing that we are blessed even when we can't see the benefits.

When we embrace the fullness of God, we don't have to see it all to be thankful. We can shout and praise God merely based on promises:

Standing on the promises of Christ my King.
Through eternal ages let his praises ring.
Glory in the highest, I will shout and sing.
Standing on the promises of God!

When we are thankful before we see the benefits, when we serve without conditions and strings attached, when our service is Holy Spirit motivated – when we cease aggrandizing our service, God will get the greatest glory from our lives. We must learn to reject the idea that everything has to be about us and for us – it's not all about us. Christian service is not motivated by what's in it for me – it's all about what's in it for God, what's in it for the kingdom. Count your many blessings and serve thankfully before the Lord.

1. Joyful v1
2. Together (All Lands) v1
3. Focused on God v3
4. Thankful Before Benefit v4

Focus with me on Psalms 100:5, "For the LORD is good; his mercy is everlasting; and his truth endureth to all generations."

We should **embrace the generations**, walking into the progressive future with God. Our selfishness often distracts us from the past and future – fragmented fractured faith leads to fear and paranoia as we panic within the light of the past and quake with thoughts of the future.

Some of us limit God, but I need you to know that we serve a mighty God – hmmm, what a mighty God we serve, our God is powerful from generation to generation. We never have to capitulate to negative thinking when God is in the process – no matter the season, God is great. We can't get out of the Gospel alone, Jesus has sent us as priest to the world – praying, serving, giving, and leading others to Jesus through the Good News. Now if we really believe that God can bless every generation – then we should have faith to see the glory of God shining through every age.

Far too often we fail to think or care ahead. The Swedish teenage conservationist and environmental activist Greta Thunberg has given voice to future generations, as she sounds the alarm at the degradation of our environment. She reminds us that the earth we leave behind, is the earth for future generations. We must serve thinking beyond our age, beyond out time, beyond our generation – committed to resounding love that transcends time and space. We must follow Christ and be committed to service.

I'm hallelujah happy that Jesus leads us to serve, illustrating true love while we were yet sinners, Christ died for us. Christ leads us to serve, leads us to the cross and presents unconditional love with selfless sacrifice.

Come, oh come to the cross with me and serve as Matthew 16:24 reminds us that Jesus beckons us to take up the cross and follow – through the tough times follow, in lean sad seasons – we must follow Jesus in service.

They crucified our Lord, yet Jesus served. The thief on the cross admonished Jesus to save Himself – but He would not come down to save Himself. We must serve like Jesus served! Ready for service!

Ready to suffer grief or pain,
Ready to stand the test;
Ready to stay at home and send
Others if He sees best.

Ready to go, ready to bear,
Ready to watch and pray;
Ready to stand aside and give

Till He shall clear the way.

Ready to speak, ready to think,
Ready with heart and mind;
Ready to stand where He sees fit,
Ready His will to find.

Ready to speak, ready to warn,
Ready o'er souls to yearn;
Ready in life or ready in death,
Ready for His return.

Ready to go, ready to stay,
Ready my place to fill;
Ready for service lowly or great,
Ready to do His will.

Thank God for Jesus, I wonder is there anybody here ready for service, ready to joyfully follow Jesus, focused on God, not worried about what you'll get out of it, embracing the collection of humanity from generation to generation – holding firm to the faith given by God the Father, Son, and Holy Spirit. Glad that God leads us into service! Anybody glad for Jesus, glad to have the opportunity to follow?

As I run to my seat – I remember back in grade school, I moved from private school to public school and I didn't know the ropes in my new academic environment. So, first few days I met a couple guys that took me into their family.

We all stuck together, they were biological brothers but they claimed me as their middle brother. Now our older brother Shawn could beat most anybody, and when he couldn't alone – we all could together – because us little guys tried to act like him. Everybody knew we were brothers, don't mess with them – their big brother will tear you up! We were so close that my mother once came to teacher-parent conference and was baffled when asked about her other two sons.

We were known by the family; our big brother could not be beat – and we tried to act just like him. We were glad that he let us hang around – just glad to watch him be a tough guy. Well don't you know we all have a Big Brother that's been fighting for us, protecting us, keeping us in the family, teaching us to fight and survive – we should be glad just to follow Jesus, just to be in the company of His word. But then, nevertheless, we have some little brothers and sisters and we have to teach them as we are learning from Him. When we want to act up, we've got to remember that little brothers are watching us serve. Little sisters are watching us fast, study, and pray. We must keep our eyes on our example, while reminded that we are examples. We must serve one another as we lend shoulder to each with a shoulder to spare – ready to serve like Jesus. Glad that God sacrificed God to save us and we ought to be glad to sacrifice for each other through the power of God's great love.

RIGHTEOUS RISING

SCRIPTURE

Luke 18:9-14 And he spake this parable unto certain which trusted in themselves that they were righteous, and despised others: 10 Two men went up into the temple to pray; the one a Pharisee, and the other a publican. 11 The Pharisee stood and prayed thus with himself, God, I thank thee, that I am not as other men are, extortioners, unjust, adulterers, or even as this publican. 12 I fast twice in the week, I give tithes of all that I possess. 13 And the publican, standing afar off, would not lift up so much as his eyes unto heaven, but smote upon his breast, saying, God be merciful to me a sinner. 14 I tell you, this man went down to his house justified rather than the other: for every one that exalteth himself shall be abased; and he that humbleth himself shall be exalted.

OUTLINE

1. Don't Lift Yourself v11-14
2. Reject Self-centeredness v11-12
3. Let Go and Let God v14

MESSAGE

Luke chapter 18 summons us toward the great teaching of Jesus, as the Christ seems to focus upon the motivation that fuels communication seasoned by the intricacies of personality. Christ presents a narrative surrounding two worshipers that sojourned up to the Temple to pray – one worshiper seems to piously position himself before God while poisoned by his own self-righteousness, simultaneously the other worshiper stood feeling unworthy, embracing humility seasoned with adoration for God.

One man felt overly confident as he prayed with himself while focused on himself, while the other man proclaimed himself a sinner before a merciful God. Christ's parable admonishes us to consider the incongruence of righteousness and self-righteousness. I would contend that we are always faced with this duality balanced between good and evil. We are challenged today to discern both our internal and external personalities.

The Pharisee and the Publican seem to be present within each of us, while existing everywhere outside of us within the personalities of others. Good and evil present us with a continuum of choice between the goodness of God and the evil seeping from demonic darkness.

The Bible says in Matthew 6:24-33, "No man can serve two masters: for either he will hate the one, and love the other; or else he will hold to the one, and despise the other. Ye cannot serve God and mammon. 25 Therefore I say unto you, Take no thought for your life, what ye shall eat, or what ye shall drink; nor yet for your body, what ye shall put on. Is not the life more than meat, and the body than raiment? 26 Behold the fowls of the air: for they sow not, neither do they reap, nor gather into barns; yet your heavenly Father feedeth them. Are ye not much better than they? 27 Which of you by taking thought can add one cubit unto his stature? 28 And why take ye thought for raiment? Consider the lilies of the field, how they grow; they toil not, neither do they spin: 29 And yet I say unto you, That even Solomon in all his glory was not arrayed like one of these. 30 Wherefore, if God so clothe the grass of the field, which to day is, and to morrow is cast into the oven, shall he not much more clothe you, O ye of little faith? 31 Therefore take no thought, saying, What shall we eat? or, What shall we drink? or, Wherewithal shall we be clothed? 32 (For after all these things do the Gentiles seek:) for your heavenly Father knoweth that ye have need of all these things. 33 But seek ye first the kingdom of God, and his righteousness; and all these things shall be added unto you."

We must seek righteousness; we must seek the Kingdom of God and God's righteousness – in order to fully capture God's great blessings. We must avoid self-righteousness.

Focus with me on Luke 18:11-14 as it reads, "The Pharisee stood and prayed thus with himself, God, I thank thee, that I am not as other men are, extortioners, unjust, adulterers, or even as this publican. 12 I fast twice in the week, I give tithes of all that I possess. 13 And the publican, standing afar off, would not lift up so much as his eyes unto heaven, but smote upon his breast, saying, God be merciful to me a sinner. 14 I tell you, this man went down to his house justified rather than the other: for every one that exalteth himself shall be abased; and he that humbleth himself shall be exalted."

In order to avoid self-righteousness, **don't lift yourself.** The Pharisee stood praising himself, while the Publican was so abased that he refused to even raise his eyes. Both men came to the Temple, both men came to connect with God, both men were flawed, however one lost focus and lost the reality of purpose. Think about how many times we have lost focus while going through the process of motions.

We shouldn't become too judgmental while examining the actions of the Pharisee, how many times have you come to worship over your life time and lost focus when you arrived. Came to worship, should have been focused – but somebody you didn't like arrived, came to church but got too caught up in somebody's weave or the color of somebody's outfit.

Hmmm, you came, you showed up but your mind was on somebody else, something else, or yourself. Worried about bills, situations, health, the man or woman that you left in a bed of promiscuity at home – too focused on your boo to see God, to worship God, somebody ought to say amen in this church!

Yes, we need to put ourselves on pause before we go trying to raise ourselves up, like oh look at me! When we need to get somewhere out of the way and sit down – rather than looking a mess trying to be seen.

We all a little raggedy, all a bit tattered, we've all sinned and fallen short of God's glory.

None of us can stand as the Pharisee with our chest poked out telling God how good we've been. Comparing ourselves to others while secretly wishing we were more like them – that's why we hatefully give them so much of our attention.

We can't admit that to ourselves or anybody else – but most of the time it's more adoration than the hate we think we hide. Oh yeah, we need to identify the demons today – the ones that have us standing up thinking we so righteous, better than everybody else.

Perhaps we can fool each other with expensive outer garments, but God sees our dirty undergarments! What kind of stains soil your undergarments under a fine light of inspection? God sees us! We must avoid self-righteousness.

Well, let me stop meddling – focus on Luke 18:11-12 as it reads, "The Pharisee stood and prayed thus with himself, God, I thank thee, that I am not as other men are, extortioners, unjust, adulterers, or even as this publican. 12 I fast twice in the week, I give tithes of all that I possess."

We must **reject self-centeredness**, realizing that when all I see is me – I fail to see God, the great supplier of all my needs. The Pharisee thanked God that he was not like other men as he bragged that he was not an extortioner, unjust, adulterous. He proudly bragged that he fasted twice a week and tithed. This fellow was caught up in himself, centered on himself while looking down at others. We must avoid self-righteousness.

Far too often we are focused on how good we are based on how different we are from someone else. But I guarantee you if you take your eyes off of other people long enough to catch a glimpse of self – you may be surprised at the monster lurking within your own personality.

I sure hope you all don't have eggs and tomatoes in your pockets and purses today. But you know I'm right about it. Self-righteousness can render us stupid, we see their mess and we think that's what we smell, when in fact if we just look down – we're standing in our own. You never have to look away to find a sinner, never have to leave home to find a mess.

Self-centeredness greatly limits our view of both God and each other. Our capacity to love lapses within the isolation of selfishness. We must learn to care about more than ourselves. We must look out and love all of humanity, God's great creation.

Doug DiPreta penned the words that Louis Armstrong sang:

I see trees of green
Red roses, too

I see them bloom for me and you

And I think to myself, "what a wonderful world"

I see skies of blue
And clouds of white
The bright blessed day the dark sacred night

And I think to myself, "what a wonderful world"

The colors of the rainbow, so pretty in the sky
Are also on the faces of people going by
I see friends shaking hands saying, "how do you do" They're really saying "I love you"

I hear babies cry
Watch them grow
They'll learn much more than I'll ever know
And I think to myself, "what a wonderful world"
And I think to myself, "what a wonderful world"

There is so much more to see and care about, outside of our selves.

Look now with me at Luke 18:14 it says, "I tell you, this man went down to his house justified rather than the other: for every one that exalteth himself shall be abased; and he that humbleth himself shall be exalted."

We should avoid self-righteousness, don't lift yourself, reject self-centeredness, and **let go and let God.** Although these two men showed up at the Temple at the same time – they arrived with different experiences and traditions.

The Pharisee was more like us, they worshiped regularly, they studied God's law and way, they prayed and fasted, they looked like all was well on the outside but God sees us inside and out. The Pharisee felt so good about his religion that he lost sight of true worship – the Pharisee's religion blocked his full view of his redeemer.

On the other hand, the Publican knew he was messed up, he wouldn't even come close to the zenith of the Temple as he stood far off in humility. I wonder can anybody relate?

I came to Jesus just as I was,
I was weary, wounded, and sad;
I've found in Him a resting place
and He has made me glad!

We've got to show up in the presence of God with what we have. Sometimes we may have joy and laughter, but then there are times all we can do is take our tears, fears, sins, hate, promiscuity, lies, and sadness and say – here I am Lord, all that I am, all that I am not, here I am Lord, I'm yours, completely yours.
We must avoid our own filthy righteousness to embrace an abundance of appreciation toward God – worthy to be praised, let bells of joy ring throughout eternity for our Great God!

The Publican, was a tax collector like Matthew. Publicans were known as rough, tricky swindlers that acted on the behalf of government and self. They were anti-movement, they were in it for the money, they would fight, confiscate by force.

These were the rough and tumble tough guys. Yes, but don't you know that God can save anybody. The text said that the Publican just came and humbled himself at the mercy of God.

The Publican said, "God be merciful to me a sinner." Not puffed up with pride or drunk off his own wine – he simply says have mercy – I confess, I'm a sinner and I need your mercy. God have mercy on me. We should be filled with praise, because God hears our faintest cry our silent tears – God hears us. God answered our necessity for mercy out on Calvary – when God sacrificed God, while represented as Jesus. Yes, while we were yet sinners, Christ died for us.
We cannot afford to miss real true righteousness while focused on ourselves. We must realize that God, and God alone, is the source of all righteousness.

The Bible says in Isaiah 64:4-6, "For since the beginning of the world men have not heard, nor perceived by the ear, neither hath the eye seen, O God, beside thee, what he hath prepared for him that waiteth for him. 5 Thou meetest him that rejoiceth and worketh righteousness, those that remember thee in thy ways: behold, thou art wroth; for we have sinned: in those is continuance, and we shall be saved. 6 But we are all as an unclean thing, and all our righteousnesses are as filthy rags; and we all do fade as a leaf; and our iniquities, like the wind, have taken us away."

We must seek God's kingdom and righteousness – while continually realizing that we are not righteous in and by ourselves. We must embrace God the Son, the one who adorned human flesh to save us all, walked in human mortality to bring us the joy of life everlasting within the power of God immortal, invisible, and everlasting to everlasting – God is great. Hallelujah!

We've been redeemed by the Righteous One who died at Calvary, was buried, and arose on the third day to give us entry into the Holy family – but we can never forget that we didn't do it for ourselves or by ourselves – we are here because of Jesus. Here to serve, here to love, here to worship.

Two men came to the Temple, two men came to pray, the Pharisee and the Publican came to communicate with God – and humility won the day, the request, the call for mercy! One man embraced self-righteousness, abasing himself, lowering his potential for justification while exalting himself.

Two men came to the Temple, two men came to pray, the Pharisee and the Publican came to communicate with God – and humility won the day, the request, the call for mercy! Thankfully, one man humbled himself to seek mercy and departed for home justified, he left better than he came, he left exalted as he let go and let

God – he confessed while embracing God, embracing God's mercy.

When we come to worship, two personalities arrive inside of us, one good and one evil. When we arrive to communicate with God, when we come to the altar to pray, there are two personalities within. We struggle with our inner Pharisee and Publican – who will we be today, good or evil, the good girl or naughty chick, the good guy or the bad boy?

We must reject self-righteousness through continual prayer. We must choose good over evil – we must choose to be evil, bad, fair, good, or great. There are two voices acoustically arranged to capture our attention. Which voice will you hear? Whose report will you believe?

We must choose God, everybody ought to know who Jesus is, the Son of God – I know too much about Him, you can't make me doubt Him. Choose today, to surrender to God – choose good over evil, choose to be great! Choose to change the world as Jesus did, choose to serve the poor and love the human family – I'm so glad Jesus choose us, oh happy that the blood chose us, elated that we can leave here justified through God's great mercy – now leave here and tell the world! Leave here and spread the Gospel, the good news. Leave here with faith and works – be actively alive in Jesus.

There is work to do, let us humble ourselves and follow Jesus through the Holy Spirit into all truth and righteousness. Led to love, led to serve, and led to go!

We've got to go serve the least and the lost, we've got to feed, visit, and clothe. We must give relief to the thirsty and take in the stranger as Jesus taught – we must love one another.

Avoid self-righteousness and embrace, seek after God's righteousness and great blessings will be added, given to you. Blessed by God's great righteousness – in season and out – blessed by God! The Lord is righteous and God alone is worthy – leading us to justification, leading us to a better way! The Publican left exalted, left better than he came – now go away from here better than you came, you came to worship, came for mercy, now depart to serve.

Lovely Day

SCRIPTURE

Jeremiah 31:27-35 Behold, the days come, saith the LORD, that I will sow the house of Israel and the house of Judah with the seed of man, and with the seed of beast. 28 And it shall come to pass, that like as I have watched over them, to pluck up, and to break down, and to throw down, and to destroy, and to afflict; so will I watch over them, to build, and to plant, saith the LORD. 29 In those days they shall say no more, The fathers have eaten a sour grape, and the children's teeth are set on edge. 30 But every one shall die for his own iniquity: every man that eateth the sour grape, his teeth shall be set on edge. 31 Behold, the days come, saith the LORD, that I will make a new covenant with the house of Israel, and with the house of Judah: 32 Not according to the covenant that I made with their fathers in the day that I took them by the hand to bring them out of the land of Egypt; which my covenant they brake, although I was an husband unto them, saith the LORD: 33 But this shall be the covenant that I will make with the house of Israel; After those days, saith the LORD, I will put my law in their inward parts, and write it in their hearts; and will be their God, and they shall be my people. 34 And they shall teach no more every man his neighbour, and every man his brother, saying, Know the LORD: for they shall all know me, from the least of them unto the greatest of them, saith the LORD: for I will forgive their iniquity, and I will remember their sin no more. 35 Thus saith the LORD, which giveth the sun for a light by day, and the ordinances of the moon and of the stars for a light by night, which divideth the sea when the waves thereof roar; The LORD of hosts is his name:

OUTLINE

1. Our Next Crop is Already Planted v27-28
2. Our Fate Doesn't Have to be Sour v29-30
3. Our Division Will be Mended v31-32
4. Our Hearts Will Motivate Us v33
5. Our Benefits Will be Mutual v34

MESSAGE

The prophecy of Jeremiah emerges from the Bible from 20 years of sermons, messages, and warnings, if you will. God inspires Jeremiah to sound the alarm toward the Southern Kingdom of Judah.

The Northern Kingdom of Israel had been ravished by Assyrians and Judah was soon to be invaded by the Babylonians as a tool of judgment in God's hand. The Southern Kingdom was a backslidden collective arranged against the way of God.

Jeremiah was commissioned by God to deliver a powerful word to tear down and build up – to uproot and plant. Tear down as judgment for sin seasoned with injustice, tear down as judgment – but build up through God's grace and mercy.

Inspired to root up corrupt sprits, yet plant the seeds of eternal love emanating from the throne of God.

The people and land had become polluted by sin, we can never act against God, the nature and essence of God – we can never go against God and embrace everlasting success. They had forgotten God, embraced foreign traditions and gods while mistreating the least of their social equation.

Jeremiah warned them, presented God's word that tough times would arrive but restoration would follow. The Southern Kingdom would be destroyed as a result of their sin, nevertheless, God promised restoration. Punishment, but then a second chance. Tear down, but build up – root up, but plant. God grants second chances, we should be glad to know that God grants second, third, fourth, and multiplied chances.

I know I've needed another chance. I know I've needed redemption, restoration, and forgiveness. We should be glad that God grants another chance!

The Bible says in Titus 3:3-5, "For we ourselves also were sometimes foolish, disobedient, deceived, serving divers lusts and pleasures, living in malice and envy, hateful, and hating one another. 4 But after that the kindness and love of God our Saviour toward man appeared, 5 Not by works of righteousness which we have done, but according to his mercy he saved us, by the washing of regeneration, and renewing of the Holy Ghost;"

We can identify with the text today, we've been foolish, disobedient, deceived, we've been raunchy, freaky, hateful, and jealous – but then God saved us. God forgave us, picked us up and turned us around, God gave us another chance.

Jeremiah delivered a word of prophecy declaring that tough times will emerge as consequences to our disconnection from God – a season of punishment, judgment, inspired repentance, and chastisement will come, but take the punishment, turn to God, repent, God will restore. The days of judgment may be dark and sad, but God will ultimately restore us to a lovely day, bring us to restoration.
The book of Jeremiah articulates impending doom throughout the parchments, yet chapters 30-33 arise like an oasis in a vast desert – providing hope and motivation as fuel toward the journey to restoration.

I've always advised parents to limit punishing and grounding children – never make your children feel that redemption is unachievable. When redemption is erased, perpetual punishment will either break the individual or the individual will break the system. God provides us with correction not condemnation – redemption flows from the love of God not retribution.

Both the Southern and Northern Kingdoms disappointed God, judgment was necessary to dispense the love of God as we are reminded by Hebrews 12:6 that God corrects those whom God loves. Jeremiah chapter 31 brings us to a glimpse of brighter days boldly shimmering in the future, beyond the corrective measures of punishment. Lovely days will arrive, God will restore us beyond our repentance as grace massages time on our behalf.

Look with me at Jeremiah 31:27-28 as it reads, "Behold, the days come, saith the LORD, that I will sow the house of Israel and the house of Judah with the seed of man, and with the seed of beast. 28 And it shall come to pass, that like as I have watched over them, to pluck up, and to break down, and to throw down, and to destroy, and to afflict; so will I watch over them, to build, and to plant, saith the LORD."

Better times, lovelier days are coming because **our next crop is already planted**, God has already planted for our future. God has a plan for each of us, our creator, grand architect, and eternal sustainer – has a plan. God has already worked it out, already has prepared provisions for us.

Jeremiah provides a word of comfort and restoration. Yes, your bad actions have landed you in the hot seat, but you don't have to stay there. We may go through tough challenging times, we mess up some time, we mess up big time - but God is there with a hand of relief – ready to extend forgiveness, ready to pick us up out of the muck and mire. God lifted me out of the slimy pit, out of the mud and mire; He set my feet on a rock and gave me a firm place to stand, as the psalmist pens in Psalm 40.

Don't fret, don't throw in the towel. God has already planned your release and prepared for your return home. Like the Prodigal Son, when we turn toward home – God like a great parent is patiently waiting our return with open arms. Our next crop has already been planted. Just hold on, the next crop has already been planted, your next season is already secure.

Focus with me on Jeremiah 31:29-30 it reads, "In those days they shall say no more, The fathers have eaten a sour grape, and the children's teeth are set on edge. 30 But every one shall die for his own iniquity: every man that eateth the sour grape, his teeth shall be set on edge."

Our fate doesn't have to be sour, as Jesus has redeemed us to walk in the unique familial relationship with God, motivated through personal priesthood.

See, we don't have to go through anybody to get to God – Jesus opened the door and left it open for us to enter in through Bible study, prayer, and the guidance of God the Holy Spirit. We may momentarily reside within the same environment – but in the ultimate translation of time we must be individually accountable to God.

We may collectively support each other through prayer and ministry – nevertheless, we will have to give a personal account for our lives within the eschatological dispensation of time, old folks used to say "every tub must set on its own bottom."

At the moment we might be affected by Washington politics, we may be sad at times, the economy may be depressing, the moral fabric of society may be tattered by violence, and we may feel some stress from policies and behaviors – but trouble won't last always.

Ultimately, like birds freed from the slithering serpents – we will fly away to the individual peace that will bring us into the collective of the saints as we enjoy the everlasting love of God. Every day will be lovely, we will be at peace throughout all of eternity, our teeth will not be set on edge from the actions of others. We will be judged on our relationship with the reality of all righteousness, our Great God is worthy of our attention, worthy of our praise.

Aren't you glad that you have a personal relationship with God, glad God knows your name, knows the number of hairs on your head? God knows you and God loves you. Our fate does not have to be sour as God so loved the world that God gave us Jesus, the greatest gift of love. God sacrificed God for us.

Look with me at Jeremiah 31:31-32 it reads, "Behold, the days come, saith the LORD, that I will make a new covenant with the house of Israel, and with the house of Judah: 32 Not according to the covenant that I made with their fathers in the day that I took them by the hand to bring them out of the land of Egypt; which my covenant they brake, although I was an husband unto them, saith the LORD:"

Better days are coming, **our division will be mended.** Jeremiah addressed a broken, fractured kingdom – as the Northern and Southern kingdom were results of the division of one kingdom into two. We should be able to identify with fractured/broken people and a fractured/broken society. Our ideological positions have polarized us more and more as sinister politicians seek to exploit our differences as calculated resources.

We have rogue, inattentive gunmen killing innocent people in their homes presumably by mistake – while it seems that brown boys are at risk on community sidewalks. Our world is fractured, our world is all mixed up, topsy-turvy as we increasingly fear the people charged with public security. Our world is broken, when our national leaders seem to protect themselves while exposing us to harm.

Our society is broken just as Jeremiah was surrounded by the torn remnants of Israel and Judah, weakened by division. There was fighting in the family, distance between cousins, unrest in the tribe – yet God prepared for a family reunion.
When we're at our worst, God is at God's best. Whatever is torn, God can mend – there's no situation too difficult and no problem too hard for God. Often, we think of the impossibilities, while God is creating possibilities. Your next crop has already been planted; plans have already been made on our behalf. God will mend relationships that have been broken.

The idea of a human family reunion, may seem like a sad fantasy, it may seem like a weak notion on the surface – but it's a statement of exponential proportions. Mark 3:25 reminds us that Jesus said, "A house divided against itself cannot stand." We lose standing when we embrace isolationism, separatism, and nationalism.

When we belong to the restored/mended family of God – we stand with power, unmovable, unshakable because of our mighty God dwelling in the united family through the Body of Christ and continued presence of the Holy Spirit. When we stand together in the power of God's delightful presence, we stand together to defeat our enemies. When we touch and agree, God is activated upon His children's united petitions. Better days will come as God mends our division, restoring relationships, living in a loop of lingering love.

Center now upon Jeremiah 31:33 as it reads, "But this is the agreement which I will make with the people of Israel after those days, says the Lord; I will put my law in their inner parts, writing it in their hearts; and I will be their God, and they will be my people."

Our next crop is already planted, our fate doesn't have to be sour, our division will be mended, and **our hearts will motivate us.**

Far too often we're going through the motions of life like the Tin Man featured in the Wizard of Oz movie. We can get caught up in just doing, while numb to the world. I'm here, but not feeling it – here but not into it, I'm here but disconnected.

God promises to write on Israel's heart – motivating them from the inside out. See, God loves a cheerful giver – when we come to the Lord we shouldn't come with stingy praise, quenched spirit, and parched attitude. We should exude gratitude while gripped by grace, thankful for all that the Lord has done.

Happy glad on the inside, motivated to fulfill our God-given purpose with joy filled hearts – inscribed by the love of God. A better, lovely day parades the halls of our minds as the seeds of God's word matures within our hearts – motivating us to treat everybody right.

I am going to stay on the battlefield for the Lord, I am going to stay on my bended knee, I am going to treat everybody right! Any task is easier when your heart is into it – when you love what you're doing, the sting ceases to saturate the process. It's so good to know that God is a mind fixer and heart regulator. Lovely day, a better day is on the way – let's keep our hearts motivated under the hand of God.

Lest I hold you too long, focus now with me on Jeremiah 31:34 it reads, "And no longer will they be teaching every man his neighbour and every man his brother, saying, Get knowledge of the Lord: for they will all have knowledge of me, from the least of them to the greatest of them, says the Lord: for they will have my forgiveness for their evil-doing, and their sin will go from my memory for ever."

Our next crop is already planted,
Our fate doesn't have to be sour,
Our division will be mended,
Our hearts will motivate us.

Finally, our benefits will be mutual – God is merciful, just, and equitable. There are no special positions, none of us will be given less or more. Our God is big enough and grand enough – filled with power, our God has enough to provide for us all. Pressed down, shaken together, and running over – God blesses us all without respect of person. When we walk with the Lord, our benefits are mutual – the Lord cares for us all.

When we walk with the Lord
In the light of His Word,
What a glory He sheds on our way;
While we do His good will,
He abides with us still,
And with all who will trust and obey.

God gave Jesus, God sacrificed God giving us all access to renewed life. The old song used to go, "I got shoes, you got shoes, all God's children got shoes," we are not neglected children – God prepares for us all. Your next crop has already been planted.

God gave us Jesus, the seed of David – crucified at Calvary in the person of Jesus the Christ. God planted redemptive salvation at Calvary as Jesus hung, bled, suffered, and died for us. Your next crop has already been planted, the first fruit of humanity – planted in a borrowed tomb, planted in the cover of the earth – but up from the grave He arose, with a mighty triumph o'er His foes, He arose a Victor from the dark domain, and He lives forever with His saints to reign. He arose! He arose! Hallelujah! Christ arose!

Perhaps, you been going through one situation after another. We've made some wrong turns, took the wrong path – penalized by time, stressed by life, fractured relationships, and broken heart. Tore up from the floor up, but yet holding on to God's unchanging hand – realizing that God's grace and mercy will bring restoration.

Back in 1977, Bill Withers wrote and recorded a song titled *"Lovely Day."* Mr. Withers ponders the source of a lovely day as he seems to focus on a woman, on a personal relationship or personal love – yet the words seem to articulate adoration most suitable toward God our great provider.

I've slightly altered Bill Withers words to embrace them toward my central interest – resting completely upon Jesus the risen savior.

The song melodically phrases:
When I wake up in the morning, Lord

And the sunlight hurts my eyes
And something without warning, Lord
Bears heavy on my mind
Then I look to You
And the world's alright with me
Just one look to you
And I know it's gonna be
A lovely day

When the day that lies ahead of me
Seems impossible to face
When someone else instead of me
Always seems to know the way

Then I look to you
And the world's alright with me
Just one look to you
And I know it's gonna be
A lovely day, A lovely day

It's good to know, that when we look to God – no matter how bad we've been, no matter where we come from or what we've been through – God is always there with open arms to forgive and restore, bringing us to the lovely day of Christ's return. Just one look to God and we know it's going to be a lovely day!

THERE IS A COMEBACK

SCRIPTURE

Haggai 2:1-9 In the seventh month, in the one and twentieth day of the month, came the word of the LORD by the prophet Haggai, saying, 2 Speak now to Zerubbabel the son of Shealtiel, governor of Judah, and to Joshua the son of Josedech, the high priest, and to the residue of the people, saying, 3 Who is left among you that saw this house in her first glory? and how do ye see it now? is it not in your eyes in comparison of it as nothing? 4 Yet now be strong, O Zerubbabel, saith the LORD; and be strong, O Joshua, son of Josedech, the high priest; and be strong, all ye people of the land, saith the LORD, and work: for I am with you, saith the LORD of hosts: 5 According to the word that I covenanted with you when ye came out of Egypt, so my spirit remaineth among you: fear ye not. 6 For thus saith the LORD of hosts; Yet once, it is a little while, and I will shake the heavens, and the earth, and the sea, and the dry land; 7 And I will shake all nations, and the desire of all nations shall come: and I will fill this house with glory, saith the LORD of hosts. 8 The silver is mine, and the gold is mine, saith the LORD of hosts. 9 The glory of this latter house shall be greater than of the former, saith the LORD of hosts: and in this place will I give peace, saith the LORD of hosts.

OUTLINE

1. Remember How it Was v3
2. Courageously Wait v4

3. Look to the Lord's Latter v9

MESSAGE

Last week's lectionary/scripture portion brought us encouragement from the lengthy anthology collected from 20 years of Jeremiah's sermons, nevertheless this week encouragement emanates from the brief prophetic words of Haggai.

Thankfully God speaks to us in different ways while imparting the same word. The Bible presents God's message of redemptive love birthed through Jesus and sustained by the Holy Spirit as we are led into all righteousness. Sometimes we need many words like the prophesies of Jeremiah and Isaiah – then there are times when our cognition operates best with less, we think better when given smaller sets of data. There are times when we need the point, don't beat around the bush – just bring it. We don't need heart surgery - a cardiovascular thump is enough to get us jump started.

Approximately 500 years before Christ, Haggai seems to be the brief word of encouragement positioned for Israelites returning from exile. You may recall from last week we talked about the judgment of God falling upon the backslidden nations as the Assyrians and Babylonians attacked and forced them into captivity. Now the Persians have taken charge, granting exiles to return home.

You know how it is when you've been ejected from your dreams, goals, and aspirations —you've been through some struggles on your journey.

There are times when life sends us a disconnection notice – we become disconnected from God, each other, reality, and vitality. We've all experienced life's disconnection notices and after a long disconnection from God – we become excited once an opportunity for a comeback is presented.

I don't know about you, but I've had some downs and outages, sometimes when an outage of love, outage of peace, outage of justice, or an outage of joy has darkened my life –I needed God to fully restore services in my life. Desperate times move us to yearn for a comeback as life frequently comes with setbacks.

I wonder is there anybody here waiting for a comeback? You've been through the storms of sin, tossed and driven by angry winds. Anybody here in need of reconnection, desperately needing a comeback? Somebody ought to praise God right now, hallelujah.

Let us look at Haggai 2:3 as it reads, "Who is left among you that saw this house in her first glory? and how do ye see it now? is it not in your eyes in comparison of it as nothing?"

We should **remember how it was**, as far too often our forgetfulness weakens us. Our faith is built stronger upon our experiences with God and each other. We cannot afford to forget God and all that God has done for us.

The prophet Haggai prompts them to remember how things where before exile, remember their prior experience with God – remember how it was. Remember your life, remember our community, remember the marketplace, yes remember how it was.

Well, Hebrews 13:8 reminds us that Jesus Christ is the same yesterday, today, and tomorrow – God sacrificed God to save us and we must never forget. Just as Jesus came back from the grave – we can always expect God to lead a comeback in our lives.

Focus now on Haggai 2:4 as it reads, "Yet now be strong, O Zerubbabel, saith the LORD; and be strong, O Joshua, son of Josedech, the high priest; and be strong, all ye people of the land, saith the LORD, and work: for I am with you, saith the LORD of hosts:"

We must remember how it was and **courageously wait**, just as the prophet reminded them to remember, they needed to wait while appreciating the presence of God. Yes, we can courageously wait when God is present. Haggai spoke to Zerubbabel and Joshua the government and faith leaders – the prophet reminded them that they were on a comeback and could not neglect to keep God at the center of their rebuilding.

Haggai 1:7-9 says, "Thus saith the LORD of hosts; Consider your ways. 8 Go up to the mountain, and bring wood, and build the house; and I will take pleasure in it, and I will be glorified, saith the LORD. 9 Ye looked for much, and, lo, it came to little; and when ye brought it home, I did blow upon it. Why? saith the LORD of hosts. Because of mine house that is waste, and ye run every man unto his own house."

The old city was being rebuilt, yet the building of the Temple was being neglected. God granted them renewed access, brought them back home again, forgave their sins – and they became more mindful of their own property over the Temple, the House of God.

We must embrace God in every season of our lives, no matter how our journey is mapped – we cannot reach glory without God. We cannot successfully move without the Lord – when you don't know what to do or where to go, wait with courage upon the Lord, and again I say wait upon the Lord. No matter how times, politics, people, and economics change – wait on God. No matter how many times the road may darken – wait on God.

We especially need God in a comeback – don't quickly forget, embrace God's restoration with appreciation. Don't forget how you lost it all, don't forget where you've been, don't forget you're struggle – rejoice for God's great grace, rejoice for redemption, rejoice for a comeback!

Center now on Haggai 2:9 as it reads, "The glory of this latter house shall be greater than of the former, saith the LORD of hosts: and in this place will I give peace, saith the LORD of hosts."

Thank God for a comeback, remember how it was, courageously wait, and finally **look to the Lord's latter** – as Haggai encourages them to embrace the beautiful hope matured within faith upon our great God.

Sometimes we go through a lot, the world is going through so much – from injustice to hatred, the world profoundly is damaged by sin, in need of redemption.

When life seems to get you down, when sad, depressing times emerge, we must hold to our faith even the more. We must reject fear as we embrace God's presence and peace. God will never leave us neglected, never leave us in eternal unrest – God will always deliver, always love, always redeem – I'm glad God is a God of a comeback and our latter will be greater than our former.

Hold on, God has shown us the greatest comeback of all time! There was a comeback at Calvary, as enemies of peace gathered for a public execution – the world needs a comeback of hope.

Anybody need a comeback? There was a comeback at Calvary, as God sacrificed God for our great comeback. Jesus seemed set back when arrested without cause like many minorities that wait trial today without the benefit of bail. Many innocent people went to sleep last night, held over for the weekend, wrongly arrested yet too poor to pay the bail.

We must resist becoming judgmental as sometimes our assumptions are misdirected as we rush to judgment. Some may have rushed to judge Jesus, yet wrongly accused He was arrested and carried from judgment hall to judgment hall. Falsely accused, seemed like a setback – but don't you know that God can always bring a comeback.

Jesus suffered, bled, and died out at Calvary – it seemed a setback for humanity, they buried Jesus. God spoke to God out on Calvary as love and mercy emerged to bring redemption to humankind. They buried Jesus, buried, caught by the grave for three days – but God raised God, with all power.

Jesus brought us a comeback, as He arose from the grave leading us to know Him in the fellowship of His sufferings and the power of His resurrection – leading us to victory over the depressions of life.

No matter what you're going through – God can bring us to a comeback.

When life is disconnected
Time is drenched with sadness
Despair dances with the day
Dancing like a dervish of doom

Setbacks saturate the journey
Trials, temptations, secret snares
Bothered, betrayed, and bent

Wait on God, with faithful heart
Wait on God through strain and struggle
Wait on God – never forget the comeback at Calvary, where Christ demonstrated love to save us, encouraging us to remain focused on God. There is always another move for God, there is a comeback.

TROUBLE DON'T LAST WITH A TURN IT AROUND GOD

SCRIPTURE

Isaiah 65:17-25 For, behold, I create new heavens and a new earth: and the former shall not be remembered, nor come into mind. 18 But be ye glad and rejoice for ever in that which I create: for, behold, I create Jerusalem a rejoicing, and her people a joy. 19 And I will rejoice in Jerusalem, and joy in my people: and the voice of weeping shall be no more heard in her, nor the voice of crying. 20 There shall be no more thence an infant of days, nor an old man that hath not filled his days: for the child shall die an hundred years old; but the sinner being an hundred years old shall be accursed. 21 And they shall build houses, and inhabit them; and they shall plant vineyards, and eat the fruit of them. 22 They shall not build, and another inhabit; they shall not plant, and another eat: for as the days of a tree are the days of my people, and mine elect shall long enjoy the work of their hands. 23 They shall not labour in vain, nor bring forth for trouble; for they are the seed of the blessed of the LORD, and their offspring with them. 24 And it shall come to pass, that before they call, I will answer; and while they are yet speaking, I will hear. 25 The wolf and the lamb shall feed together, and the lion shall eat straw like the bullock: and dust shall be the serpent's meat. They shall not hurt nor destroy in all my holy mountain, saith the LORD.

OUTLINE

1. Forget the Old Stuff v17
2. Get Happy v18

3. Get Ready to Build v21-22
4. Get Ready for Answers v24
5. Get Ready for God's Ecology v25

MESSAGE

One of the old songs emerging from our tradition rests within the simplistic words melodically arranged within "Trouble Don't Last Always." We come to worship to praise God, nevertheless, we also encourage one another.

Carlton Pearson tells the story of visiting an elderly woman that presented him with the question, "Are you yet holding on?" Pastor Pearson said he replied, "I'm yet holding on," and the lady said, "Well, keep on keeping on."

We love God and we love each other, so we encourage each other through the tough, rough, tragic times. We love each other through pain and sorrow, stress and strain – we love each other through the ups and downs.

When we love like Christ, we are empowered with eternal endurance through the everlasting presence of the Holy Spirit. When we love like Christ, we see past today, past now to prophetically see that in the pattern of God – trouble don't last always.

We can walk in fearless love as Christ did when we trustingly focus on God. Love is not always safe, love is not always comfortable – love can cause us some troubles and woes, but Christ testifies that trouble don't last always.

We can love the least, worst, and lost when we trust in the power that God has given us. Like Christ, we walk in the love that motivates us to turn to the pain of humanity, love that turns us toward those that hunger and thirst, love that turns us to visit hospitals, prisons, and nursing homes. Love is remaining even after realizing that living like Christ can bring the troubling pains of the cross – but trouble don't last always with a turn it around God!

Look with me at Isaiah 65:17 as it reads, "For, behold, I create new heavens and a new earth: and the former shall not be remembered, nor come into mind."

We need to **forget some old stuff**, as trouble don't last always – but our memories can often sustain conditions that have long been over. Still mad about something you should have let go of a long time ago – we get stuck on sad. We cling to the clashes, becoming used to drama – when we could have been free of trouble a long time ago, just let it go.

Trouble don't last always; we don't have to wallow in the dross and guilt of sin. God grants forgiveness to the repentant, as captives to sin are set free through the movement of Christ. Oh, the blood that was shed for me, oh the blood that has set us free.

Trouble don't last always with a turn it around God, don't give up, don't give in – trouble don't last always! Are you yet holding on? Keep on keeping on – you've been forgiven, you've been set free. Let your old thinking, old ways, old selfishness, and hatred go. Give God your pain, give God your hatred, sadness, sickness, and malice – trouble don't last always!

We can trust God through it all, the Lord will eternally take care of us. We don't have to lose rest over the past – God grants us strength and renewal. We need to forget some old stuff, issues driving us crazy, things people say, things people do – all the stuff we internalize that we need to release.

Give the past to God, all the negative stuff people have said, the pain of childhood, rejections, even the depressing things we say to ourselves – we need to give it all to God!

Look now with me at Isaiah 65:18 it reads, "But be ye glad and rejoice for ever in that which I create: for, behold, I create Jerusalem a rejoicing, and her people a joy."

Trouble don't last always – forget some old negative stuff, then **get happy**. The prophet Isaiah reminds the Children of Israel to rejoice through the process.

The prophet experienced the presence of God – Isaiah knew the power of God, the prophet stood before God in chapter 6 as he was transformed from lying lumps to coal cleansed words purified by God.

Isaiah knew that God could pick you up and turn you around – he knew that God could change anybody, he knew that God would turn it around. Isaiah knew that trouble don't last always, he knew that God can take us from sad to glad, from mad to happy, and from hate to love.

See part of holding on and moving on – rest within our ability to embrace the life jacket of hope while abandoned on the angry seas of life. We can joyfully jog through life when focused on God, as no problem will over cast God. Trouble is temporary while God is eternal. Trouble don't last always; God grants grace and mercy in the midst of our struggles – God's attributes sustains our faith and heals our half-hearted hope.

The Children of Israel suffered the consequences of their sins as judgment emerged through cruelties issued by first the Assyrians and then the Babylonians – yet God forgave the nation's sin, turned their situation around, defeated their enemy, and gently brought them to restoration – trouble don't last always.

We should be thankful that God will make us glad – when I think about the Lord and all that's been done for us, my soul is made glad.

Focus with me on Isaiah 65:21-22 as it reads, "And they shall build houses, and inhabit them; and they shall plant vineyards, and eat the fruit of them. 22 They shall not build, and another inhabit; they shall not plant, and another eat: for as the days of a tree are the days of my people, and mine elect shall long enjoy the work of their hands."

Trouble don't last always, **get ready to build** – God will restore to build again – we must repent and turn from our way to God's way, realizing that God is a creator, a builder leading us to build. We must learn to make the world a better place, always building for the promise of God's love to arise before a hope deprived world.

We must build through love in action, by getting out to vote, participating in the 2020 Census, and caring about our neighbors.

We must build through social justice while holding government accountable with our tax dollars – we must correspond to the conditions of humanity with love by writing letters, emailing, and calling our government leaders to encourage justice for all seasoned with mercy. We must be builders, building relationships for the Kingdom of God.

Our God is a builder and creator – God tears down to build and roots up to plant. Jesus came through the womb of humanity to build His divine Kingdom – Jesus came building the temple of the soul, preparing the way for the indwelling of the Holy Spirit.

God leads by example, leading us to build upon the cornerstone of Jesus, building with the solid stones of love, peace, mercy, and forgiveness. God is a builder, always building us up as we should choose to follow the divine pattern – purposefully building others.

Ephesians 2:19-22 says, "Now therefore ye are no more strangers and foreigners, but fellowcitizens with the saints, and of the household of God; 20 And are built upon the foundation of the apostles and prophets, Jesus Christ himself being the chief corner stone; 21 In whom all the building fitly framed together groweth unto an holy temple in the Lord: 22 In whom ye also are builded together for an habitation of God through the Spirit."

Inspired in the mid-1700s by God our great creator, Pastor James Relly penned the poetic words:
The Stone the Builders did refuse,
Which human Wisdom nee'r will choose,
Is here the Head-stone seen:
Brought forth with Joy to make all fast;
Christ is the first Stone and the last;
The Church is safe between.

The spacious Roof, extended wide,
Lock'd in secure on ev'ry Side,
Braves all the Storms that fall:
Christ is that Cov'ring, suited well,
To shelter Man from Storms of Hell;
O Christ! thou art our All.

Focus with me on Isaiah 65:24 as it reads, "And it shall come to pass, that before they call, I will answer; and while they are yet speaking, I will hear."

Trouble don't last always – **get ready for answers**, God has the answers to all the questions of humanity and beyond. Whatever you've been asking God has already been answered. The Lord reveals to Isaiah that our petitions are already heard before we call and while we yet speak.

Oh, did anybody hear me in this church? The emergency 911 department makes a recording after you call – God is prepared and waiting before you call. In fact, 911 didn't take care of all the hidden snares and depressed dangers – God has handled more of our problems than we will ever know.

If you could look back over your life and see the footprints in the sand, you'd realize that there are very few times when we are walking with God – most of life, God has been carrying us. God knows us before we call, hears us before we finish, and has the power to fix every situation.

When we get connected to God, the worrisome questions of life pave the path to peace, as we gain divine strength to walk over the stress on the journey to Glory. God has the net out before we fall, God knew us before the womb, your questions, your needs, your struggles and your uncertainties have already been heard and answered by God.

This prophetic voice essentially says, "It is already done" – we have favor! God says, "I hear you." Maybe that isn't very important to you in this age of rude people continually ignoring each other.

Nevertheless, I can tell you that it's not amusing to be ignored. God doesn't ignore us. Many of us are occupied by so many things and digital devices – we hurtfully ignore each other. We should be grateful when someone is talking to us, eating with us, dating, or taking an interest in us.

In this digitally addicted society, it's easy to feel left out and alone – but God! Oh, say it with me "but God!" No matter the time, season, or reason – God hears us! Before we call, while we're still talking, God is acting and answering.

It's good to know that God cares, in spite of our past, no matter how poor, no matter our social status – God loves you and me. We should be glad for favor. God favors you; God favors us – Ephesians 3:20 reminds us that God is able to do exceeding abundantly above all that we ask or think. God has the answers, God is the answer.

The African-American hymnist Cleavant Derricks corralled the instructional words:

Now let us, have a little talk with Jesus,
Let us, tell him all about our troubles,

*He will, hear our faintest cry,
And he will, answer by and by.
Now when you, feel a little prayer wheel turning,
And you, know a little fire is burning.
You will, find a little talk with Jesus makes it right.*

*Sometimes my path seems drear, without a ray of cheer,
And then a cloud of doubt may hide the light of day.
The mists of sin may rise and hide the starry skies,
But just a little talk with Jesus clears the way.*

Look with me at Isaiah 65:25 it reads, "The wolf and the lamb shall feed together, and the lion shall eat straw like the bullock: and dust shall be the serpent's meat. They shall not hurt nor destroy in all my holy mountain, saith the LORD."

Forget the old stuff, get happy, get ready to build, get ready for answers, and **get ready for God's ecology**.

Think about it, many of us can't keep a plant alive, some of us can't keep fish swimming in water – but God knows how to organize and arrange. God is the grand and great architect – fruit somehow grows on trees as benefits of sun, water and soil.

Fruit changes colors to signal readiness and darkens then shrivels to indicate expiration – serving animals with nutrition. What a mighty God we serve.

There is a circle of life, one stage feeding the other, one sphere resting within another – God's ecology is always balanced and only disturbed by man through God's permission. God gives us the grace to experience sin, failure, and transgression as academies of appreciation. God fixes up, while we often tear up.

We are living in an increasingly divisive society, to the extent that our disrespect for the unity of life slowly anaesthetizes us to our own suicide. Our actions are killing us, from what we eat to what we do.

The first job that God gave to humanity was to maintain stewardship over the animals and earth. We cage animals and call them pets, we wear them and call it fashion, as we eat them and call them dinner. Blood is shed, cruelty is fueled from game hunting to slaughter, and yet we remain hungry while some starve under the over-consumption of the greedy.

From deforestation to the depletion of natural ground water reserves, big business and gluttony with polluted water momentarily quenching thirst. The world is in trouble, the world is in crisis – sound the alarm.

While many of us ignorantly ignore our environment, while some of us irresponsibly deny climate change – the environment is killing us. Heat stress, depleted food resources, water shortages, along with the complexities of extreme weather will ultimately kill us.

Our ecological arrangements will kill us, our selfishness, self-centeredness, and environmental separatism will kill us. But trouble don't last always.

We struggle with racism, xenophobia, and hatred – embracing division will ultimately destroy us. Jesus reminds us that a house divided against itself cannot stand. Division will ultimately destroy us – fighting against each other over lies, while ignoring the truth, it will destroy us. While we're focused on fighting each other, enemies prepare at the borders while watching us weaken ourselves with civil stupidity.

God's way is not like our ways, God's ecology calls together all of creation to honor the greatness of our great God. Sub specie aeternitatis, in the light of eternity the day will come when peace shall capture time as a revelation of God's manifested plan.

The gospel hymnist Thomas A. Dorsey penned the words of faith beautified by hope:

There will be peace in the valley for me.
Well, the bear will be gentle.
The wolf will be tame,
And the lion shall lay down with the lamb,Oh yes
And the incomprehensible from the wild will be led by a
child, I'll be changed from this creature that I am. Oh, there
will be peace in the valley for me, I pray.

No more sadness, no more trouble there'll be. There will be
peace in the valley for me, for me

Trouble don't last always with a turn it around God, naw – trouble don't last always! Perhaps the enemies to humanity rejoice over the dark seeds of discord, hoping that we all continue in our transgressions, but God ready to sacrifice God gave us Jesus.

True trouble, the problem of death and sin, the questions of death and sin were answered at Calvary as Jesus died for us, God the Son surrendered blood for us, God loves us, in that, while we were yet sinners, Christ died for us.

The cross reminds us that trouble don't last always. The day drew dark, the journey of agony and pain as Jesus was crucified – but trouble don't last.

Jesus, the solid rock we stand upon – Jesus the rock was placed in a rock, buried in a tomb, but trouble don't last always with a turn it around God.

Jesus remained in the grave three days and arose with victory - the greatest testimony that trouble don't last always.

Trouble fades into God's glory when we learn to reject self-absorption to center and focus on God alone. During the 1800s the French preacher Theodore Monod articulated the selfless petition to God:

O The bitter shame and sorrow
That a time could ever be
When I let the Saviour's pity
Plead in vain, and proudly answered:
All of self and none of thee!

*Yet he found me; I beheld him
Bleeding on th'accursed tree,
Heard him pray: Forgive them, Father!
And my wistful heart said faintly:
Some of self and some of thee!*

*Day by day his tender mercy,
Healing, helping, full and free,
Sweet and strong and, ah! so patient,
Brought me lower, while I whispered:
Less of self and more of thee!*

*Higher than the highest Heaven,
Deeper than the deepest sea,
Lord, thy love at last has conquered;
Grant me now my spirit's longing:
None of self and all of thee!*

DON'T GIVE UP

SCRIPTURE

Luke 20:27-38 Then came to him certain of the Sadducees, which deny that there is any resurrection; and they asked him, 28 Saying, Master, Moses wrote unto us, If any man's brother die, having a wife, and he die without children, that his brother should take his wife, and raise up seed unto his brother. 29 There were therefore seven brethren: and the first took a wife, and died without children. 30 And the second took her to wife, and he died childless. 31 And the third took her; and in like manner the seven also: and they left no children, and died. 32 Last of all the woman died also. 33 Therefore in the resurrection whose wife of them is she? for seven had her to wife. 34 And Jesus answering said unto them, The children of this world marry, and are given in marriage: 35 But they which shall be accounted worthy to obtain that world, and the resurrection from the dead, neither marry, nor are given in marriage: 36 Neither can they die any more: for they are equal unto the angels; and are the children of God, being the children of the resurrection. 37 Now that the dead are raised, even Moses shewed at the bush, when he calleth the Lord the God of Abraham, and the God of Isaac, and the God of Jacob. 38 For he is not a God of the dead, but of the living: for all live unto him.

OUTLINE

1. Don't Give Up on Resurrection v27
2. Don't Give Up on Family v36
3. Don't Give Up on God v37-38

MESSAGE

We often fail to follow through as our lack of faith facilitates the fading of our future. Sometimes we grip our disbelief more fervently than our belief. We tell ourselves we can't, when we can – we say no, when we should be saying yes. We miss many opportunities as we struggle with the faith to believe that all things truly are possible with God.

Far too often we allow materialism to barricade us from the truth that things are temporary. The Sadducees were wealthy believers, elite intellectuals that rejected resurrection. They believed that the only way to live on was to have children and your future life was carried on through your offspring. They believed, when you die, you die – with the understanding that your afterlife was invested within the lives of your children.

These unbelievers or partial believers challenged Jesus with a question – how many times have faithless questions arrested our future, fate, and foundation?

This text arises during a season in the life of this church whereby we have been examining this past year, the scriptures that have emerged from the lectionary over the past weeks have reminded us to keep the faith, remember the seasons of the sanctuary, as God has reminded us through the liturgical symbolism parading through the wonders of worship like saints shouting for joy.

We are reminded that Christ was born, baptized, blessed, betrayed, bound, buried, and brought back from beyond by our bountiful God.

The church calendar cycle reminds us that Christ came to us as a gift from God, as an example of purity through the waters of Baptism. Jesus came to us as the power of humility bowed to beckon humanity to the cross – but up from the grave Christ arose and ignited the everlasting fire of God the Holy Spirit in each of us.

The year has passed, the case for Jesus, the Gospel is presented – now what will we do?
Christ came and saved us, God the Holy Spirit resides within us – yes God is with us, we cannot give up. God has blessed us and continues to compose the majestic melodies of love chorded with jubilant joy.

I'm glad that you believe God, nevertheless the Sadducees believed God, but not everything – they didn't believe in resurrection. They had a form of godliness, yet they missed and denied the power of God as described in 2 Timothy chapter 3.

They don't stand alone in history, as all of us have fallen short of God's glory – all of us have failed at faith, while embracing fear.

It's easy to give up when you live with weak faith – but when you truly believe in God, when you truly trust that God sees and knows much more than we do –

when we trust God, we never have to give up, because God will always follow through with manifested truth.

Don't give up, God sees more. We're limited but God is superiorly unlimited, don't give up – trust God. Look with me at Luke 20:27a it reads, "Then came to him certain of the Sadducees, which deny that there is any resurrection"

Don't give up on resurrection, as the power to rise is foundational to faith as we harness hope to follow Jesus. Calvary reminds us that God has the power to save us from any situation. Don't give up, Jesus came up from the grave – you have hope, you have favor. We have the history and testimony of Jesus – the Resurrection is real.

The Sadducees could see God now, they could understand the present, they could understand and believe God on the easy stuff, the stuff easy to see – but they couldn't see a resurrecting, renewing, refreshing, regenerating God. They had the mentality poised to issue idiotic ideology like, "God is good, but He's not that good."

God can keep us while we are here on earth, but there is nothing past this, nothing past what we can see, nothing past Jesus – that's foolish thinking. Some people are so pessimistic, if things aren't going well, then they will never go well – so folks are quick to cry, "God has left us." Rather than focus on God's departure – we should center on God's return.

Don't give up, can you hear Jesus speak from the text, "Destroy this temple and I'll raise it up again in three days." Don't give up through the night, hold on proclaiming like Job, "Weeping may endure for the night, but joy comes in the morning." Don't give up on resurrection.

Focus with me on Luke 20:36 it reads, "Neither can they die any more: for they are equal unto the angels; and are the children of God, being the children of the resurrection."

Don't give up on family, we are children of God – we are in God's family. I can assure you that there is no better family than God's family, no better DNA pool, no better family traditions, no better heritage, and no better parent than our great Heavenly Parent.

Don't give up – you don't belong to a family of quitters. Don't give up on the family – pray for me and I'll pray for you. All of you all that know the worth or prayer, pray for me and I'll pray for you just like all God's children should do.

We're in the family, don't give up. A football coach would never call for a kicker on first and goal – even the worst team can get that much faith, what about us? We are on the best team, we're always first and goal and grace keep resetting the clock – we're in the family! Don't give up.

We never have to give up, we are in the family of the Most High. We are in the family of the One that stepped out before there was a when or a where, uttered a syllable to add boom to words that materialized from sound to solids, from musical melody to material matter. Good God, I wish I had time to preach this!

We are in the family of the Great Creator, the One that met Moses on the backside of the mountain while a fire danced from a bush that didn't give up. It was on fire, but wouldn't give up. I'm glad that there was a tree at Calvary adorning the cleansing fire of all generations – Jesus.

Don't give up, you're in the family, a part of the royal priesthood, in the family – positioned to save the world, born to love, saved, sanctified, fire baptized. We are in the family, never give up, God didn't make you that way – better days will arrive. Cassius Clay, Muhammad Ali used to say he was "pretty" – he had a high self-esteem, we need to have a high spiritual self-esteem.

Greater is the power that resides within than he that is in the world, in my Heavenly Parent's house there are many mansions, I am wonderfully made, I am the head and not the tail, I am redeemed, I am saved, and I am in the family. Don't ever give up, you are in God's family.

Lest I hold you too long, I've got to get out of the way for the preacher. Look at Luke 20:37-38 it says, "Now that the dead are raised, even Moses shewed at the bush, when he calleth the Lord the God of Abraham, and the God of Isaac, and the God of Jacob. 38 For he is not a God of the dead, but of the living: for all live unto him."

Don't give up on resurrection, don't give up on family, and finally **don't give up on God** – God hasn't given up on you. God sees you. God knows you and God the Holy Spirit will never leave you. God sees us when others have counted us for dead, God is the God of the living, God cares and God is with us.

God will never leave us, we never have to give up with God and God the Holy Spirit will never leave us, John 14:16-17 says, "And I will pray the Father, and he shall give you another Comforter, that he may abide with you for ever; 17 Even the Spirit of truth; whom the world cannot receive, because it seeth him not, neither knoweth him: but ye know him; for he dwelleth with you, and shall be in you."

The Sadducees were focused on the things and actions of the worldly, they could only see the things and people of this world, they were limited, they could only see the temporary.

They couldn't see the big picture, they couldn't see God's big plan, and they lacked the faith to trust that which they could not see. I wonder is there anybody here that knows that you can trust God, yes you can trust God even though you can't trap, trace, or trail God.

They came with what they knew, detailing the legacy of Moses – Jesus met them on their level and enlightened all of humanity while lifting the words of Moses. The Sadducees attempted to use Moses to prove their belief that there was no resurrection – but Jesus used Moses to settle the matter.

Essentially, Jesus said – even Moses could testify that God don't stop, that God can do things you never seen, God can work things out you never will understand. Come here, Moses, what did you say – Jesus said that Moses called the Lord God of Abraham, Isaac, and Jacob. Hmmm, he didn't say He **was** the God of Abraham, Isaac, and Jacob – Moses said He **is** the God of Abraham, Isaac, and Jacob.

God is a help in a time of trouble and a shelter in a time of storms. God is our God on every level, both coming and going. When we are transformed and lifted from this earth – God will still see us, when others will have bid us goodbye. Christ died to deliver us into the family, so that we may be resurrected with Him. No matter what the season may look like – hold on, don't give up, and don't give up on God. Better days are coming.

The hymnist Thomas A. Dorsey penned the lamenting articulation:

I was standing by the bedside of a neighbor
Who was just about to cross a swellin' tide
And I asked him if he would do me a favor
Kindly take this message to the other side

Well if you see my Saviour tell Him that you saw me, when you saw me I was on my way, you may meet some more friends who may ask about me but tell'em I am comin' home some day

Well, you have to make this journey on without me, sooner or later sooner or later it's a debt that must be paid. When you reach that golden city think about me, but don't forget to tell my Savior what I say.

You may chance to meet my mother and my father Or some friend that I can't recall. You may chance to meet my brother and my father but don't forget to see my Saviour first of all

I was standing by the bedside of a neighbor Who was just about to cross a swellin' tide And I asked Him if He would do me a favor Kindly take this message to the other side.

I don't know, in fact I don't think we can send messages like that – but I do know that we can pray and God will answer us, I do know that God will turn it around, God will make it better, and you don't have to send a message, just live like Christ, live right and some day you can carry your own message. Someday God will call and we must answer. Don't give up, hang in there and wait on God and again I say wait on the Lord.

BE READY: THE KING IS COMING

SCRIPTURE

Matthew 24:36-44 But of that day and hour knoweth no man, no, not the angels of heaven, but my Father only. 37 But as the days of Noe were, so shall also the coming of the Son of man be. 38 For as in the days that were before the flood they were eating and drinking, marrying and giving in marriage, until the day that Noe entered into the ark, 39 And knew not until the flood came, and took them all away; so shall also the coming of the Son of man be. 40 Then shall two be in the field; the one shall be taken, and the other left. 41 Two women shall be grinding at the mill; the one shall be taken, and the other left. 42 Watch therefore: for ye know not what hour your Lord doth come. 43 But know this, that if the goodman of the house had known in what watch the thief would come, he would have watched, and would not have suffered his house to be broken up. 44 Therefore be ye also ready: for in such an hour as ye think not the Son of man cometh.

OUTLINE

1. We Don't Know When v36
2. We Have Examples v37-41
3. Be Ready v42-44

MESSAGE

Life comes with change as the winds of time come with many situations. The events of life often bring surprises and expectation mixed throughout the seasons of life. There are times when we are more than faithful and times when we are faithless – as life comes with ups and downs paralleled within nearly every component of vitality.

There are times when the world seems so dark, intensified by poisoned hope exterminated by fear. Many of us feel void of hope, as faith is weakened by our blindness to God's way. This world, our society, will drain, depress, and deprive hope from our hearts. We are in desperate need of a revived, regenerated, and renewed relationship with God.

We are confused and confounded by many issues, from alliances, nationality, sexuality, ideology, and deportment – people call the truth lies as they lie while adding to the lie and calling it truth. It doesn't take long to get trapped in a conundrum of doom while feeling arrested by poisoned truth developed from partial accuracy. Things look bad at times.

Crime is on the rise, illness is pervasive, drug dependency is epidemic, and morality seems bankrupt. Thinks look bad, things are bad and times are getting tough. We need hope, we need a vision of a greater lovelier future. We need to overcome disease, hatred, and corruption. When the road gets rocky and the going gets tough, hope motivates us toward better days. The world may seem to be in shambles, nevertheless I've come today with a declaration that the King is coming! Not just any king – but the King of Kings.

Look with me at Matthew 24:36 as it reads, "But of that day and hour knoweth no man, no, not the angels of heaven, but my Father only."

We don't know when the King is coming – we must be ready. God requires readiness as a lifestyle and not a diet. People often diet for small, quick, temporary changes – but a changed lifestyle is necessary for long term, permanent, stable transformation.

Many of us are suffering from anxiety, depression, and over stimulation with the rapidly changing news cycles, deficient resources, and political pollution. It may seem like there is no light at the end of the tunnel, like hope unborn has died – but the King is coming, we may not know when but we know that the King is coming.

We need to calm down and get ready. We need to look to God and let peace abide. When motivated by readiness we can overcome our fear with firm faith. When we focus on the King, on our God – anxiety, fear, depression, mental stress and strain will dissolve as peace emerges. The more of God we see, the bigger God becomes in our lives – the smaller our problems become. The more we look at God the less we focus on situations. The closer we get to God the further we get away from our problems.

God our King is so great, we don't need to know when the King is coming to get excited – the fact that the King is coming should ignite joy within the heart of the faithful. Hallelujah.

When we immerse ourselves into God's word, give our time over to prayer, communicating with God brings us to peace. The presence of God covers us in peace, protection, and provision. The Bible teaches us how to wait on the King, how to wait on God.
We can walk in joy when we learn to be transformed by the renewing of our minds. We renew our minds through studying God's word, continuing in prayer and meditation. It's not what you see, it's how you see it.

When we look through the lens of God the Holy Spirit, the world looks much brighter as we understand that no matter what the process may bring, utopian life will arrive when we embrace God the King.

The King is coming, nevertheless you don't have to wait to celebrate, you don't have to wait to get excited, you don't have to wait to shout – God always keeps promises and we are standing on the promises of God. Matthew chapter 24 commences with Christ leaving the temple followed by the disciples coming to show Him the buildings within the temple.

Christ walked away as they beckoned Christ's attentive return. Jesus was walking away from man-made stone upon man-made stone – they were focused on the earthly while Christ was focused on the Holy.

Jesus conveyed that the things of man are temporary, while the ways of God are eternal. He said that all the bricks could tumble and fall, the temple unrecognizably destroyed is no problem with God. Whatever the problem, no matter how broken – God can fix it. I don't know about you, but I'm glad that the things of this world are temporary, while God works in the eternal.

Time is filled with swift transition,
Naught of earth unmoved can stand,
Build your hopes on things eternal,
Hold to God's unchanging hand.

The problems and situations we stress out over are only temporary, focusing on God and the eternal blessing of God will wrap you up in joy. It will top you off with the bow of peace with a card attached signed by love. The King is coming, we don't need to know when – we simply need to be ready for God's return. Walking by faith, surrounded by celebration for our returning King.

Focus now on Matthew 24:37-41 as it reads, "But as the days of Noe were, so shall also the coming of the Son of man be. 38 For as in the days that were before the flood they were eating and drinking, marrying and giving in marriage, until the day that Noe entered into the ark, 39 And knew not until the flood came, and took them all away; so shall also the coming of the Son of man be. 40 Then shall two be in the field; the one shall be taken, and the other left. 41 Two women shall be grinding at the mill; the one shall be taken, and the other left."

The King is coming, **we have examples** – the writer scripts that we must be ready as God works on God's time and we must remain ready, living after the way of Christ. The biblical text reminds us that Noah prophetically warned the people of his day, yet they rejected the prefigured savior while embracing disconnection from God.

Noah's neighbors continued life as usual, eating and marrying – fully focused on themselves, while blind to the movement of God. Warned yet wrecked by disbelief, cautioned yet captured by faithlessness. They didn't believe Noah. They missed the moments of opportunity. The King beckoned their belief and called for their faith as Noah promulgated God's power through the prophetic voice that echoed before the flood.

We have examples of our returning, redeeming, active God – our best life is lived under the direction of God, fortified by the indwelling of the Holy Spirit. Disbelief proved detrimental once the rain commenced and puddled into fatal flood waters. The unbelievers all died separated from the ark, safety provided by our great God.

We have examples that God often works when we least expect – we must remain ready. Noah tuned into the instructive voice of God as salvation emerged floating above the floods. God moves on God's time – we can't hurry or schedule God.

Look with me at Matthew 24:42-44 as it reads, "Watch therefore: for ye know not what hour your Lord doth come. 43 But know this, that if the goodman of the house had known in what watch the thief would come, he would have watched, and would not have suffered his house to be broken up. 44 Therefore be ye also ready: for in such an hour as ye think not the Son of man cometh."

The King is coming, **be ready** – we know not the day nor the hour, just be ready. Don't let the Lord catch you with your work undone, we've been called to follow Jesus. Take up the cross and follow Jesus, be ready to live like Jesus – to know God the Son in the fellowship of suffering and power emerging from the resurrection.

Jesus died for us, sacrificed Himself for all of us to live the Kingdom life – living our best life like Jesus. Great love crucified at Calvary, was buried, and arose with great power. God is love and love is God – the grave couldn't hold love when the King called! Romans chapter 10 reminds us that we must believe that God raised Jesus up from the grave.

If God is powerful enough to raise God – then our situations are a flash for God, the Lord can bring change in the twinkle of an eye. One day and it may not be long, you'll blink your eye – the sky will open, Jesus will return and gather us for home! Be ready. Sometime during the 1800s. A.C. Palmer penned the words:

Ready to suffer grief or pain,
Ready to stand the test;

*Ready to stay at home and send
Others if He sees best.*

*Ready to go, ready to stay,
Ready my place to fill;
Ready for service lowly or great,
Ready to do His will.*

*Ready to go, ready to bear,
Ready to watch and pray;
Ready to stand aside and give
Till He shall clear the way.*

*Ready to speak, ready to think,
Ready with heart and mind;
Ready to stand where He sees fit,
Ready His will to find.*

*Ready to speak, ready to warn,
Ready o'er souls to yearn;
Ready in life or ready in death,
Ready for His return.*

The King is coming, the prophetic revelation of the New Testament projects for us that God will wipe all tears from our eyes, and there will be no more death, suffering, crying, or pain.

These things of the past will be gone forever. God is the Alpha and Omega, the beginning and the end. All who win the victory will be blessed. The God of Abraham, Isaac, and Jacob is our God, and we are

God's people – the greatly powerful I Am that I am. Joy forever and peace without end.

Matthew takes us back through the annals of time as he presents the words of Christ, reminding us that the King is coming and we will not know the day or hour. We may stroll through Biblical history, to realize that we've never known all of God's business.

Oh, come here, Job, remember you had a conversation with God and were informatively chastised toward the revelation that we don't know the when and we don't know the where of God. Where you there from the first blade of grass or privileged to see trees before years of growth clothed them in green leaves and brown bark?

Were you there when God raised land up from the sea, where you there when He taught sea bass how to swim or ducks how to fly?

Were you there for the dog's first bark, the cow's first moo, or the rooster's first cock-a-doo-dal-doo? What about the frog's first leap or the kangaroo's first hop – where you there for man's first breath, when God scooped up dust and breathed into it without blowing it away, Oh, I wish I had some honest folk in this church?

We don't know the when, where, or how – and we've never known, we don't need to know. All we need to know is that in every season, through every age, through time and change we are blessed.

When we stop focusing on when and focus on Who, then we'll be free from the stress of spiritual impatience. We need to stop worrying about details that are out of our control, stuff we can't change – focus on Who, focus on God.

Well, as I run to my seat – I'm reminded of something you've probably already heard broadcast across the land of nursery rhyme, news media, or from some gossiping teacher – words articulated in a single quatrain with a trochaic meter about an anthropomorphic egg.

Rumor has it that, Humpty Dumpty sat on a wall, Humpty Dumpty had a great fall; all the King's horses and all the King's men, couldn't put Humpty together again.

The king's horses were not able and the king's men don't have the same power as the king. There are sometimes that we have to bypass the horses and the human folk – we need the king.

There are times in life where we feel like Brother Dumpty, fallen, cracked, damaged, and downtrodden.

Times when we feel helpless and alone, times when the world seems so lost with violence and corruption rampant throughout our social universe, sickness, sorrow and pain – situations on every hand, but I'm here to tell you the King is coming.

There is no situation too hard for the King, the King can put Humpty together again, the King can put you together again – the King is coming!

READY FOR A NEW WORLD ORDER

SCRIPTURE

Isaiah 10:1-10 Woe unto them that decree unrighteous decrees, and that write grievousness which they have prescribed; 2 To turn aside the needy from judgment, and to take away the right from the poor of my people, that widows may be their prey, and that they may rob the fatherless! 3 And what will ye do in the day of visitation, and in the desolation which shall come from far? to whom will ye flee for help? and where will ye leave your glory? 4 Without me they shall bow down under the prisoners, and they shall fall under the slain. For all this his anger is not turned away, but his hand is stretched out still. 5 O Assyrian, the rod of mine anger, and the staff in their hand is mine indignation. 6 I will send him against an hypocritical nation, and against the people of my wrath will I give him a charge, to take the spoil, and to take the prey, and to tread them down like the mire of the streets. 7 Howbeit he meaneth not so, neither doth his heart think so; but it is in his heart to destroy and cut off nations not a few. 8 For he saith, Are not my princes altogether kings? 9 Is not Calno as Carchemish? is not Hamath as Arpad? is not Samaria as Damascus? 10 As my hand hath found the kingdoms of the idols, and whose graven images did excel them of Jerusalem and of Samaria;

OUTLINE

1. Watch the Stump (Opposed to the Tree Tops) v1
2. Righteousness Will Rule v3-5
3. Perfect Peace Will Emerge v6-10

MESSAGE

The world is increasingly changing, as the globe turns it seems that social and political systems are spinning out of control with seemingly changing power structures. It's nearly impossible to navigate the ideology of government leaders – motivations are at times for us and at times against us.

For ages we have lived amidst the haves and have nots – the rich and powerful seem to control the world. The poor are often neglected and exploited within the halls of oppression. The world order tends to favor the rich and disregard the poor.

It often seems like the bottom will never rise, peace will never abound, and love will never linger – however Jesus said that the first shall be last and the last shall be first. There is the hope of change – someday there will be a new world order.

For centuries upon centuries the world order has been dominated by the greedy oligarchs across the world – ultimately the system of wealth has given nefarious luxury to racism, hatred, and greed.

Unfortunately, it seems that the age of technology, robotics, artificial intelligence, and smart machines will make matters worse before they become better – nevertheless God's order will prevail.

We are moving into an age that may ravage our current social system and debilitate humanity. We have failed to

completely regulate technology, which will certainly bring exponential consequences in the future.
Jobs will be lost. Lives may be lost within the learning curve of mechanical innovation. Legislators are often focused on the minors while missing the majors or entranced in self-absorbed issues.

The wicked, wayward, and wretched will ultimately be cut down like grass as God ushers peace into our collective experience. Oh, if you don't believe – then gather at the testimony service of Psalm 73, as Asaph recounts his experience with the wicked.

The fableist Asaph seemed nearly bitter as he pontificated the seeming prosperity of the wicked – but then he entered the sanctuary, went to the church, walked into the place of worship, and received revelation of God's ultimate sovereignty.

It's easy to become discouraged, depressed, and bitter – but the presence of God brings order to chaos as peace is infused. No matter how the world seems now, God will usher in a new world order – a world filled with peace seasoned by love yet continually void of evil.

I wish there were some excited people, glad to know that trouble don't last always – God will bring order to the universe. God our God, most powerful and supreme architect of all creation.

The prophet Isaiah articulates our favor filled path into the future. Isaiah's community was very much like our own – people were in need of hope and enlightenment to fuel motivation toward purposeful survival. I wonder do you know that God has a plan, yes – God has a plan! Look with me at Isaiah 10:1 as it reads, "Woe unto them that decree unrighteous decrees, and that write grievousness which they have prescribed;"

Watch the stump, a new world order is on the way. Hmmm, watch the stump – just because things may seem dormant, there is life where God resides, when God is in the narrative, God in the plan, God in the order of things! Watch the stump! Leaves may have shed, bark may have long been gone and the trunk split by ax or nature, yet watch the stump.

The prophetic text reminds us that God creates the order of things, brings life to whatever God chooses – in fact God can sustain life and bring the dead back to life. Oh, somebody ought to ask the Shunammite woman's son from 2 Kings chapter 4 – he was dead and the power of God brought him back through Elisha.

Come here, Lazarus, lying in the grave swaddled by the stench of death – God the Son called Lazarus, oh Lazarus and Lazarus walked away from death like waking up from a nightmare at midnight – Oh, God can bring new order!

God can turn it around, fix it up, change it up, God can do that which is impossible for us. God is the strength and hope of our lives. I know you know the greatest testimony of all time, Jesus – yes Jesus, God raised God from the dead, after the crucifixion there was a resurrection! Somebody ought to say amen in this church – hallelujah for the Lamb that was slain from the foundation of the world to save us all!

Praise God, come to God with your broken heart, come with your languish, come with your sadness and God will carry you through – I'm satisfied with Jesus, satisfied with Jesus in my heart.

Look now with me Isaiah 11:3-5 as it reads, "And shall make him of quick understanding in the fear of the LORD: and he shall not judge after the sight of his eyes, neither reprove after the hearing of his ears: 4 But with righteousness shall he judge the poor, and reprove with equity for the meek of the earth: and he shall smite the earth with the rod of his mouth, and with the breath of his lips shall he slay the wicked. 5 And righteousness shall be the girdle of his loins, and faithfulness the girdle of his reins."

Righteousness will rule within the new world order. Sin has plagued humankind nearly since the dawn of creation. Those captured by the wrongs of this world will ultimately find that righteousness shall prevail.

Isaiah 40:3-5 says, "The voice of him that crieth in the wilderness, Prepare ye the way of the LORD, make straight in the desert a highway for our God. 4 Every valley shall be exalted, and every mountain and hill shall be made low: and the crooked shall be made straight, and the rough places plain: 5 And the glory of the

LORD shall be revealed, and all flesh shall see it together: for the mouth of the LORD hath spoken it."

God will get the glory as the right will always prevail over the wrong.

Look with me at Isaiah 11:6-10 as it reads, "The wolf also shall dwell with the lamb, and the leopard shall lie down with the kid; and the calf and the young lion and the fatling together; and a little child shall lead them. 7 And the cow and the bear shall feed; their young ones shall lie down together: and the lion shall eat straw like the ox. 8 And the sucking child shall play on the hole of the asp, and the weaned child shall put his hand on the cockatrice' den. 9 They shall not hurt nor destroy in all my holy mountain: for the earth shall be full of the knowledge of the LORD, as the waters cover the sea. 10 And in that day there shall be a root of Jesse, which shall stand for an ensign of the people; to it shall the Gentiles seek: and his rest shall be glorious."

Perfect peace will emerge – as the glory of God facilitates a new world order. It seems feasible to believe that there are secret coalitions to consolidate countries under one government – the ultimate power force. Humankind has been trying to be God since Adam and Eve; collective agendas have been around ever since the Tower of Babel catastrophe.

Humankind can attempt world consolidation – but it will never work without God. Our creator and redeemer has a plan, there is a plan for us! We will never be able to change the world on our own and it's foolish to think that we can. Yet with God, all things are possible.

Rich folks are exploring space and alternative bio-domains, but I've got news for them – Jesus is the way, the truth, and the life. Jesus is the way to God, the good news.

Even if man could bring man together, they can't do what God can. In the fullness of God's plan all of creation will come to peace. The tension between the lion and the lamb will give way to triumphant coexistence – babies will play with snakes.

Yes, God is going to change the world order. Isaiah warned the people of his day that God will bring consequences to the wicked, especially those that mistreat and exploit the poor. God has a plan to love, liberate, and lift us from the old decaying world of Adam's legacy.

A new world order will come with the returning Christ. In Matthew 24:24 we are reminded that we must be ready when Jesus returns as the Kingdom of God becomes visible beyond faith.

Isaiah reported the unusual, the holy city of Jerusalem became vulnerable as a result of sin. The Assyrians and Babylonians persecuted them, took their stuff, and enslaved them – but the prophet encouraged focus

upon God's power. We will someday see God as God and life will change forever.
Well as I run on, it's time for us to get out of here.

Isaiah told them that they would be cut down like a tree. Yes, in my world the Lord giveth and Lord taketh away, don't nothing move without God.

Well I know you know to watch the stump. Hope seemed lost but God has a plan. A new world order is immanent – Jesus said the last shall be first and the first shall be last.

Keep the hope, keep the faith, and stay in the movement for love.

There may be times when you feel like giving up, times when all you can see are the crucifixions of life – but we must follow Jesus through the lowness of the grave to reach glory, wait and again I say, wait on the Lord.

No matter how things seem today – a new world order is on the way, when all God's creation will exist with abundant peace. Just hold on through what it looks like, through the rough, tough times – Jesus once wore a crown of thorns, nevertheless the crown of victory rests upon the work of God the Son at Calvary.

In 1820 Thomas Kelly posed the words:
The head that once was crowned with thorns
is crowned with glory now;
a royal diadem adorns

the mighty Victor's brow.

The highest place that heav'n affords
is his, is his by right,
the King of kings and Lord of lords,
and heav'n's eternal Light:

The joy of all who dwell above,
the joy of all below,
to whom he manifests his love,
and grants his name to know.
To them the cross, with all its shame,
with all its grace, is giv'n;
their name an everlasting name,
their joy the joy of heav'n.

They suffer with the Lord below,
they reign with him above;
their profit and their joy to know
the myst'ry of his love.

The cross he bore is life and health,
though shame and death to him;
his people's hope, his people's wealth,
their everlasting theme.

JUST WAIT

SCRIPTURE

James 5:7-10 Be patient therefore, brethren, unto the coming of the Lord. Behold, the husbandman waiteth for the precious fruit of the earth, and hath long patience for it, until he receive the early and latter rain. 8 Be ye also patient; stablish your hearts: for the coming of the Lord draweth nigh. 9 Grudge not one against another, brethren, lest ye be condemned: behold, the judge standeth before the door. 10 Take, my brethren, the prophets, who have spoken in the name of the Lord, for an example of suffering affliction, and of patience.

OUTLINE

1. The Field is Planted v7
2. Reject Frustration (Grumbling) v9
3. Embrace Examples v10

MESSAGE

We often lack the patience to wait for anything in this instant, microwave world. Everything has to be quick - fast food, fast cars, fast lane, and fast women.

It truly is a rat race at times, life moving quickly - leaving us by the wayside. Nevertheless, the old adage may be more than true, good things come to those who wait.

Look with me at James 5:7 says, "Be patient therefore, brethren, unto the coming of the Lord. Behold, the husbandman waiteth for the precious fruit of the earth, and hath long patience for it, until he receive the early and latter rain."

The field has been planted, as we see in the text the caretaker has the patience to wait on maturity. You have been preapproved for blessings – already plugged into your future.

The challenge to follow Jesus, demands that we embrace patience, learning to wait for the crown, wait for reward, wait for the resurrection!

Instant gratification is the way of the world - God's divine way leads us to hold to the ideology of Jacob in Genesis chapter 32, hanging on to departing blessings.

I'm going to stay right here and study myself. Waiting on the Lord, praising and worshiping as I go. Look at the text - our blessings have already been planted.

The harvest truly is plentiful, the field was planted long ago as God set life in motion with the sound of His voice. Think about it, God empowered your earthly father to plant a seed.

When the seed was planted, you were far from the uniquely distinguished personality that you are today. No nose, no mouth, no teeth or hair. But you had potential the day you were planted.

We aren't born adults; we grow into adulthood. Hmmm, we get planted then we grow from there – everything you are now, was programed into your DNA from conception.

God programed us with purpose while we were yet in our mother's womb. We have built-in blessings and benefits; we just have to wait for our season of maturity. Come on now, you know that babies get happy when they learn to walk and get tall enough to reach things.

We were glad when we got old enough to walk to school without supervision. Glad when we matured enough for a first date, glad when our bodies formed muscles and other defining characteristics.

Childhood has its advantages – but I wouldn't trade adulthood in for the helpless vulnerability of childhood. It feels great to grow up, glad to have some autonomy – childhood can kick rocks!

But, wait – think about it, we can be just as excited over spiritual maturity. It's good to get spiritually mature enough to appreciate God's word. God's word is a lamp unto my feet, and a light unto my path. Glad to grow up in prayer, continual communication with God – pray without ceasing.

Just wait, the Apostle James reminds us that God waits for us like a caretaker waits for fruit to mature on the branch. God loves us and gracefully bestows abundant mercy upon us, allowing us to mature under the influence of God the Holy Spirit. Change will come if we wait on the Lord – just wait.

Look now with me at James 5:9 as it reads, "Grudge not one against another, brethren, lest ye be condemned: behold, the judge standeth before the door."

We must **reject frustration** as we wait on the power of God to bring us complete peace. When our faith fades, frustrations often season our faithlessness. Yes, we become frustrated when we fail to completely trust God.

James chapter 5 reminds us that we are best benefited when we walk within judgement free zones to remain free of personal condemnation. Judging others is like wrestling a muddy pig – some mud will get on you. Pig wrestling is a messy business – just like judging others.

The Bible says in Galatians 6:7-9, "Be not deceived; God is not mocked: for whatsoever a man soweth, that shall he also reap. 8 For he that soweth to his flesh shall of the flesh reap corruption; but he that soweth to the Spirit shall of the Spirit reap life everlasting. 9 And let us not be weary in well doing: for in due season we shall reap, if we faint not."

Jesus is recorded to say it like this in Matthew 7:1-2, "Judge not, that ye be not judged. 2 For with what judgment ye judge, ye shall be judged: and with what measure ye mete, it shall be measured to you again."

Hmmm, same measure – let's park here for a moment. Many times, our frustration comes from feeling like we are superior, feeling like the whole world is about us and centered around us – everybody is wrong except you. We go off halfcocked while intoxicated on our own idiotic self-aggrandizing ego.

See, Jesus essentially says – don't get yourself in trouble dishing out that which you don't want served to you. Judgment by the same measure is immeasurable by us. We may think we know all the facts, we may think we are fair in our approach, but only God knows all the facts, God knows the background to the background. God is the only fair judge, because God is the only one that knows it all.

When we choose to be judge, prosecutor, and jury all of our surface judgment will return to testify in our personal trial. The same faulty process we used will be the same process used against you. The same shallow process that you used on someone else will be used on you.

We have to be careful with our judgments as we may be judged by the same measure. God's judgment utilizes pure truth, grace, mercy, and eternal love. Our judgment is based on what we know and we don't know much.

Don't let frustration capture you, avoid the pitfall of becoming stuck in somebody else's business while your life remains unkempt. Avoid rushing to conclusions, rushing to judgment and condemnation – just wait on God. Trust God through the process, trust God to fight the battles, just wait – believe God's final work and complete the journey with the love of Christ.

Focus on James 5:10 as it reads, "Take, my brethren, the prophets, who have spoken in the name of the Lord, for an example of suffering affliction, and of patience."

Just wait, the field is planted – God has a plan, the old account was settled long ago, the Lord has pre-ordered provisions for us.

Just wait, reject frustration – grumbling and complaining while spewing poor judgment through ignorant impatience.

Finally, **embrace examples** – the Bible is like a bag of resources, a tool belt equipped for purpose. The Bible provides us with examples, from the prophets to the Gospels – we have examples on how to live and how not to live.

We can learn the perils of impatience from our Biblical ancestors, the text is a treasure trove of truth emerging from case like studies. If we study to show ourselves approved before God – life will become sweeter as we become stronger through God's enriching word.

We must wait while committed to the way of Christ. I wonder is there anybody here, glad because God's grace and mercy provides us with time to mature as God patiently waits on us.

The field has been planted, all that we need has already been provided. God planted the crop for our salvation long ago. Jesus shed blood on Calvary while we were yet sinners.

Jesus was crucified then buried – the seed was planted so that we might be saved. With great testimony, Jesus arose from the grave as the Sprout of Humanity.

Yes, Jesus suffered, bled, and died – was buried, got up from the grave, ascended into the Heavens, and some day our Savior God will return for us – just wait.

In the early 1900's Jennie Wilson wrote:
Time is filled with swift transition,
Naught of earth unmoved can stand,
Build your hopes on things eternal,
Hold to God's unchanging hand.

Trust in Him who will not leave you,
Whatsoever years may bring,
If by earthly friends forsaken
Still more closely to Him cling.

Covet not this world's vain riches
That so rapidly decay,
Seek to gain the heav'nly treasures,

They will never pass away.

When your journey is completed,
If to God you have been true,
Fair and bright the home in glory
Your enraptured soul will view.

Hold to God's unchanging hand,
Hold to God's unchanging hand;
Build your hopes on things eternal,
Hold to God's unchanging hand.

SELFLESSNESS

SCRIPTURE

Matthew 1:19-25 Then Joseph her husband, being a just man, and not willing to make her a publick example, was minded to put her away privily. 20 But while he thought on these things, behold, the angel of the Lord appeared unto him in a dream, saying, Joseph, thou son of David, fear not to take unto thee Mary thy wife: for that which is conceived in her is of the Holy Ghost. 21 And she shall bring forth a son, and thou shalt call his name JESUS: for he shall save his people from their sins. 22 Now all this was done, that it might be fulfilled which was spoken of the Lord by the prophet, saying, 23 Behold, a virgin shall be with child, and shall bring forth a son, and they shall call his name Emmanuel, which being interpreted is, God with us. 24 Then Joseph being raised from sleep did as the angel of the Lord had bidden him, and took unto him his wife: 25 And knew her not till she had brought forth her firstborn son: and he called his name JESUS.

OUTLINE

1. We Should Reject Exposing Others v19
2. Is Fearless When God is Involved v20
3. Fosters the Miraculous v25

MESSAGE

It seems more than fitting that we examine this idea of selflessness during Advent season. It is easy to fall into the trap of materialism and miss the main focus for our celebrations during this season of good tidings. When we look into this particular chapter, we can see that many births take place in the first few verses.

It seems only fitting that we begin with a list of births, as childbirth seems to be the most selfless act that humans under take, for nine months mother caries an embryo, a baby in a selfless act.

God leads us to life, creation, and productivity - we must selflessly give of ourselves to bring God's plan of activated salvation seasoned with graceful majesty and love.

Matthew chapter one narrows our focus toward the betrothal, the engagement of Joseph and Mary as selflessness emerges center stage.

Look with me at Matthew 1:19 as it reads, "Then Joseph her husband, being a just man, and not willing to make her a publick example, was minded to put her away privily."

We should selflessly **reject exposing others**, as the Bible reminds us that we must reap what we sow, what goes around comes around. There are times when you could say something, but you shouldn't, times when you could pull the covers off the whole thing, times when you could keep it real with somebody else's business - but you shouldn't.

Times when you know they owe you money, times when you saw them creeping around town, times when you saw them come into work late - but you need to let it go because you're glad God let you go, glad for grace and mercy in your life.

Joseph knew that he hadn't known Mary, he knew that he hadn't turned out the light as Teddy Pendergrass would suggest. Joseph didn't need a DNA test. He knew she was pregnant but he also knew he was not the father - but he didn't expose her.

Joseph was selfless and silent to the situation, he didn't go running his mouth, he didn't walk out on her and she wasn't even pregnant with his baby. Joseph let God have what was supposed to be his and he did it without the exposure of complaining. We must reject exposing others.

Look with me at Matthew 1:20 as it reads, "But while he thought on these things, behold, the angel of the Lord appeared unto him in a dream, saying, Joseph, thou son of David, fear not to take unto thee Mary thy wife: for that which is conceived in her is of the Holy Ghost."

We can be **fearless when God is involved**. See, we often think in survival mode, it's all about the survival of the fittest – self-preservation. We attempt to work life out on our own, while blind to the fact that we need God to do anything eternally great.

We live in an overly anxious society as life is more than uncertain when we selfishly reject God's way.

Antithetically, when we embrace God in every part of our lives - there is no reason to fear.

Joseph was assured of God's presence and power, therefore, Joseph could grip faithful grace in spite of the circumstance of his pregnant fiancée. Perhaps many of us would have told him to leave Mary without deliberation. She can't be trusted - but Joseph trusted God. Have you ever been in a situation whereby you had to trust God against the facts, against today, against this season?

God gave, but it seemed faulty, God blessed but it felt like a curse, we receive but the gift seems like a loss – we know God did it, and we believe, but we can't fully appreciate God's work while our faith is fading. We must selflessly believe while trusting God's way.

Focus with me on Matthew 1:21-25 as it reads, "And she shall bring forth a son, and thou shalt call his name JESUS: for he shall save his people from their sins. 22 Now all this was done, that it might be fulfilled which was spoken of the Lord by the prophet, saying, 23 Behold, a virgin shall be with child, and shall bring forth a son, and they shall call his name Emmanuel, which being interpreted is, God with us. 24 Then Joseph being raised from sleep did as the angel of the Lord had bidden him, and took unto him his wife: 25 And knew her not till she had brought forth her firstborn son: and he called his name JESUS."

We should reject exposing others, be fearless when God is involved, and finally **we should foster the miraculous** through our selflessness – as we walk in the miraculous when we walk with God. Every day is a day of thanksgiving and praise when we look around and see all that the Lord has done for us. Just to wake up this morning was miraculous as all of humanity should be thankful for air to breathe, water to drink, food to eat – registered through the complexities of our bodies.

One drop of blood is miraculous, and if we take our eyes off of ourselves long enough and take a selfless non-entitled look at God – we should become humble in worship as we bring adoration to our great God. Look at us, we were never worthy of God's blessings and love – who are we that God should call us friend?

Joseph accepted the word and way of the Lord – followed divine instruction and God used Joseph to help save the world as his obedience proclaimed the immaculate work of God's maternity room.

I'm glad that Joseph and Mary were obedient enough to let go and let God, to surrender to God's blessed way, as we're all benefactors of Christ's birth, life, and death – realizing that if we selflessly take up the Cross and follow Christ we shall someday journey from labor to reward.

Oh, what a glorious day – as we await the return of God the Son to transform us forever from this mundane mortality to celestial celebration as we walk in the greatness of God's manifested glory. Is there anybody here glad to be in the service of the Lord, glad to be favored, glad just to walk in the presence of the Lord?

Let's not fall into the trap of self-centered absorption, our God is too great for us to try to take center stage. We must let the glory of God shine through every part of our life – use us Lord, use us to do Thy perfect will.

Our greatest desire should be to live in selfless service to God. Bill Withers the secular lyricist penned a petition to God as he wrote:

If You can use anything Lord You can use me
If You can use anything Lord You can use me
Take my hands, Lord and my feet
Touch my heart, Lord and speak through me
If You can use anything Lord You can use me

Lord, You called Moses from the wilderness and You put a rod in his hand. You used him to lead Your people over to the Promised Land.

Lord, I'm willing to trust in You so take my life Lord and use it too. Yes, if You can use anything Lord come on and use me

When David fought Goliath and that mighty giant fell
He proved to his people that God was alive in Israel
Lord, I'm available to You and I'm waiting to be used

*After the multitudes heard the words that Jesus said
He took two fish and five loaves and the multitude was fed
Lord, what I have may not be much but I know it can
multiply by Your touch*

*So, If You can use anything Lord You can use me
If You can use anything Lord You can use me
Take my hands, Lord and my feet
Touch my heart, Lord and speak through me
If You can use anything Lord You can use me*

HOW TO ACTIVATE THE GUARANTEE

SCRIPTURE

Psalms 24:1-10 A Psalm. Of David. The earth is the Lord's, with all its wealth; the world and all the people living in it. 2 For by him it was based on the seas, and made strong on the deep rivers. 3 Who may go up into the hill of the Lord? and who may come into his holy place? 4 He who has clean hands and a true heart; whose desire has not gone out to foolish things, who has not taken a false oath. 5 He will have blessing from the Lord, and righteousness from the God of his salvation. 6 This is the generation of those whose hearts are turned to you, even to your face, O God of Jacob. Selah. 7 Let your heads be lifted up, O doors; be lifted up, O you eternal doors: that the King of glory may come in. 8 Who is the King of glory? The Lord of strength and power, the Lord strong in war. 9 Let your heads be lifted up, O doors; let them be lifted up, O you eternal doors: that the King of glory may come in. 10 Who is the King of glory? The Lord of armies, he is the King of glory. Selah.

OUTLINE

1. Embrace the Lift v7,9
2. Know the King v8
3. Get Ready for Company (The King Shall Come In) v9-10

MESSAGE

Psalm 24 emerges as the last of the great worshipful trilogy. Psalm 22, 23, and 24 provide us with the prefigured literary illustrations of the past, present, and future.

Psalm 22 leads us to the Suffering Savior / My God, My God, why hast Thou forsaken Me? As Psalm 23 presents the God that is with me – The Lord is my Shepard, finally Psalm 24 brings us to the world to come as the earth is the Lord's and the fullness thereof.

Psalm 22, 23, and 24 – representing the God who was, the God who is, and the God who is to come. Our Great God - everywhere present like the wind that guides the air that we breathe.

The Lord created, cares for, and will sustain us throughout eternity in spite of what things look like today, we have a guarantee that God will take care of us materialized through God's infallible word.

We are guaranteed by the God who was, is, and forever more shall be, we have eternal divine assurance from our God, the same yesterday, today, and forevermore – God has promised never to leave or forsake us. We need to make sure that we've activated the guarantee as Romans chapter 10 reveals belief, faith in the risen Son of God is prerequisite to the benefit of salvation.

Activation of our guarantee should bring us to praise, worship, and adoration. The guarantee paid for through the sacrifice of God the Son, enforced by love – God sacrificing God to gift us with the great gift of Love. We must be in relationship with God our great heavenly parent.

Look with me at Psalms 24:7-9 as the passage reads, "Lift up your heads, O ye gates; and be ye lift up, ye everlasting doors; and the King of glory shall come in. 8 Who is this King of glory? The LORD strong and mighty, the LORD mighty in battle. 9 Lift up your heads, O ye gates; even lift them up, ye everlasting doors; and the King of glory shall come in."

We activate the guarantee when we **embrace the lift**, as the text admonishes them to lift the gates and open the doors to let the King in. Not just any king, the King of Kings, the King mighty in battle, the Eternal King of all ages, here to reign forever – raise up the gates, open the door.

Lift up your gates, lift up the door, lift up the everlasting door – let the King of Glory come in. You must connect with God, you must let God into your heart, open the gates of your heart. Open the gate, the big door, the open the door, the little door – give God access to every part of your life. Open the gates!

We must connect with God through Bible Study, prayer, meditation, personal time with God – we must keep the door lifted for God. Hospitality toward God the Holy Spirit is essential to a God approved lifestyle.

Yes, lifestyle, this is not a diet – this is an absolute redirection as God hasn't provided us with a warranty.

God has not given us a time limited guarantee or warranty – God gave us a forever stamp, an eternal guarantee that will endure all the seasons of time and multiplied eons upon eons. God is great and greatly to be praise!

Lift the gate, open the door – I'm glad that Jesus is the way and the life, Jesus is the door. Jesus from the lineage of Abraham, Isaac, and Jacob – see, Isaac was married to Rebekah and the Bible says in: Genesis 24:60, "And they blessed Rebekah, and said unto her, Thou art our sister, be thou the mother of thousands of millions, and let thy seed possess the gate of those which hate them."

They will be the gate possessors, the gate keepers – Jesus is the door, Jesus is the way!

In John 10:9, Jesus says, "I am the door: by me if any man enter in, he shall be saved, and shall go in and out, and find pasture."

Then Christ goes on to say in John 12:32, "And I, if I be lifted up from the earth, will draw all men unto me."

Oh, I wish I had some worshipers in this church today, glad that Jesus is the way! Glad that God the Holy Spirit is lifted within your heart – ready to lift Jesus before the world, glad to have God the Holy Spirit as a permanent resident. Motivated to tell the world forever – ready to lift the door!

In the mid-1800s Johnson Oatman, Jr. arranged the informative words:

How to reach the masses, people of ev'ry birth,
For an answer Jesus gave the key:
"And I, if I be lifted up from the earth,
Will draw all unto me."

Oh! the world is hungry for the Living Bread,
Lift the Savior up for them to see;
Trust him, and do not doubt the words that he said, "I'll draw all men unto me."

Don't exalt the preacher, don't exalt the pew,
Preach the Gospel simple, full and free;
Prove him and you will find that promise is true, "I'll draw all men unto me."

Lift him up by living as a Christian ought,
Let the world in you the Savior see;
Then men will gladly follow him who once taught,
"I'll draw all men unto me."

Lift him up, lift him up,
Still he speaks from eternity:
"And I, if I be lifted up from the earth,
Will draw all men unto me."

Focus now on Psalms 24:8 as it reads, "Who is this King of glory? The LORD strong and mighty, the LORD mighty in battle."

We should embrace the lift and **know the King,** as David provides articulated feedback – somebody said open the door, lift up the gates for the King, an interrogative emerges as someone asks "Who is this King?" then finally the answer rises like the rhythm of an ancient melody, The LORD strong and mighty, the LORD mighty in battle!

I wonder does anybody here know the King? The Lord strong, mighty, powerful – the King of glory!
Grand momma's walking cane, the One that created us from dust and set us in the path of paradise, the One that met Moses at the bush and Red Sea, the One that strengthened Elijah beneath the juniper tree, the One that blessed Ruth at the foot of Boaz, the God that woke you up this morning, put clapping in your hands, and running in your feet.

As Pastor Rufus Johnson from our family church in Carolina says, "God blessed us with eggs to scramble, bacon to flatten, and toast to butter on both sides, now that's blessed!" When you know the King, the guarantee of ultimate peace bursts through the acts of grace and mercy. The Lord with us forevermore.

Who is this King, the text says – the one that's mighty in battle? In context, this passage relays that the King has just won and is on the way in the gate. The war is over, this is the King retuning from the last battle – open the door!

Who is this King, the One that can beat all of yawl! The One that can take care of any situation great or small – the King of Glory! Does anybody know my Jesus? Anybody know the King?

"Who is this King of glory? The LORD strong and mighty, the LORD mighty in battle. Lift up your heads, O ye gates; even lift them up, ye everlasting doors; and the King of glory shall come in. Who is this King of glory? The LORD of hosts, he is the King of glory. Selah." (Psalm 24:8-10)

See there it is, "And the King of glory shall come in" that's verse 9. And the King of glory shall come in – **get ready for company!** The King will come in if you just open the gate, open the door – God stands with gifts of love, peace, and joy.

Trouble don't last always! Things may seem empty and bleak at the moment, but wait with hope – God will bring us to victory. Walk in assurance, guaranteed that God will take care of you.

Be not dismayed whate'er betide,
God will take care of you;
Beneath His wings of love abide,
God will take care of you.

God will take care of you,
Through every day, o'er all the way;
He will take care of you,
God will take care of you.

All you may need He will provide,
God will take care of you;
Nothing you ask will be denied,
God will take care of you.

Revelation 3:20 says, "Behold, I stand at the door, and knock: if any man hear my voice, and open the door, I will come in to him, and will sup with him, and he with me."

Open the door and get ready for company, God will dwell with us as love streams like mighty rivers from our soul. God's presence is resource rich – "Blessed are those who walk not in the counsel of the ungodly, nor standeth in the way of sinners, nor sitteth in the seat of the scornful. But his delight is in the law of the LORD; and in his law doth he meditate day and night. And he shall be like a tree planted by the rivers of water, that bringeth forth his fruit in his season; his leaf also shall not wither; and whatsoever he doeth shall prosper." Psalm 1:1-3

God's presence is resource rich; we can trust in the power of God. We are so blessed with the light of God's word. Psalm 22 reminds us that God sacrificed God as the Suffering Savior cries out, "My God, My God why hast Thou forsaken Me?" Psalm 23 reminds us that God the Holy Spirit is forever with us to guide us into all truth and righteousness, "The Lord is my Shepherd, I shall not want."

Finally, Psalm 24 emerges with hope as the doors open, the victorious, glorious, marvelous King emerges across the horizon of our lives. Lift them up! Lift up the gates, Lift them up – the everlasting doors.

The King is coming! Open the doors! We can be assured of victory, assured of the King's return, open the doors we have a guarantee from the blood-stained garments at Calvary, an empty grave is there to prove that our Savior lives.

Our blessed assurance is not in earthen vessels, clay and stone – but in the everlasting fact that our God is King, Jesus has defeated the ultimate enemies of humanity, the blood of Christ has established perpetuation for peace.

I'm glad today that the resurrection of Christ stands as the ultimate symbol of our guarantee. We are blessed in every season by God's love from Calvary.

We needed Jesus to seal the deal for us. Psalm 24:3 says, "Who shall ascend?" In Hebrew this word is "ala" – we need access to move on up a little higher. The earth is the Lord's declared David, and the fullness thereof, everything and anything in the world – everything belongs to God! David acknowledges God's great sovereignty, reminds us that everything belongs to God. Now how do we get access? Who can negotiate for us?

Oh, listen, won't you listen – just as Isiah heard the call in his own private worship, who will go for us? God, responded to God at the need to save us. God veiled within the humanity of Jesus Who came to give us assurance through the sacrifice that provides hospitality for God the Holy Spirit to reside with us all. We have the guarantee, we have blessed assurance.

Blessed assurance, Jesus is mine!
O what a foretaste of glory divine!
Heir of salvation, purchase of God,
born of his Spirit, washed in his blood.

Perfect submission, perfect delight,
visions of rapture now burst on my sight;
angels descending, bring from above
echoes of mercy, whispers of love.

Perfect submission, all is at rest,
I in my Savior am happy and blest,
watching and waiting, looking above,
filled with his goodness, lost in his love.

HOW TO LIVE IN EVERY SEASON

SCRIPTURE

Ecclesiastes 3:1-13 To every thing there is a season, and a time to every purpose under the heaven: 2 A time to be born, and a time to die; a time to plant, and a time to pluck up that which is planted; 3 A time to kill, and a time to heal; a time to break down, and a time to build up; 4 A time to weep, and a time to laugh; a time to mourn, and a time to dance; 5 A time to cast away stones, and a time to gather stones together; a time to embrace, and a time to refrain from embracing; 6 A time to get, and a time to lose; a time to keep, and a time to cast away; 7 A time to rend, and a time to sew; a time to keep silence, and a time to speak; 8 A time to love, and a time to hate; a time of war, and a time of peace. 9 What profit hath he that worketh in that wherein he laboureth? 10 I have seen the travail, which God hath given to the sons of men to be exercised in it. 11 He hath made every thing beautiful in his time: also he hath set the world in their heart, so that no man can find out the work that God maketh from the beginning to the end. 12 I know that there is no good in them, but for a man to rejoice, and to do good in his life. 13 And also that every man should eat and drink, and enjoy the good of all his labour, it is the gift of God.

OUTLINE

1. Recognize the Time and Season v1
2. Know the Yield (What All Comes from God) v9
3. Enjoy the Gift v13

MESSAGE

Hebel, hebel, hebel – it's all hebel. The writer, teacher, preacher of Ecclesiastes uses the Hebrew word hebel to vocalize reality as a vapor, an intangible distraction. Chapter 1, verse 2 translates hebel into the word vanity – nevertheless, the etymological depiction may be best seen with the idea of trying to capture smoke in your hands.

Smoke possesses a kind of vanity that gives the appearance of tangible matter while completely escapable from human grasp. Hebel, hebel, hebel – vanity, having a physical appearance while maintaining a fading fantasy, never to be clasped in reality.

Hebel, hebel, hebel – fluff! Nothing but fluff! The writer, teacher, preacher of Ecclesiastes emerges to remind us that much of what we see as important is against the reality of time.

Think about it, the most important two days of life rest within the day we were born and the day that we will die. Everything between birth and death merely provides substance for the review of those two days. Only two questions demand our attention in the end – how were you born and how will you die? Where did you start and how will you end?

Ecclesiastes reminds us that we often embrace the distracting substance sandwiched between life and death. We focus on our bodies, our things, our riches or our poverty. We focus on vacations and travel, work and rest — we focus on clothes and rags, hair, nails, muscles, and shoes with matching outfits.

Hebel, hebel, hebel — focused on everything except that which is important. Seasons will change, we will go through ups and downs — good times and bad, nevertheless, in the end we will remain judged against our commitment to the way, love, and life of Christ.

There is a time and a season for everything under the sun — and we must not become distracted by the ups and downs of many days, as in the end we will be judged upon the indelible acts that we presented as emulating Jesus. Only what we do for Christ will last.

Time and change will dissolve some things and experiences — but a relationship with God is eternal. You may be flossing today, doing great, wealthy and wise — but how will you exist through eternity? We must be ready to live in every eternal season.

Look with me at Ecclesiastes 3:1 as it reads, "To every thing there is a season, and a time to every purpose under the heaven:"

Recognize the time and season as we must know the season to realize our mode of operation. People living in the Mid-west understand, as any region experiencing all four seasons understand, that each season comes with necessary preparation and behavior unique to the season. Winter clothes must be reserved for after fall, bathing suit are needed for summer and raincoats for spring. The climate gives us an indication as to possible weather conditions.

Although we may know the weather today, any anomalies or rare temperature days cannot be allowed to change our perception about the climate.

Life will come with some odd days, perhaps some odd seasons – nevertheless, we have to learn to survive in spite of the complexities of change.

In Paul's letter to the Philippians chapter 3, he says, "That I may know him, and the power of his resurrection, and the fellowship of his sufferings, being made conformable unto his death; 11 If by any means I might attain unto the resurrection of the dead. 12 Not as though I had already attained, either were already perfect: but I follow after, if that I may apprehend that for which also I am apprehended of Christ Jesus. 13 Brethren, I count not myself to have apprehended: but this one thing I do, forgetting those things which are behind, and reaching forth unto those things which are before, 14 I press toward the mark for the prize of the high calling of God in Christ Jesus. 15 Let us therefore, as many as be perfect, be thus minded: and if in any thing ye be otherwise minded, God shall reveal even this unto you."

We cannot become so distracted by the race that we forget to run, forget to win. We cannot get distracted by other participants, we cannot get so distracted by our gear and shoes that we forget to win the race. We must stay focused on the prize that is set before us; we must stay focused on Jesus – we must stay focused on the ultimate season of eternity.

To live in every season – we must know the season, but most importantly we must know the conductor of every season – we will never win the ultimate race without divine connection.

Don't get distracted by scenery, keep on keeping on. The sun will set and rise, you will win some and lose some – but don't lose the ultimate prize of eternal life with God.

Don't ever give up or give in based on hevel, based on what things look like, based on the vapor - smoke and mirrors. Stay focused on God's reality while rejecting man's fantasies. We cannot afford to take our eyes off the prize of everlasting life, enjoyed within the glories of God's great promise.

I'm pressing on the upward way,
New heights I'm gaining every day;
Still praying as I'm onward bound,
"Lord, plant my feet on higher ground."

My heart has no desire to stay
Where doubts arise and fears dismay;
Though some may dwell where those abound,
My prayer, my aim, is higher ground.

I want to live above the world,

Though Satan's darts at me are hurled;
For faith has caught the joyful sound,
The song of saints on higher ground.

I want to scale the utmost height
And catch a gleam of glory bright;
But still I'll pray till heav'n I've found,
"Lord, plant my feet on higher ground."

Lord, lift me up and let me stand,
By faith, on Heaven's tableland,
A higher plane than I have found;
Lord, plant my feet on higher ground.

Focus on Ecclesiastes 3:9 as it reads, "What profit hath he that worketh in that wherein he laboureth?"

We should **know the yield** – far too often we labor and toil without plans and goals. If you leave home without a plan you could end up anywhere. If you plant seeds without knowing what you're planting – the outcome will be uncertain. Far too often we operate without plan, purpose, and partnership.

Verse 9 reminds us to check the profit margin. What do we get out of work, what is the yield? We get jobs and work for a car that will ultimately rust, we work for houses that will crumble and fall in time, we work for clothes that will turn to rags, we work for so many temporary things. We work for food and we'll be hungry again in about an hour or two. What are we working for? Most of life is spent working for the temporary while ignoring the eternal. What are we working for, what is the yield? Think about everything that you do and work for everyday and now let's prioritize, out of everything that you work for, everything that you have, every relationship that you are connected to, what will remain 1000 years from now? Are you prepared to live beyond the seasons of humanity - beyond the seasons of physical bodies and flesh? Are you prepared to depart labor to accept reward in that day when God will gather us to our everlasting homes?

We must know the yield, know the risk – realizing that everything will pass away and we will be left with the singularity of soul, we must love God with heart, soul, and mind. Although life has many components, nevertheless we must prioritize our relationship with God as we seek to live like Jesus. In the final season the material universe will not matter against the weight of your soul.

We must acknowledge the time and season. We must know the yield to live in every season – holding to faith with glorious hope lifting us into the presence of God. Look now at Ecclesiastes 3:11-13 as it reads, "He hath made every thing beautiful in his time: also he hath set the world in their heart, so that no man can find out the work that God maketh from the beginning to the end. 12 I know that there is no good in them, but for a man to rejoice, and to do good in his life. 13 And also that every man should eat and drink, and enjoy the good of all his labour, it is the gift of God."

In every season recognize the time and know the yield – realizing everything comes from God we should **enjoy the gift**.

God so loved the world that God gave God's son Jesus to save us. We've been given a great gift – the greatest gift ever given. Now there is some nice stuff – it's easy to get caught up in hevel, vapor and smoke, chasing dreams that keep disappearing, distracted by suboptimal stimulation – when we would be best served to simply enjoy the greatest gift.

Jesus said in Matthew 6:25-33, "Therefore I say unto you, Take no thought for your life, what ye shall eat, or what ye shall drink; nor yet for your body, what ye shall put on. Is not the life more than meat, and the body than raiment? 26 Behold the fowls of the air: for they sow not, neither do they reap, nor gather into barns; yet your heavenly Father feedeth them. Are ye not much better than they? 27 Which of you by taking thought can add one cubit unto his stature? 28 And why take ye thought for raiment? Consider the lilies of the field, how they grow; they toil not, neither do they spin: 29 And yet I say unto you, That even Solomon in all his glory was not arrayed like one of these. 30 Wherefore, if God so clothe the grass of the field, which to day is, and to morrow is cast into the oven, shall he not much more clothe you, O ye of little faith? 31 Therefore take no thought, saying, What shall we eat? or, What shall we drink? or, Wherewithal shall we be clothed? 32 (For after all these things do the Gentiles seek:) for your heavenly Father knoweth that ye have need of all these things. 33 But seek ye first the kingdom of God, and his righteousness; and all these things shall be added unto you."

Every season requires consistent connection with God. Completely focused on God our great redeemer, our savior forever. While we were yet sinners, God planned for our future seasons as God the Son sacrificed life and blood for all of us. The greatest gift sacrificed at Calvary brings eternal love, joy, peace, and liberation. Prepared for ever season by God – sacrificed at Calvary to save our seasons.

No matter what it looks like today, hold on as a testimony arises from the tomb – Jesus was crucified, buried, and arose from the grave with victory and triumph. We can live in every season under the protection of God.

In 1906 Jennie Wilson penned the hope inspiring words:
Time is filled with swift transition,
Naught of earth unmoved can stand,
Build your hopes on things eternal,
Hold to God's unchanging hand.
Trust in Him who will not leave you,
Whatsoever years may bring,
If by earthly friends forsaken
Still more closely to Him cling.

Covet not this world's vain riches
That so rapidly decay,
Seek to gain the heav'nly treasures,

They will never pass away.

When your journey is completed,
If to God you have been true,
Fair and bright the home in glory
Your enraptured soul will view.

Hold to God's unchanging hand,
Hold to God's unchanging hand;
Build your hopes on things eternal,
Hold to God's unchanging hand.

Hebel, hebel, hebel - everything between birth and death merely provides substance for the review of those two days. Only two questions demand our attention in the end – how were you born and how will you die? Where did you start and how will you end?

GOD DOES NOT FORGET

SCRIPTURE

Exodus 5:22-6:5 And Moses returned unto the LORD, and said, Lord, wherefore hast thou so evil entreated this people? why is it that thou hast sent me? 23 For since I came to Pharaoh to speak in thy name, he hath done evil to this people; neither hast thou delivered thy people at all. 6:1 Then the LORD said unto Moses, Now shalt thou see what I will do to Pharaoh: for with a strong hand shall he let them go, and with a strong hand shall he drive them out of his land. 2 And God spake unto Moses, and said unto him, I am the LORD: 3 And I appeared unto Abraham, unto Isaac, and unto Jacob, by the name of God Almighty, but by my name JEHOVAH was I not known to them. 4 And I have also established my covenant with them, to give them the land of Canaan, the land of their pilgrimage, wherein they were strangers. 5 And I have also heard the groaning of the children of Israel, whom the Egyptians keep in bondage; and I have remembered my covenant.

OUTLINE

1. You Will See v1
2. God Can Work While Nameless v3
3. God Hears Us Through Bondage v5

MESSAGE

Memory rests within our ability to retain, store, and subsequently recall information and past experiences.

There are times when our ability to recall becomes diminished as days dissipate into history. People highlight forgetfulness as "having a senior moment." That thought quickly forgotten between the family room to the kitchen, moments when silence becomes the sharp sound of forgetfulness.

We forget events, but even worse is how we forget each other. We become so self-absorbed in personal orbits that we forget to maintain relationships with God and each other. We tend to easily forget – too busy to care, too busy to remember. We become so focused on our world that we forget the pain and suffering waged against humanity thriving through global terrorism from the White House to the Kremlin. Oppression seasons our society, often draining joy from humankind.

We're living in the cabinet of corporate greed, with minds harvested for data like Florida oranges pressed for juice. Oppression on every hand! The Apostle Paul writes in 2 Corinthians 4:8-10, "We are troubled on every side, yet not distressed; we are perplexed, but not in despair; 9 Persecuted, but not forsaken; cast down, but not destroyed; 10 Always bearing about in the body the dying of the Lord Jesus, that the life also of Jesus might be made manifest in our body."
Oh, don't you see – oppression is real and where we forget, God remembers. God does not forget.

Focus with me on Exodus 6:1 as the verse reads, "Then the LORD said unto Moses, Now shalt thou see what I will do to Pharaoh: for with a strong hand shall he let them go, and with a strong hand shall he drive them out of his land."

God does not forget, **you will see**. The text provides that God communicated to Abraham that devastation would arise spanning four hundred years – his descendants would suffer the pangs of enslavement as foreigners in a strange land. I wonder is there anybody here – who ever walked through the halls of enslavement as elements of poverty lunged for vitality and life? Living pay check to paycheck, hand to mouth and thankful – yet physically enslaved just the same.

Abraham had warning – God warned him that life was going to come with some oppression but time would deliver the manifestation of hope from slavery to a land flowing with milk and honey. God forewarned tough times, yet promised victory and eternal blessings. God does not forget.

Exodus chapter 5 floods with the sadness of oppression as the desire to worship is exchanged for wickedness – as they requested a religious respite to worship God, antithetically Pharaoh the Egyptian, forced them to labor the more, challenged to make brick without straw. God does not forget!

We are working longer hours for less pay – just like being asked to make brick without straw. Companies lay off three workers and give you the tasks of five without an extra dime, vacation, or break. Many of us are tired from being tired – wondering when relief is coming, wondering how long will this morally depressing season extend into the history of human lamentation. Well, I stopped by to tell you – God does not forget.

God guides Moses to Egypt with the powerful message, "Let my people go." Nevertheless, the message seemingly took a moment to manifest, somebody should say amen in this church. God's time can be uncomfortable for us – as God often works when we least expect.

They were slaves, Moses was sent with a word – but the word did not immediately produce a release from slavery. God works on God's time – but know this, God does not forget. Pharaoh's heart was hardened by God's providence to insure evidence of God's hand. With all the great things God has done, miracle after miracle to include waking us up this morning – I don't know about you, but it's a miracle just to wake up. We see God work, we see God heal, we watch God deliver – then forget.

We quickly forget the hand of God, yet God does not forget. God reassured Moses; God confidently proclaims, "Now shalt thou see what I will do to Pharaoh." God does not forget, just hold on God hasn't forgotten your trials, tribulations, terrorists, and trauma – God does not forget.

It may seem like God has forgotten but God does not forget. God reassures us that we will see what He will do to our enemies, we will see how God will handle our oppressors, we will see how the Lord deals with our Pharaoh types. Just wait and see what God will do with Pharaoh – just wait and see!

Look with me at Exodus 6:3 reading, "And I appeared unto Abraham, unto Isaac, and unto Jacob, by the name of God Almighty, but by my name JEHOVAH was I not known to them."

God can work while nameless – as God's powerful work is limitless, never restricted by our missing elements. We are often dumb enough to think that things change because we don't fully understand, we can't call it, we can't name it, we can't explain it so it must be invalid. Please – who do you think you are? God can work however and whenever God wants to work. Who among us has the power to check God? Only the fool embraces a heart that denies God.

God is God, God's ability to be God is not based on our knowledge of God – our theology is but raggedy worn threads within the great tapestry of God. God can, you don't hear me – that's all need be said, God can. I don't need to know how, I don't need to know all the terms and the switchboard of heaven all I need to know is that God can – then pair that up with God does not forget, then the question arises "Who can stand before our God, if God be for us – then who can stand against us?"

Oh, let me move on – before something gets started in here. Somebody should just shout hallelujah one time – God can, come on – hear the Spirit today, God can. Now pair it with God does not forget! So glad for God.

Center now upon Exodus 6:5 as it reads, "And I have also heard the groaning of the children of Israel, whom the Egyptians keep in bondage; and I have remembered my covenant."

God does not forget, you will see the Lord will show up and show out - God can work while nameless, God's power is limitless.

God hears us through bondage, nevertheless oppression can be so debilitating that it muffles pleas for help. Yet no matter how muffled our pleas become, God hears us through our bondage. The song writer Cleavant Derricks pens the laudation that God will hear our faintest cry, and will, answer by and by:

Sometimes our path seems drear, without a ray of cheer, and then a cloud of doubt may hide the light of day. The mists of sin may rise and hide the starry skies, but just a little talk with Jesus clears the way.

We may have doubts and fears, eyes be filled with tears, but Jesus is a friend who watches day and night.

I go to God in prayer, God knows my every care, And just a little talk with Jesus makes it right!

God hears through the clamor of bondage - God does not forget. God remembers God's covenant and will uphold every promise. Isaiah 55:11 reminds us that God's word will not return void but will accomplish exactly what it was sent to do.

God does not forget! Through the rains and through the storm – we can move with peaceful faith, enriched by fortified hope as we hear the song of saints worship the Rock of Ages – our great God. You have not been forgotten; we have not been forgotten!

God the Son, Jesus saved us through sacrifice at Calvary, redeemed our testimony upon exit from the grave – fortifying victory forever. God does not forget – just hold on, keep on holding on. Trouble don't last always – on this last Sunday of the year let it go, let all the negative gnarly, nasty notes from the past, reaching for the new, the positive, reaching for God's great blessings. Trust in God who will never leave nor forsake us. God does not forget us - we should not forget God. God remembers us, we should remember God.

Reverend Doctor Carolyn Winfrey Gillette, modern hymnist and preacher articulates the powerfully poetic reminder:

Remember me—the God who saves—
For back in Egypt you were slaves;
Then by my hand I set you free.
Now keep my law. Remember me.

Remember me in bread and wine
Whene'er you share this meal of mine.
I gave my life to set you free.
With thanks and praise, remember me.

Remember me in all you do,
For I'm alive! I walk with you.
I was, I am, and I shall be.
O church I love, remember me.

Our God, we hear! We're called and freed!
Your Spirit gives us memory.
Now send us out that we may share
Your love's great story everywhere.

God remembers us, let us remember God.

HOLAM BOOKS & MEDIA
www.holambooks.com

Holam (חוֹלָם) is a Hebrew niqqud vowel sign represented by a dot above the upper left corner of the consonant letter. For example, here the holam appears after the letter mem (מ): מֹ. In Modern Hebrew it indicates the close-mid back rounded vowel, and is transliterated as an "o".

www.ingramcontent.com/pod-product-compliance
Lightning Source LLC
Chambersburg PA
CBHW031419150426
43191CB00006B/329